About the author

Tamara is the author of ten books; they are novels, stories and fairy tales for children; all of them are published in Russia. She is a member of the Writers' Union of the Russian Federation and a member of the International Writers' Guild. In 2011 she became a laureate of the nomination 'The Small Prose' at the International Literary Festival of Literature and Art, 'Russian Style' (2011, Germany). This autobiography was published in 2011 in Moscow as 'Трава, пробившая асфальт', which can be translated to English as 'The Blade of Grass that Broke the Asphalt'. In 2018, the British Broadcasting Corporation (BBC) included Tamara Cheremnova's name in the list of the one hundred most prominent women in the world. Maria Arbatova, a Russian novelist and a famous public figure, wrote about this autobiography: 'Tamara Cheremnova instantly became a star after publication of her honest, scary, shrill, and at the same time, very positive book.'

This is a work of creative non-fiction. The events are portrayed to the best of the author's memory. While all the stories in this book are true, some names and identifying details have been changed to protect the privacy of the people involved.

THE BLADE OF GRASS

TAMARA CHEREMNOVA
Translated into English by Albina Leibman-Klix

THE BLADE OF GRASS

Vanguard Press

VANGUARD PAPERBACK

© Copyright 2022
Tamara Cheremnova

The right of Tamara Cheremnova to be identified as author of
this work has been asserted by her in accordance with the
Copyright, Designs and Patents Act 1988.

All Rights Reserved

No reproduction, copy or transmission of this publication
may be made without written permission.
No paragraph of this publication may be reproduced,
copied or transmitted save with the written permission of the publisher, or in
accordance with the provisions
of the Copyright Act 1956 (as amended).

Any person who commits any unauthorised act in relation to
this publication may be liable to criminal
prosecution and civil claims for damages.

A CIP catalogue record for this title is
available from the British Library.

ISBN 978 1 91090 375 9

*Vanguard Press is an imprint of
Pegasus Elliot MacKenzie Publishers Ltd.*
www.pegasuspublishers.com

First Published in 2022

**Vanguard Press
Sheraton House Castle Park
Cambridge England**

Printed & Bound in Great Britain

Dedication

I dedicate my autobiography to Julia Kristeva, one of the greatest psychoanalysts and feminists of our time, whose approach to disability aims to bring the disabled and non-disabled together, ending the marginalization and isolation of people marked by a stigma.

Acknowledgements

It is a great pleasure to thank all those who helped me with the English translation of my autobiography. I want to thank Albina Leibman-Klix for her hard work with her Russian-English translation, who accomplished this work to the best of her ability. I would like to thank John Klix and Sherry Wolf for their meticulous proof-reading of the English text. My deep appreciation goes to my friend Vyacheslav Lopushnoy for writing the preface to my book which he titled 'Ascension of Saint Tamara' — a great compliment to me though I must say I am not a saint. Maybe I will become a saint, but after my death…

Ascension of Saint Tamara
(Preface to the Autobiography by Tamara Cheremnova)

When I read this book, I immediately realized that even the toughest man would hardly suppress his tears reading this bitter and life-affirming autobiography. I am sure this book will find readers in any country of the world: it has a great potential to be translated to English, Italian, Chinese, to any language! For this book will find a response in any soul, as we feel the same everywhere... The Russian writer Tamara Cheremnova lives — I will repeat after Pushkin — "in the depths of the Siberian mines," — in Kuzbass. I am also from this area, and I am proud to be Tamara's friend.

Tamara was born in 1955. She was disabled from childhood and suffers from the most severe form of cerebral palsy (CP is the group of permanent movement disorders that manifests itself in early childhood). I attended this festival and asked their committee to entrust Tamara's award to me. In her native town there was a great celebration in Tamara's honor, where she received a warm reception from her friends and colleagues and was presented with awards. As a messenger, I reported the words of Maria Arbatova, a well-known Russian writer, who was a member of the jury at the Festival in Germany. I told how highly Arbatova praised Tamara's works. I also told that one of the largest bookstores in Moscow had been selling very successfully Tamara's autobiographical novel, 'The Blade of Grass that Broke the Asphalt', and now Tamara has many readers. In my speech, I said how much I admire the strength, vitality, and heroic attitude towards life of this seemingly defenseless woman.

I said, "God gave her an unbelievable strength of character, natural intellect and a great talent, and as they used to say in old days, a subtle spiritual organization. Her tragic story, I believe, has no precedents anywhere in the entire world... With her great infirmity, she was like Don Quixote, leading her constant battle against the windmills of our medical system, demanding to cancel the stigma which was given to her more than half a century ago: the diagnosis 'oligophrenia at the stage of debility'.

In fact, it was a death sentence to an individual, who was denied existence as a normal human being. It was impossible to eliminate this diagnosis even when Tamara had published her books… But she won! Fortunately, she met good people, those who recognized her and were reactive in promoting her works. Tamara's story is really fascinating. She has perfect Russian and keeps her self-oriented perfectionism even when she writes her emails. Because of her physical condition, her writing required a great deal of physical efforts and maneuvers; nevertheless, she mastered the computer. And this is the person who does not have any formal education! Tamara is self-taught, as education in these 'sanatoria' for the disabled, well known for their bad reputation, did not exist.

Now I understand why she ended her fabulous narration with the words: "I have succeeded in life!"

There is an article in English about Tamara on Wikipedia. I hope an article in Russian will be published on Wikipedia as well. I believe Russia, Tamara's native country, should honor her first hand.

Alexander Pushkin predicted his fame with accuracy:

"Слух обо мне пройдет по всей Руси Великой
И назовет меня всяк сущий в ней язык…"

"My fame shall cover all of Russia's vast expanses
And set astir the many tongues of all who speak…"

I hope the spirit of the poet will not be offended if I take the liberty of paraphrasing his two lines to divine Tamara's destiny:

Her fame shall cover all of the world's vast expanses
And set astir the many tongues of all who speak!

Vyacheslav Lopushnoy, poet and writer, city of Kemerovo

Part 1
The Bachata orphanage

The Last Night at Home

When I lived at home, I was so fond of the evening when all went to bed. Only the kitchen remained illuminated; as my mother and grandmother were about to finish their cleaning, a cozy strip of light, revealed through the delicate curtains, fell into the dark room.

I was lying in my bed listening to the silence. The muffled voices in the kitchen penetrated my dream, gentle and light… If I had a feeling that my home would soon disappear from my life, I would try to remember every detail — even thin lines on the wall facing my bed, every flower in our garden, every petal…

One autumn day I noticed a box of colored pencils and a notebook on my dresser. I asked, "Mother, is that for me?"

My mother was making my bed at the time. She slowly turned to me and said, embarrassed, "We bought them for you. Soon you will go to school. You will learn how to read and write…"

I felt some chill inside me; something in her intonation was alarming. I tried to imagine the school, but I had no idea about it, and how it would be to go to school.

Later my father went to the orphanage for the handicapped children to see what needed to be taken there. He and my mother wanted to bring my bed to the orphanage, but they were told there were proper beds there.

My parents decided to take only two things to the orphanage — the stroller and the walker. During the day I used to spend most of my time sitting in the stroller. It was just the regular, lightweight stroller, but slightly reconstructed by my father as I continued to grow.

My family members started acting in a peculiar way. My grandmother grew distant: she would leave the house for the entire day. I did not understand why she behaved that way. As an adult, I realized that they had all known about the plan to send me to the orphanage, and what kind of life the helpless child would have *there*. They felt guilty and ashamed, but the decision had already been made…

Where Did They Take Me?

It was a somber October when my parents moved me. Now there is no clear picture in my memory about this day, except some fuzzy, gray, and blurred remnants, looking like a page which has been erased… Late at night, my father and I reached the Bochata station, near which the orphanage was located.

I remember my father was holding me close to his breast as we left the station. I was silent with fear. We walked up to a dark, wooden barrack; my father knocked on the door. I heard rattling sounds then the two side doors opened.

I was brought into the room and put in a dirty bed. It was the waiting room, and everyone who worked that day ran to see me. This specialized orphanage had been established recently, and every child that arrived at the orphanage aroused great curiosity among the staff. And here they were witnessing young and healthy parents, delivering a child whose arms and legs did not look so strange at first sight — it was just a six-year-old girl, looking ordinary, but frightened.

Lying in the reception room bed, I was looking at dirty walls, which had not been whitewashed for a long time, calmly waiting for my father. I still hoped he would take me in his arms, saying, "Well, daughter, now let's go." And then we would go to the station, take a train, and soon we would be home.

But it did not turn out that way. The people around me split up in opposite directions, giving way to my mother, who entered the waiting room. She was wearing a shabby institutional gown, made of cotton with patterns in color, which were worn away and barely visible. She started undressing me in a hurry, turning her head away from me. My father leaned over to kiss me, but accidentally I knocked his hat off with my hand. I still remember this minute detail: he hesitated, lifting his hat from the floor. When he was leaving, everyone noticed tears were running down his cheeks. I did not remember this episode, and I could not see my father's face; it was one of the nannies who told me this story when I grew up.

Then my mother took me in her arms and carried me down a long, grey corridor. She went into the ward, put me on a free bunk, asked someone from the personnel to move another bunk close to that one in which she put me, so I would not fall on the floor, and left in silence. And then they turned off the lights. In darkness I could recognize some silhouettes. There were a lot of beds, and they were occupied by unanimated children who appeared to me like ghosts. Then I detected a big girl running around. Her coiffure looked like that of a sheep whose fleece was just removed. Her hair was cut in shreds — there were pockets of hair coming out like little islands, surrounded by bare skin. Because I was completely unfamiliar with this environment, I understood nothing and felt nothing. I even imagined myself dead, but my eyes were still functioning; they studied involuntarily this completely incomprehensible place.

It was a dark autumn night; it became quiet in the room, and this foreign silence, very different from the silence at home, helped me to get out of my stupor. All night, looking into the darkness, I was waiting for my mother to come quietly, sit on my bed and comfort me. I was so unhappy!

In the morning, as soon as the nannies checked the children to see who had urinated in bed, suddenly I realized I was abandoned, and I started crying bitterly. The big girl with the sheep's head, who had been rushing around the ward the night before, started running like a mad beast through the aisle between the beds. She looked so wild and bizarre in this gray, institutional ward that I could not imagine anything that would be more terrifying for me than these surroundings.

Nannies stopped by my bunk and started consoling me. "Why are you crying? Look how many girlfriends you have here. Do you see Luda? She is just like you, and she is lying in bed and not crying."

The nannies picked up Luda and led her to my bunk. She was a little girl who could not walk without help. When she was supported by the nannies, I noticed that she was stepping only on her toes. Looking at her face, I realized that they rarely approached her, and even more rarely took her from her bed. Luda smiled at me, but it made me even sadder; I turned away and started crying again. I have never cried for so long, and this crying made my mouth and lips dry.

After a while, the nannies came back into the room and started delivering breakfast. A woman came to me with a bowl of cereal, but I turned my head. The woman went away indifferently, not even offering me some tea, which I would not have refused at that moment.

I did not have any tears: I ran out of tears. I cried it all out, and I was just howling like a grief-stricken puppy. And then this big girl who resembled a sheep, whose woolen fleece was just sheared, jumped up to my bunk and barked, "Why are you yelling? All day she is screaming and screaming! They brought her to give us a headache!"

I felt like a stone had been thrown at me; no one at home had ever been so angry with me. My howl immediately stopped because of fear, but my body continued to shudder silently. I do not know if I suffered until lunch and had a meal or if I fell asleep.

All I remember is when my mother finally showed up, the minute I saw her, I started crying again. She put me on her lap, trying to calm me down, rocking me and saying, "Don't cry; look how many girls are here, and none of them is crying. Your father and I will visit you here; we'll take you home on weekends…"

"I don't want you to visit me! I want to go home!" I was screaming, drowning in tears.

My mother seemed to me to be a different person, maybe because of the shabby robe which she was wearing in the orphanage, or maybe because she was talking to me in a new way. She gave me water; she offered me lunch, but I refused it stubbornly. I would not let my mother go away, and she could not remove my crooked fingers from her.

"Toma, I have to finish my work on your stroller; I have to upholster your stroller. If I don't do this, how will you sit in a bare stroller? I want to cover it, and then you'll be very comfortable sitting in it. I have to go home; there's Olga alone. She misses me too, and she is crying without me."

While I was being consoled by my mother, I noticed that she called me not Nemka as they used to call me at home, but Toma. Apparently, the beloved Nemka stayed at home, and the unwanted Toma was sent to the orphanage. Either I was completely weakened by my sobbing, or I agreed with the arguments of my mother, or I was sobered by the new name 'Toma', which substituted 'Nemka', but I let her go.

The dinner was over; the nannies took away dishes. And then my father showed up at the door of the room. He did not come to me but stood, leaning against the door frame. I saw him smile. I wanted to squeal, but I did not have any strength left. I just stared at him until I had pain in my eyes. The teacher came and started complaining to him. "Your daughter cries all the time. She doesn't want to eat anything!"

"She's so inventive, she can use any piece of paper to invent a game," my father said. Then he turned around and left.

***

By evening, they brought me my stroller, which was already improved by my mother. It was a regular promenade stroller for children; for comfort it was covered on all sides by a dense material. At that time, wheelchairs for invalid children probably did not exist in Kuzbass, or they were accessible only to a few people.

"Where is my mother?" I asked the nanny.

"Your mother and father left. Your mother asked me to put you in the stroller. If you wish, I can put you there."

I nodded in agreement. She put me in the stroller and left. I protruded my neck to see better what was outside the window. All was just grey — a melancholic autumn… I saw in the distance a wooden house — it was exactly like our house! I started crying again. And in spite of my young age, I firmly realized that in my position, nothing could be changed. Nothing at all! If I could walk, I would get up; I would leave this place. I would run to get out of here! But I was helpless…

The normal patient, not the chronic one, knows that some time will pass and he will recover and enjoy life again. For example, my aunt, my father's sister, whom I called Nanny, had an accident when she was in the eighth grade. Her leg was cut off by a tram, but she mastered the prosthesis and achieved such perfection that she ran like she had her own two legs. But for me there is no exit when I can change nothing, and I have to exist in this condition forever; it is my only life form. And for the first time, I tried to understand — why is it so with me? Why? For what?

My thoughts were interrupted by the arrival of a hairdresser. Without asking my permission and not reacting to my protests, she quickly cut all my hair off. Nadia came in — the one who had scared me with her 'sheep haircut' and her bestial running through the ward — and she asked in a sympathetic manner, "Why are you crying? You feel sorry for your hair?"

I did not think any more that Nadia was that bad. The nanny had told me that she was not completely mentally normal; she had been taken from the 'school for fools' (from the auxiliary school), and her haircut was so ugly because they had cut it not with a hair clipper but with scissors.

My whimper was heard in the hallway; a staff member came to the room, and then he called a boy who was older than I. "Take this girl down the hall; she needs some entertainment."

The boy came to my stroller and started rolling it with joy, while I was sitting in it, immersed in my thoughts.

***

At night I came up with an interesting idea: what if I took off my skin? This skin is so bad, it keeps me from normal functioning. Under the bad skin there is another skin, the good one — this good skin will not arrest my movements, and certainly having a new skin, I will be able to get up and walk. But how can I do that?

Everyone fell asleep, and like a frog in a fairy tale who transformed into a princess, I decided to work on my transformation. I wanted to remove my skin which I believed was the cause of my trouble. Under the blanket I started scratching my kneecaps with my fingernails until I felt the pain. After a moment of reflection, I realized that my skin was the only one and there is no other skin underneath. And the hopelessness pressed me down again as if I were beneath a stone slab.

Being half asleep I had a vision: as my bunk carried me to the station, it climbed itself onto the train; then, like an intelligent and obedient horse, it carried me safely to our yard. My grandmother came outside from the house, took me from my bed-horse and said, "Thank you."

I exclaimed with joy, "Here I am!"

Then the vision disappeared, and I returned to my grim despair. God forbid I should experience such despair again!

***

The orphanage where I was taken was a specialized institution for children with physical and mental disabilities; it was located in the village of the Bachata Belovo District, near the Bochata station. I was six years and ten months old. This is how these names are written: the name of the station is written with an 'o' (Bochata), the name of the settlement with an 'a' (Bachata). These two names sound similar, but they have a different spelling, because they are derived from different words. 'Bochata' means a barrel, and 'bachata' means 'pit' in the local dialect. And me — I was caulked inside a barrel and thrown into a pit.

I was destined to spend twenty long years in this orphanage.

***

Getting acquainted with my surroundings, I quickly understood what kind of life the orphanage is. You might like it or not; you have to accept it, but for some things you might have to fight.

At that time, I did not know that my father left my mother with the same lightheartedness as he put me into the orphanage. Probably to justify his action regarding me, he chose a lame woman as his wife. At the court, where my parents had their divorce procedure, my father said, "I betrayed one person; I do not want to betray another one…"

The Tasteless Soup

When I woke up in the morning, I did not want to leave my wonderful dream in which I was coming home. But when I realized it was just a dream, I cried again. No one came up to me, and they did not give me breakfast when they saw me crying and shaking my head negatively.

The nannies were already rattling dishes in the hallway in preparation for lunch when a young teacher in a snow-white robe came to the room. She looked at me attentively, approached my bed, sat down on its edge, and asked me cheerfully, "What is your name?"
I stopped crying and became alert. She examined me, smiling, and repeated her question. "So, what is your name?"

"Toma Cheremnova…" still sobbing, I answered.

"Toma, I will bring you lunch; I will feed you."

I frowned. "Where is my mother?"

"Your mother is at work; she will come to see you during the weekend," the teacher answered and got up. Then she left the room. Very soon she came back with a bowl of soup.

I sniffed and was ready to refuse to eat the soup, but the teacher scooped up the hot soup with a spoon, blew on it and brought it to my mouth. I obediently opened my mouth. What I swallowed had nothing to do with soup. It was thickly cooked millet, seasoned with potatoes and canned fish. I felt a fish bone on my tongue; I spat it out on the towel with which the teacher had covered my breast, so I would not spill.

"Well done! Good soup?" the teacher asked me.

I made a face. This soup was very strange. It was the first meal I tasted in the orphanage. Later I got used to it.

After many years, when my request was approved and I could transfer from the department for children with chronic psychological problems to the institution of a general type, I swore to myself that if I ever left the institution and had my own home, I would make my own soup as my first meal in my own home. But my destiny, alas, denied me the happiness of my own home. And it seems it would continue that way.

The first impressions of the orphanage have been sealed in my memory forever: dull gray walls, windows without curtains and long waits for nannies. But the most terrible was silence. It is scary to imagine a silent room full of children, and there was no conversation and laughter between the visits of nannies; it was just moaning and whimpering.

That young teacher — Zinaida Stepanovna Yeskova — worked in the orphanage from the day of its opening until 1968. Having seen *our* suffering, she must have been so frightened of her *own* suffering. She hanged herself when her first child, her son, was born with hydrocephalus.

Roommates, Teachers, Nannies

The next day I continued crying, and again refused to eat. Probably everybody got tired of that. Children who could walk left the room immediately after breakfast; those who stayed in bed were quiet, and I had nothing to do but cry until lunch, alone and digesting my misfortune. However, that day they did not let me accomplish my crying. The new teacher, Dina Vasilevna walked in the room; she took me in her arms and carried me into the hallway. Caressing me, she tried to comfort me. "Why are you crying?"

"I want to go home!" I answered in a hoarse voice.

"Why is she crying like that?" a woman, who was sitting in the hallway, waiting for the chief physician, asked.

"They brought her here recently; she misses her family. I have a daughter; she is the same age. When I work too late, she misses me too," Dina Vasilevna explained to the woman. She said to me, "Tomochka, let's have a deal; you will not cry any more. I will walk with you, and then your mother will come."

I sobbed, but I stopped crying. Dina Vasilevna carried me in her arms to the hall, then she took me back to my room. She wanted to put me in bed, but I clung to her and whimpered.

"Toma, you promised you would not cry," she said gently and patted my back. "Is there something wrong?"

I had wanted toilet help, and the nanny was angry with me, I complained in a whisper.

I told her that this morning, when the nannies walked in and started changing wet sheets from the girls' beds, I had asked one of them to put me on the pot, but she did not react. Maybe she did not hear me? And when she came closer to my bunk, I screamed at the top of my lungs, "Nanny, I need to pee!"

The nanny turned her head in my direction. "You think you are the only one here, and I will serve you like a queen? I have too many things to do here," she declared grimly and left.

When I was a little girl, I never wet the sheets, and I would never imagine myself doing this in bed! And the realities of this institution, which were that you do your business in bed, and wait until they change your sheets — were unknown to me. I explained all this to Dina Vasilevna. She took the pot under the bunk and put me on it. Then she called the nannies; the three of them immediately came. She strictly said to them, "This girl has always to be put on the pot; she doesn't do it in bed. So come to her more often. She understands everything, and she speaks very well."

The three nannies, with their hands on their hips, looked at me with surprise. One of them, the most boisterous, began to make excuses. "You know, we are always busy. If we are not around, she can ask the girls to put her on the pot. For example, Nina can put her on the pot."

"Nina, can you put Toma on the potty?" Dina Vasilevna gently asked the girl whose bed was next to mine. She looked like an adult girl.

"Okay, I can do it," Nina, the quietest and most reliable girl in the ward, agreed meekly.

The nannies stood by, staring at me, took me from the pot, put me in my stroller and left the room. I heard their unhappy voices behind the door, and I realized they were angry with me.

***

One bed away from me, there was an adult-like girl of about fourteen. After Nadia, with her hairstyle resembling that of a sheep whose fleece was just cut, she was for me the second scariest girl. She had a very unpleasant manner — she would come to a person, putting her hands behind her back, sticking out her lower lip, rolling her eyes to her forehead and twanging, "Well!"

I was frightened by her resemblance to Baba Yaga, depicted in the book which I left at home. I remember one night my parents had to go somewhere. They put me to bed, and for my entertainment they gave me the first illustrated book they picked up, not even looking at it. When I opened it, I saw an illustration of Baba Yaga, flying through the air above the forest in a giant mortar (a bowl for grinding food), with her knees almost touching her chin, using the pestle (the grinder) as a rudder. I started to examine her carefully, looking at every detail, and I strained my eyes so much that it seemed to me that Baba Yaga started moving. I threw the book away in such agitation that it landed under my parents' bed. I put the blanket over my head and I was so afraid that I did not dare to crawl out of there. So I fell asleep under the blanket and did not hear when my parents returned home.

And now this animated Baba Yaga tortured me with her attention and with her nasal voice saying, "Well!" If this had happened at home, I would have immediately shown her my tongue, but here I was, scared and I just pressed my body to the back of my stroller and looked imploringly: please leave me alone.

Then they brought my things — a notebook and a box of colored pencils. When I opened the box and looked at the pencils, I felt a lump of tears stuck in my throat. I recalled the time when this box was on the dresser in my room at home, how I opened it for the first time, how vivid these pencils appeared to me, but here they looked different — all their colors vanished.

When my walker was brought in (my mother covered it with the material in the same way as she did it with the stroller), they reintroduced it to me. It was not possible to make movements as I used to do in the past: with my arms I was holding the frame, while my little body was hanging in the air. I did not dare to use my feet as they would betray me immediately, so weakened was I after a long period of sitting in the stroller and my constant, inconsolable crying.

Being a little girl, I could not find a verbal expression of what had happened to me. I did not yet know the word 'betrayal'. I felt like I had been pushed into a deep, terrifying abyss, at the bottom of which, swarming and moving around, struggling to survive, were children such as myself, who were different from other children, who were invalids.

The Distribution of Gifts and my Mother's Visit

Two weeks passed as one long nightmare; days were dull and similar to each other. I hoped in my naïveté that I would be taken home, but that is how the man lives, because he does not know what his future is.

Two weeks later, the second building was opened in the orphanage, and we children were divided. Those in bad physical condition who never left bed, and those with mental problems, stayed where they were, and the others, including me, were transferred to the new building. Once again, I was introduced to a new settlement: a grey, oblong room, with the two rows of beds like in a soldiers' barracks, with five windows and a small stove.

My bunk was behind the stove. At night I looked at its fire, cried quietly and panicked because of the open windows. In our house, the windows were always covered at night by shutters, for the sake of safety and protection against intruders.

Three days after our settlement, after they woke us up in the morning and I was already sitting in my stroller, the teacher came in with two big boxes and said, "Girls, I brought you presents. Now I am going to give each of you a gift, but if someone does not behave well, I will take back the gift. Well, should we start?"

She put one box on the floor and started pulling ribbons and combs from another box. After handing out ribbons and combs to the girls standing first in line, she bent down to the box on the floor and began to sort through the items in it. She fished a little doll out of the pile of wrapping paper and handed it to me. I made a displeased face — I never liked dolls, and I did not play with them at home.

"Why are you so unhappy?" she said, surprised.

"I would like to have a ribbon." I found courage to say this.

"What are you going to do with the ribbon? Will you put it around your ears?" She frowned at me, pointing at my bald head. She put the doll in my stroller and left the room.

The girls were trying on bright ribbons and playing with large combs, which were intended for long hair. I was sitting in my stroller with the undesirable doll on my knees, and I envied their gifts and their hair.

There was nothing good about this doll — she had a white dress covered with tiny red flowers, a rough-painted face and her head was painted brown, indicating hair. I did not regret it a bit when in one hour she disappeared; I think one of the nannies took her home for her daughter.

Then two days later, we received blankets of poison-green color; they were also presented as gifts. In the 'dead hour', so they called the time of siesta, these blankets were hanging on the backs of our beds, and I, unable to sleep during the day, looked at them until I felt pain in my eyes.

***

One morning, I looked through the window and saw snow on the roof of the building facing our building. Winter came. The snow on the roof was so fluffy, like it was in my home courtyard.

It was a mild winter day. After lunch, children who were able to walk and who had warm clothes ran outside, and I was sitting in the hallway in front of the window, looking at the closed gate of the orphanage and dreaming that my parents would come to me, bringing my little black coat and white hat, and my father would carry me to the station.

After three or four days, my mother came, and I begged her to take me outside. She made excuses, saying that I had nothing warm to wear; all my winter clothes were at home. But I was supported by the girls, telling her to wrap her daughter in a blanket. Sitting with my mother outside, I was at first afraid to ask when I would be taken home. But then I dared to ask.

"We'll take you home when your father and I come here together. Alone I cannot carry you to the station," my mother answered guiltily. She looked ashamed and turned her eyes away from me. Finally, I was convinced that I had been consigned there for a long time.

After my mother's visit, I came down with a temperature, and in the morning, I had a pink rash all over my body. The chief physician thought it was chicken pox and was about to send me to the infirmary, but I said I'd had chicken pox at home.

"Aha, then it must be a nervous reaction," the chief physician concluded indifferently; then she left.

***

After my mother's visit, I began to wither and melt like I was made of snow. The nannies did not put me in my stroller any more; they spoon-fed me in bed, but I ate almost nothing.

Probably because of the expansion of the orphanage, new employees were recruited. New nannies came, and among them was Anna Stepanovna Livshina, the sister of our chief nurse; she was hired because of this kinship.

When Anna Stepanovna saw me, she asked me my name. I gave her my name, but she pretended she did not understand it. She asked my name again, then again; she did it about ten times. I sensed she understood me perfectly — she just tried to dominate and confuse me. She wanted me to be afraid of her.

Anna Stepanovna started her night shift by sending everyone to bed; she did not let anyone sit even quietly. During her night shift, the children hid in fear under the blankets, covering their heads. She walked from one room to the other, trying to listen attentively for anyone who was moving. Most of her rude shouts fell to my lot because of my hyperkinesia (uncontrolled movements of arms and legs); I could not lie still. And when this sadistic woman heard me moving in bed, she would immediately scream with her sonorous voice, "Cheremnova! What are you doing under the covers?"

With fear, I would shrink, and tears would come to my eyes. Sometimes I had a strong need to go to the toilet, but had to endure and wait for the official hours, between eleven in the evening and midnight, when the nannies started lifting everyone and offering to 'go to the pot'. If only someone could hear how I persuaded myself to endure until the official hours. Sometimes, I would fall asleep before the official hours assigned for the procedure to 'go to the pot', and then I would wake up after midnight when the official procedure was over. I suffered tremendously, because it was not possible for me to empty my bladder. By which pain scales can the suffering of a sick child be measured? Why should a child lie with a full bladder? Is it really difficult to put a child on the potty when needed but not on command?

To be fair, the chief nurse was a completely normal and kind woman. But her sister, this Anna Stepanovna, turned out to be a refined inquisitor. Why did she become a nanny? Such nannies only damage the psyche of children.

Anna Stepanovna stuck in my memory for many years. Four decades later, I wrote a fairy tale: 'A Puppy Walking in Autumn'. One of its characters was a nasty cleaning lady who ruthlessly chased the helpless puppy with a mop. Of course, the name of this lady was Anna Stepanovna. In my story, she was easily brought to her senses and reminded that her job was to wash the floor, but not to chase the puppy. But there was no one in the orphanage who would restrain the real Anna Stepanovna.

I Wish to Die...

The teachers requested that in spite of my apathy, the nannies should dress me every morning and put me in my stroller to arouse any interest in life. But sitting in the stroller, I felt the same as I did before — I was weak, indifferent, with my eyes half closed. I just quietly tried to force myself to die; I did not want any more to be in this alien world, forcibly imposed on me.

Very soon, naughty children turned all the nuts off my stroller, and it became impossible to use it. There was an extra bed in the playroom; the nannies started bringing me to this bed. They would lay me down and forget about my existence. And I was happy about it; I did not need anyone's attention, because I decided to leave this cold, hungry, filthy, vile and degrading place. And I knew the only way I could escape from this place was by dying.

The buildings in which we lived would be better to call constructions. Before they established the orphanage for sick children, there was a forestry school inside these constructions. It consisted of two wooden barracks with stoves heating them. Each room had a stove that was heated during the day by a worker. At night, the stoves were supposed to be tended by the night nannies, but they neglected to do this, so by midnight the stoves in all rooms were barely warm, and our blankets, which were shabby and not thicker than sheets, did not help — we were dreadfully cold.

But the worst and most shameful of all was that there was no bathroom in our barracks, where children like me could be washed at least once a week. And I was a very clean person; when I lived at home my cousin Sergei and I were bathed every week. During my two months at the orphanage, I had never been washed. In the building where I was received upon entering the orphanage, the bathrooms were subsequently installed to wash the weakened children, but in our building, there was no place to put them. There was a long row of hand-washers with cold water; we could be washed only there. The children who were able to walk did not take a bath either, because not everyone had winter clothes.

This unsanitary condition had its effect immediately — everyone in the ward had scabies. To me, it was a real torture — mostly I wanted to scratch my back — the spine and the scapula — but with my paralyzed hands they were out of reach. Imagine that your skin itches and you cannot scratch it.

To add to my troubles, I was the smallest in the orphanage, and there were no clothes of my size, and they put on me whatever was found. They could dress me in a garment of enormous size, putting it on me from any side. I could wear it through the neckline, or the armhole, or any opening beneath — I could pass through any opening, I was so small.

To this day, I still have nausea when my memory brings me episodes of my experience with farina porridge. The cooks were too lazy to stir farina wheat during the cooking, and the result of their carelessness was farina porridge with lumps. I hated those lumps — they would put a spoon of lumps into my mouth, and I could do nothing about it. I was not strong enough to chew these lumps. I also found them disgusting, and had the urge to vomit. I could not spit them out — if I did it, the nannies would immediately start screaming at me, "Why are you spitting out your porridge? If you don't want to eat, just say so!"

Dealing with the evil Anna Stepanovna Livshina was especially strenuous. Then I developed a strategy. When I was being fed, they put a towel on my chest, so I would not spill the food on my clothes, and I managed to spit out farina lumps in that towel. So I was able to eat some liquid porridge and to avoid the screaming of these nannies. But then, when they tossed the towel, the lumps came out, and they screamed at me anyway.

I was horrified to see how the nanny on duty was eating this lumpy porridge without any signs of displeasure; I saw her jawbone movements were in agreement with her appetite. What can I say? A healthy country woman, who became hungry during the day, she could eat anything. And I, unable to cope with farina porridge, was starving at night; it seemed that my stomach was glued to my spine. There was nothing inside me; I was like an empty sack.

Then I learned to hide pieces of bread in the hem of my immense dress and eat them at night. We had nannies who were handing out the rest of the bread to the children who wanted it, but there were others who would throw all leftovers indiscriminately inside the bucket and hand them to the pigs.

And these nannies fed me differently. One nanny would wait until the food cooled a little bit, then she would carefully bring the spoon to my mouth, waiting for me to swallow the food, and she would not spill a drop. But Anna Stepanovna would put a bowl of soup on the nightstand and start feeding me with it, shoving spoon after spoon into my mouth, not paying attention to the fact that the soup was extremely hot. And I could cry, saying that my lips were on fire and it hurt. She would say, "It's okay! It will warm your belly!"

After such barbaric feeding, pieces of food were found everywhere — on my clothes, on my bed linen, on the floor. During her shift, I always refused to eat, and I just wanted to die.

What Happened to my Family?

Nothing goes unpunished. By getting rid of a sick child, my parents had untied a knot holding my family together. My father felt liberated from all his duties; he started to live anew, from a clean slate. And while I was crying in the orphanage, another tragedy was being played out in my own home. The fact that I was placed in the orphanage did not bring my parents the relief they expected. My father went on vacation to the village where he was born; there he met a crippled limp girl and she became his new wife. Perhaps he expected she would worship him for choosing her in spite of her physical condition, that she would respect him and obey him unconditionally. Or perhaps he just became tired of the complicated and tedious relationship with my mother. It is also possible that my father really fell in love. Going forward, my father's second marriage would prove to be more successful than his first marriage: he would have a third (after me and my little sister Olga) daughter; they would get a separate apartment and live happily.

When my mother had learned of my father's decision to leave the family, she took little Olga and moved to her sister's. Thus, our comfortable room in the house of my grandparents became empty.

When I became an adult, I wondered why none of my family had prevented me from being institutionalized. My grandmother? My grandfather? My aunt Tamara, after whom I was named and whom I gently called nanny? My aunt Valentina?

I was not related by blood to my grandmother. My grandfather, when he was young, came from the village close to Novokuznetsk. He married a young woman, and then one day, the son from his previous marriage came to him from nowhere. This son from my grandfather's first marriage was my father. And after a while, he brought his pregnant girlfriend — this was my mother. My grandmother did not dare to contradict her husband; she gave her stepson and his wife the room of her own daughters. I can imagine how hard it was for her, that concession! It was especially difficult for her, considering that one of her own daughters, the one-legged Tamara, continued to live in the house of her parents, just on the other side of our room wall.

However, my grandmother became attached to me, and I was attached to her too. Eventually I learned that my grandmother and I were not related by blood, but I still considered myself to be her granddaughter. As a little girl raised at home, I had been loved and pampered by my parents; I felt that everything at home was fine, harmonious, and just wonderful.

Like any child, I loved my family, and I never questioned if they loved each other. Sometimes I saw my mother and father arguing, but my grandfather always took the side of his daughter-in-law. I watched them from my bell tower, and I did not understand much. And I had no idea that these people who lived under the same roof hated each other for so long.

Then I recalled that it was very often when my father came home from his work at night in a special mood. He would lie in his bed and turn to the wall, and my mother would always say that Father was tired. Maybe he was not just tired; maybe he was already planning his new life and trying to figure out how to start it? After he had married the lame woman, he wanted to bring her to his parents' house, but my grandmother objected to her stepson. "If you hadn't done this behind our backs, and so vilely, I would let you in. But you left without telling anyone that you were going to divorce. So, go and live wherever you want."

And they went to live with one of my father's half-sisters, and lived there until they got an apartment. So, after I was sent to the orphanage, the family was smashed to smithereens, and the fragments flew in all directions. In a way, justice was done, but it did not make me happy; I hurt.

I would never go back to my house, and I would never see my little garden… Every year the winter would cover the road to my home with snow, the snow drifts would grow, and then the spring streams would cover up the treacherous steps of my father when he carried me out of the gate to throw me in the orphanage.

The New Year's Eve at the Orphanage

It was the New Year of 1963, my first New Year's Eve out of the house. It was the first time in my life when I observed how children dressed in masquerade costumes, how girls performed the snowflake dance and how Santa Claus and teachers distributed presents. At night, I dreamed that next year I would wear a masquerade costume too.

At that time my parents did not visit me: they were too busy discussing their affairs. Perhaps because they left me alone, my weakened body became a little bit stronger; gradually I became more animated and more interested in life. Nothing was more disappointing than my mother's visits, with her eyes not looking at me and leaving without a kiss goodbye.

There was another pleasant change: the nannies became tired of waking us up at night, and now the girls could get up at any time to go to the toilet, and I could ask them for help instead of waiting until midnight. Only the evil Anna Stepanovna remained faithful to the ritual. Besides the harsh treatment of the children, she had a nasty habit of making gossip about employees. And when it came to decide who was on duty with whom on the night shift, the nannies were bitterly sighing if they had to work with her, and behind her back she was called only by her last name.

All nannies, except Anna Stepanovna, felt themselves at home at the orphanage. Not only did they allow us to sit in the hallway after the lights were out, and give us the rest of the bread, but they also dined in our room, keeping an eye on us. And they would not object when I asked them if I could join the girls in their beds. I remember they would move three bunks together, and we all slept together; in this case it was not so cold, and we did not feel so lonely.

There were also 'bosses' among the girls, those who liked to dominate. For example, Nadia, the one with the 'sheep haircut', liked to command. One night I had to go to the toilet. I started waking up Nina, who always helped me. Probably my voice woke up Nadia.

"Why are you yelling? You woke up the entire ward! Don't you dare wake me up again!" she barked at me and scared me to death.

After that, I had to lie down and endure my desire to go to the toilet until one of the girls got up for her own needs and she would help me out.

Spring Came and I Learned the Word 'Coffin'

Spring showed its rites more and more. It was my first spring in the orphanage, where so much grief and so many human vices gathered together. Here useless, sick children were thrown into the abyss, and those who had thrown them into it distanced themselves.

We even had our own cemetery; it was separate from the village cemetery, a tiny one for crippled children, as if after their death they would infect the others.

The higher death rate was not in our building, but in the other building — children did not survive to be older than ten years old. What was the difference between these two buildings? In our building there were children who possessed some intelligence and had the ability to explain themselves. The other building was called 'the building for the feeble' or 'the weak quarter', where the children who were placed there were unable to move independently and with serious mental retardation: simply speaking, idiots who were bound to bed. You can imagine what kind of care they received in the orphanage! And they were never brought outside or taken for promenades; I even do not know how many children lived there.

In our building, many children survived with varied success to the age of eighteen; after that they were sent to adult homes for the disabled or to psycho-neurological boarding schools, the so-called PNBS. The first batch of grown-up children from our unit was taken in six months after I had arrived in the orphanage.

I learned the word 'coffin' very early. New coffins were brought in an open truck and loaded into the morgue — our orphanage had its own morgue — and this usually happened in the presence of children walking around. The coffins with the dead were taken by a horse carriage behind the railway line to the deserted woodland — the most isolated orphanage cemetery.

Trains ran very close to the orphanage, and in the brightly lit windows of the passenger train cars it was possible to recognize passengers — I see a man, now I see a woman, now I see a boy, I see a girl. Alas, these trains with their rattling wheels reminded me of my home for too long…

In Summer on the Porch

I did not notice when summer came. It warmed up, and the grass and trees became green. They started taking me outside. At first, they would put a blanket on the grass in the garden and bring those children who could not walk, but soon mischievous children broke the fence and trampled the grass. At that time, some children had their own strollers; other children could sit on the bench. Just for me, they put a blanket on the porch.

In our building there were two exits to the street; one of them was through the spacious hall with the stone porch. They used to bring me to this porch, where they placed me on a thin cotton blanket. It was all right, but one terrible circumstance forced me to slide from the blanket onto the cold stone steps of the porch.

The problem was that the violent child Victor was locked inside the hall; he would pound on the door leading to the porch. And as I lay on the blanket, very close to the door, which shook under Victor's blows, I was terrified that the door would fall off the shattered hinges and crush me. But much as I tried to persuade the nannies not to put my blanket close to the door, they stubbornly put it on this very spot, assuring me that the door was sturdy and Victor could not tear it down. They said if they put me far away from the door, on the edge of the porch, I could fall off and kill myself.

What an iron logic these nannies had! It never occurred to them that all my bones were cold because I was placed on this porch, and that later I would get diseases which had developed in my early childhood, particularly on this very porch.

Probably none of them could imagine that this pathetic freak, who constantly experienced seizures and convulsions, would live to mature. And nobody could believe that this poor thing would grow up and recover, would get rid of the wrong diagnosis of 'oligophrenia', would write books for children and journalistic articles for adults and would become a member of the Union of Writers of Russia… What they had in front of them was a small cripple who desperately tried to survive the unjust cruelty of adults.

After dinner, the children walked outside for another hour, and I was already lying on my bed staring at the opposite wall, which was becoming sinister red from the setting sun. I would close my eyes and felt an incredible nostalgia and longing. At times like that, I tried to recall the smallest details of my room at home, my yard, my bed, all my old world, where there was no place for my exhausting longing…

I Want to Have Bird Cherries!

In my bitter memories, I see the road between two rows of wooden houses on the outskirts of Stalinsk, which would be renamed Novokuznetsk again. And the smoke is coming from the chimney of one of them; this is the little house I was born in.

Our house was not a new building — after my grandparents got married, they bought it, and it was ready to live in. Our house was nice and comfortable with a yard, a vegetable garden and a flower garden. This was my childhood environment, and as a child I liked to laugh, and I was playful, naughty, and capricious like all children. The only difference from other children was that I had limited access to the world. At that time, I did not think much about how a handicapped child would perceive the clutches of physical constraint and how she should cope with those constraints. I did not wonder whether it was convenient for the child to live such a limited life. I did not think about what exactly the little disabled person was in our society.

I will try to recall some details of those years — probably the happiest years of my life, because later my life will turn into years of war for a place in the sun, for the right to be HUMAN with all the consequences, which include its linguistic meaning and its significance referring to God's plan. It was the struggle for my legitimate rights, which were diminished by human indifference.

***

So, there is a dusty unpaved road along the wooden houses. The wooden logs of some houses have not turned dark with age — they have been constructed recently. One of the houses with a low picket fence displays a small garden whose greens and luxurious dahlia flowers hang in abundance through the fence and bow to the road.

I stand inside the garden, looking at broken flowers. I know I would be scolded if they find me here. I try to bend over and pick up the broken dahlias, but my walker will not let me do it. I look with hate at the narrow gate of the garden that I triumphed through just three minutes ago. I want to try to sneak out, even though all the members of my family would find out, as I am the only one who could break the flowers; somehow, I have to get out of it, but how…

"Tomka, who helped you to get here?" My father is shaking his head. "Look, you broke the flowers again, and your mother took such great care of them. And how did you get in?"

"You showed me how to get here," I mumble back, gasping and preparing to cry.

"When did I show you how to get here?" My father is so surprised, he stops being angry at me.

"When my mother went to weed strawberries," I say and I see the astonishment on my father's face.

On that day, my father developed photographs, and I was hanging around him and getting in his way. Once I shook the table, then I pushed his hand. Then because of my intrusion in the process of developing photographs, two or three of them became blurry. My father lost his patience; he dragged me to my mother who was working in the garden. This was how I learned how to squeeze with my walker through the narrow gate to the garden.

Being very clever, I did it on my own by lifting one side of my walker, and I gradually squeezed myself through the unfortunate gate of the garden. I got stuck for a moment, but when I shook my walker, I got out. It was intended to make the gate to the garden narrow, keeping in mind that I could not get through it without help.

My father angrily grabbed my walker from behind me and dragged it out along with me, while I was screaming loudly. "I want bird cherries!" I screamed.

"I'm going to get you bird cherries, but don't yell," my father promised, feeling uncomfortable under curious gazes of passers-by.

"I want to get them myself!" I started shrieking like a little pig.

Then I felt that my walker, together with me, slid inexorably into my father's hands and he continued walking in the direction of our house, then I gave up.

"Father, I will not do this again; let me walk!" My walker went straight to the ground.

"Toma, tell me, why do you think I put this gate in the garden?"

"So that Sergei and I will not climb," I said, bringing to my defense my cousin, a year and a half younger than me.

"Well, if Sergei comes to the garden alone, he won't break the flowers, but you'll ruin everything with your walker. Do you understand?" my father said.

I humbly nod my head.

"Walk in the yard; I don't want to see you again in the flower garden or in the vegetable garden. If I ever see you climbing up again, I'll put you in the stroller." My father set the condition.

In return, I snorted, but I didn't protest — sitting in my stroller was not a lot of fun; I could not move in it alone.

Everyone in our district knew that there was a sick child growing up in our house, although the definition of 'sick child' did not fit my personality — I was flamboyant and active. The other thing was that with all my exuberance and activity, I could not get up and walk, I could not sit down on my own and I did not have complete control over my hands. However, thanks to my walker, which managed better than my own body, I easily mastered space. And I sensed my walker as something that was inseparable from me, but not as a clumsy, bulky prop. There was a problem with food too: I managed to eat only hard food, by bringing a piece of food to my mouth, but I could not eat with a spoon or drink from a cup — I would drop them or I would splatter the liquid.

Now, as a mature adult, I see my childhood from a different perspective, and I understand how difficult it was for my parents to have a sick child at that time known for its archaic approach towards the handicapped. Even today a disabled child is often perceived by Russian society as some deficient and incorrectly programmed being. But I think Mother Nature is more intelligent than man. And if a disabled child is born, it means that Nature wants to send an important message to humanity.

In that distant Soviet era — the second half of the 50s, the six happy years starting from my birthday were the happiest period of my life. But this period ended, thanks to the two letters CP (cerebral palsy), which were nailed into my biography and stigmatized me as a child with cerebral palsy.

In my medical dossier there was a diagnosis which was considered an interminable 'disorder of CNS' (central nervous system). Now I know that 'disorder of CNS' is a very vague diagnosis, not specifying what is affected in the central nervous system. However, it was sufficient to permanently isolate the child from the wider world and place them in a specialized closed institution.

For what kind of offence, I was destined to carry my cross? Only in half a century would I able to answer this question. Nothing is given to a person without reason; each individual destiny has its own definition, its own purpose and its own logic.

The Little Pig Borka

So my father returned to the house, leaving me in the yard, and I took a breath — the broken dahlias got away with it again. And I opened my walker, trying to decide what I should do next.

The yard was empty, only outside the gate I could hear the laughing of girls, playing on the side of the road where the puddles had not yet dried up after the rain. I was observing them with envy; I also wanted to muddy my feet down to my knees and run down the wet road, squishing loudly with the soles of my sandals. At times like that I felt emptiness inside, but of course I did not realize that I would never be able to run on my feet along the road and slap my feet in the mud. I did not even wonder why I could not walk without my walker like everyone else. Envious of the girls, I attached myself to my walker and I sadly staggered to the door of the house. But I stopped by the bench when I saw a rod lying on the ground. I reached out to pick it up, though I did not know why I needed it and if I needed it at all.

At that time, the little pig, Borka, screeched in his little compartment. I waited for my grandmother to come out for this squeal, then with a rod in my teeth, I went to Borka. The little pig heard someone coming to his door; he grunted happily and stuck his snout into the slot of the door. But when he realized it was not the person who usually feeds him, that is my mother or grandmother, he hid in his compartment. I wanted Borka to come out, so I taunted him with the rod.

At first, Borka did not pay attention, but then he could not take it any longer, so he grabbed the rod with his teeth. I got so involved playing with Borka that I did not even notice that my cousin Sergei had joined me.

"Tom, Tom…" he whined, "I want to play with Borka too."

"Find your own rod and then play," I advised, importantly.

Sergei found a proper rod and joined me. We made the little pig so excited that he stood on his hind legs and showed us his snout through the slot of the door.

But then Borka ran out of patience, and he made a sharp maneuver and took the rod from Sergei and dragged it to his place. Sergei became upset.

Then I said, "Let's feed Borka; our grandmother will be happy about this."

"What are we going to give him?" Sergei stared at me.

I said, "Today I saw how Grandmother prepared food for Borka. She cooked soup with cabbage leaves for him. Some cabbage leaves are still in the shop. Can you run there and bring some cabbage leaves here? You see I can't do it."

Sergei ran off to the shop and came back with two huge cabbage leaves. We offered them to the little pig through the slot of the door and stood by, listening to how he chewed them cheerfully behind the door. After he had eaten all the leaves, Borka again stuck his snout into the slot of the door, hoping to get more cabbage leaves.

Sergei brought two more cabbage leaves, and then he brought another one, and so on, until my grandmother went outside. We did not even hear her coming out. We only looked back when we heard she was crying.

"What kind of children are you? You bring only grief! What have you done? There is no cross on you!" my grandmother lamented.

"What is going on, Klava?" my grandfather came outside and asked.

"The children must have killed Borka," my grandmother cried loudly.

"What are you talking about? Killed how?" My grandfather did not understand.

"They fed him all the leaves which were in the shop!" my grandmother cried.

My grandfather approached the shed and opened the door. Borka was lying by the doorstep. My grandfather touched him with his shoe sock. Borka opened his eyes lazily and looked at my grandfather as if he hoped to get from him more cabbage leaves, then he grunted leisurely.

"It's okay; he just ate a little bit too much," my grandfather concluded and closed the door.

My grandmother was not a stingy woman, but in those years a little pig was so expensive — like he was made of gold. Ordinary people had fled from the crumbling villages to the construction sites of the century, as there were many in Kuzbass, and where they were gladly taken as cheap labor. Village youths were especially welcome; they created families and built houses on the outskirts of the future industrial city. There were many houses like ours; long streets grew, and in such a spontaneous way that a semi-urban, semi-rustic 'city-garden' had been emerging instead of that which was planned in the thirties.

In this 'city-garden', my grandfather and grandmother as well as my father and mother, who were all descendants of the villages of the Novosibirsk region, had met. With bitter irony, I am thinking of writers who wrote books on the construction of the century, but kept silent about the details.

For example, women were loaded with bricks, like sturdy camels. For this purpose, there was a special device to carry bricks — a wooden board with straps, which was attached to the back like a rucksack, and bricks were placed on the wooden board from the waist to the back of the head. It was the norm; the woman carried the weight to the destination, and in Soviet literature it was presented as heroism. And where are the writers who so profited from their now-forgotten books? I wonder if they have a guilty conscience for not noticing human destinies ruined beneath their feet.

What is most outrageous is that women worked under such conditions and with such pressure during their pregnancy. In the early stages, when they did not know they were pregnant, and in the later stages, when they did know, they refused to do easier, less paid work, and they even hid their pregnancy to make some money doing the dangerous job.

I suppose that this behavior during pregnancy is one of the reasons for CP. Carrying heavy things during pregnancy may cause the intrauterine asphyxiation of the fetus; if oxygen is cut off even for a second, it can damage the brain. This is sufficient to cause cerebral palsy, even if the pregnancy continues without problems.

***

But let me go back to the little pig. My grandfather closed the door of the shed of Borka, then he put his palms on our heads and smiled. Our children's faces probably expressed a great surprise. I had never seen my grandmother crying like that, so I wanted to come to her and console her. But I was not able to do this because my father showed up; he sternly disconnected me from my walker and put me in my stroller. That meant my daytime adventures were over for the day. I was sitting in my stroller, resentful at everyone, grinding my discontent in my little head.

And then when I visualize my grandmother, crying so desperately for the pig we had supposedly killed, I think — did she cry that way for me when I was taken to the orphanage?

The Little Dominos

A healthy child, even if they do not have toys, immediately finds activity and entertainment in the yard. They can squat and dig in the sand, they can construct something using chips of wood and rags, or they can play mother-and-daughter. I could not do this; I could stand or move, supporting my body with my walker, but I could not bend over. Sometimes they would bring my toys outside, so I could play, but my uncoordinated movements would get in the way.

One day they gave me the little dominos created for children, and my mother, after she dressed me up to go outside, let me take this game with me. Outside, I made my way to the bench, carefully pulling the box out of my pocket; I was going to put it on the bench and open it. But as soon as I started transporting the dominos to the bench, my hand twitched, and all the pieces fell on the ground. I cried loudly, "Mother, I've spilled the dominos!"

My mother came outside to pick up the dominos, and when the dominos were assembled, the box was missing three pieces. After the second fall of the dominos and picking up its pieces, more than half the pieces were missing. Just during ten or fifteen minutes, I lost my beautiful dominos.

"Nemka, don't cry! I have to clean the house; play with something else." My mother became tired looking for dominos, and she went inside.

Playing dominos has never happened since.

Then there were no toys 'suitable for my hands', and I did not like dolls, because I could not play with them using my hands, except by carrying a doll by one leg.

Most of all I liked to play with my cousin Sergei. He would turn two chairs upside down in front of my stroller — that was the bus cabin. I would take a grocery bag, put it around my neck, and announce stops, playing the bus assistant who sells tickets and announces stops. Sergei usually played the bus driver, but sometimes he would play the role of a passenger to whom I was supposed to sell a ticket. After we finished our game, my grandmother had to pick up our tickets — pieces of the torn newspaper which were all over the rooms.

***

The medical doctors behaved strangely in those years. They were kind enough to let disabled children live, but they did not do anything for them. A disabled child is not a pet, but a human being. And in no way can it be considered that if she is fed, washed and dressed, the mission of care and education has been accomplished.

The doctors somehow assured my parents that my paralysis would go away when I became twelve years old, and my parents believed it. The magic phrase 'paralysis will go away by itself when she is twelve years old' was repeated all the time; finally, this formula put my parents to sleep. And instead of resisting my illness by all means and keeping it from progressing, my parents did nothing. And the disease took its toll: in five years, the coordination of my movements discernibly deteriorated. If in the beginning my parents were convinced that when I grew, I would be able to hold a spoon in my hand, or maybe a fork, then five years later their hope in my good progress had evaporated.

The second appointment with the doctors with the following examination ended with the diagnosis of 'irreversible damage of the CNS' (central nervous system), with the explanation 'she will never recover'. And I was put in a specialized home because my parents believed I would never recover.

But my parents should have overcome their false shame about having a child who was different from other children, the child who needed special care and medical attention. Actually, what was needed was not so much medical care but everyday ingenuity. Would it have been difficult for my parents to put my grandfather's fur coat on the floor, to place me on it and leave me alone? Sooner or later, I would have learned how to sit down on my own, and then maybe I would try to stand up. I liked movement so much!

If they had only understood what a terrible dependence on others they put on me, with their indifference! Paralyzed people understand what it is like to realize every second that your body cannot do anything, when your spirit ignores it and demands a full life on its own. One could find this practice — putting me on the floor over the fur coat and leaving me alone — cruel. But did they have compassion for me when they put me in the orphanage? By the way, this was where I learned how to sit up on my own, when I was abandoned.

My mother or my grandmother could have given me a massage in the evening, if someone had taught them how to do it; it does not require great skill. Massage and coaching courses for parents of disabled children are now widely available. But they did not think about it; they were waiting for a miracle.

Walking On My Own

It was strictly forbidden for me to go outside the gate, using my walker, because the road was busy with the traffic — trucks were running along all day long. However, I broke the ban as soon as I had learned how to lift the hook and open the gate.

It was five p.m. My grandfather came home from his work early. I saw him when he was approaching the gate.

"Oh, Grandpa's here!" I screamed happily.

My grandfather opened the gate, walked into the yard and caught me flying towards him with my walker.

"Oh, Tomka, when will you be able to run without your walker?" He sighed bitterly.

"Grandpa, let's go for a walk to the road," I screamed enthusiastically with a high-pitched voice.

"Let me rest for a while, and we'll go for a walk," my grandfather promised.

He went inside the house, and I stayed by the gate.

There was a group of teenagers; the boys were pulling a rope along the road, trying to build something. I observed them, while they were close to our gate, then they moved further. I turned my head, and my gaze caught the hook on the gate. Before this, I could not reach the hook, though I wanted so much to open the gate when I saw children running along the road; some were even younger than me. I looked around to make sure that my grandmother could not see me through the window. I reached for the hook. And I could not believe my eyes — my fingers were able to reach the hook! I was full of joy and pride. First of all, I realized I had grown a great deal, and then I recalled something… One day when I was staring at passers-by, I imagined that if I ran down the road without my walker, I would definitely learn how to run exclusively on my own feet.

I lifted the hook, opened the gate, and flew out (as far as the verb 'fly' applies to my movement with my walker) to the road. However, there was a pit by the side of the road, and I was tightly stuck in it. Children playing on the road immediately came closer and surrounded me. They were looking at me with curiosity, and I was looking at them with curiosity too. Probably it was the first time I felt terribly clumsy. But the children were looking at me with kindness, and some even tried to cheer me up; probably they saw in me their accomplice — I used to help them to tease our mutual enemy, our neighbor, the redheaded boy Valera. I shouted louder than anyone else, calling this unfortunate boy 'Valera-cholera'!

It was interesting to be outside the gate, but I cautiously looked around to see if a car was approaching. I intended to carry on my plan — to run over the road. I tried to pull my walker out, but it was stuck in the pit. And then I heard the sound of an explosion; it came from the mysterious construction of the teenagers, which continued at a distance, and then a scorched rope flew over my head. Before I recognized what it was, my grandfather grabbed me with my walker from the pit.

"Tomka, who helped you open the gate?" my grandfather asked.

"Oh, Grandpa! Now I can open it myself!" I bragged.

"Who taught you to open it?" my grandfather asked.

"I won't do it again," I whined.

"Let it be; I forgive you," my grandfather said, holding me close to his chest.

"Grandpa, let's tell everyone that I grew up!" I exclaimed.

"We will certainly tell everyone that my granddaughter has grown up," my grandfather said and carried me to the house.

My Grandfather's Apricots

I do not know why my grandfather loved me so much. One autumn, my parents harvested potatoes, digging them from the ground. They decided to dry them in the attic before they would be stored underground. After they finished their work with the potatoes, my grandfather took Sergei to the attic to show him the terrain from above. Sergei climbed the stairs, and my grandfather guarded him in order to keep him from falling. When they came down, I screamed loudly, "Father, I want to go to the attic too!"

"I'm not going to take you anywhere! Don't you see I'm tired?" my father scolded.

"Nemka! Shame on you! Sergei doesn't have a father, so your grandfather wants to teach him how to walk the stairs." My mother tried to rebuke me.

My grandfather came to my stroller, took me out, put me on his shoulders and climbed up the stairs. I could feel his hand trembling with tension. Everybody was looking at this extravagant performance. When my grandfather reached the attic with me on his shoulders, he put me on the log, sat next to me and lit his cigarette. I tried to stretch out my neck to see the city being built on the other side of the Gorbunicha River which passed our garden and went far, far beyond the water tower.

If I had known that the time would come very soon when I would be completely alone, without my mother and father, and without my grandparents… I would have pressed myself to my grandfather's breast, to absorb this human being so dear to me, to remember him forever…

***

There was another flamboyant thing — it tells of my grandfather's love for me. One day he went to a sanatorium. He came back with a suitcase full of apricots. Presenting each member of our family with one apricot, he came to my stroller, opened his suitcase and gently said, "Eat, my granddaughter! It's all for you!"

All became speechless with surprise.

"Misha! She won't be able to eat them all; she could mash them and cover herself with apricots." My grandmother became indignant.

"Shut up," said my grandfather. "Let her eat as much as she wants and we'll finish after her."

I was so happy. I climbed into the suitcase, sat with my little body over the apricots, and as my grandmother warned, I was smeared with apricots from head to foot. After a while they took me out of the suitcase and carried me for a bath, and they ate bruised apricots without me.

Dragonflies and the Taste of Rain

I was named Tamara in honor of my nanny, Sergei's mother. Perhaps it is bad luck to be named after a woman who had only one leg? There is a belief that one should not give a newborn child the name of a sick, handicapped relative or one who died tragically — it could bring a curse to the infant. And no matter how well they govern our destinies *there above*, no matter how wisely they put a special idea into each human being, it is the fact that my destiny is impregnated with too much bitterness.

Probably God makes mistakes too. Or maybe he deliberately gave such a generous portion of bitterness to an innocent child to see how he could justify the priceless gift whose name is Life...

***

I was attracted to everything new. Like all children, I was anxious to discover this magical, colorful world. One day, after pouring rain, my nanny brought me a big, shimmering, green dragonfly.

"Tomka, look what I caught!"

"Where did you get such a beauty?" I was enchanted by the dragonfly.

"There are a lot of them flying after the rain," my nanny said.

"Give it to me!" I told her.

"No. If you harm her, she will die. It's better to let her go." And she left with the dragonfly in her hand.

And after that, every morning after I woke up, I listened for rain and wished it would come.

The long-awaited rain started in a week. It was a weekend day; Sergei and I were bathed, the women had time to do the laundry, and after five o'clock in the evening they planned to go to the bathhouse. But after lunch, it rained with a thunderstorm, and everyone stayed home. I dragged my walker to the threshold, intending to open the door.

"Where are you going?" my mother asked me, surprised. "Don't you see it's raining?"

"Don't you know that there are beautiful dragonflies flying there now?" I said.

"What dragonflies?" my grandmother said.

"Tomochka, I will catch you a dragonfly," my nanny said, glancing out of her room.

"I want to see them flying. You've all seen them, only I haven't seen them," I said stubbornly.

"You will see them today. Just wait until the rain stops, let it get a little dry outside, and then you can see your dragonflies," my grandmother said agreeably.

"They will fly away then!" I continued to be stubborn.

"If you continue being stubborn, you're not going anywhere!" My father entered the kitchen.

"I'm going, and I'm going right now!" I said categorically.

"You are being stubborn; you are not going anywhere," said my father as he came to the door and closed the bolt which I could not reach.

I watched the massive bolt silently, and there were two sentiments in my soul: the resentment that I would never see beautiful dragonflies, and I would never admire the way they fly after the rain; and the understanding that it was raining outside. Beautiful dragonflies won. I pressed my forehead on the door and cried. I cried and cried until my voice became hoarse, then my grandfather could not take it any more. He got up, went to the door, opened the bolt, and took me together with my walker and dragged me outside. But as soon as my grandfather let me go, I felt my walker falling down with me into the mud. My feet were soaked right away, so I tried to move my walker, but I could not; it stuck tightly.

The sun looked out; I saw big raindrops falling down, but I did not see any beautiful, magical dragonflies. I felt guilty and looked at my grandfather, and he looked at me with his understanding eyes; we both knew very well what awaited us at home. My grandfather carried me into the house. And here my memory conveniently concealed events, which were not very pleasant, and erased all details. I only remember my grandmother taking my wet shoes off silently, and there was so much harshness in her movements…

In the evening I had a fever; there was wheezing in my chest, so they had to apply mustard plasters on my back and chest. I have a vivid memory of my father carrying me around the room in his arms, and me crying and my understanding that I was crying not so much because of pain caused by hot mustard plasters, but from guilt.

But once, my parents completely satisfied my 'rain curiosity'. I remember myself sitting in the garden, covered with an umbrella, under a warm rain which is called 'mushroom rain', and the sun bursting through a cloud. An unforgettable experience! It went on through my whole life. You cannot imagine what it means for a sick child to experience such a beautiful rain…

Learning the World

At home, the window above my bed was slightly open, and I woke up in the mornings feeling a summer sunny day, or a day with rustles of rain, which would break into my room. And in the fall, it was a barely audible touch of autumn falling leaves. And in the winter, when the window was opened just a little bit, the frost chilled my cheeks and the magical ice patterns shone on the glass.

But I kept in my memory for a long time how my beautiful mother opened the morning shutters from the outside, and I admired her portrait framed by the window with the background of sunny space behind her. This bright memory cannot be erased; even betrayal is powerless — my mother's betrayal…

No matter how many times my mother humiliated me later — some of her humiliations would bring me a bewildered fright, for this woman was in the past my loving mother, and then she became filled with ignorant cruelty —adoring moments cannot be erased from my memory.

Sometimes in the orphanage at night, when unbearable bitterness came to my throat, I wanted to howl like a little wolf, but you could not even cry; even crying was too much of a luxury.

"No one is hurting her, and she is crying! It's difficult for everyone to be here, but no one is crying!" the nannies would say with anger.

And there was something monstrous about it, though now I understood that the nannies were tired and our suffering was infectious.

So, during the nights like that, I would remove the image of my beloved mother from my mind — the real mother, the one who did not betray me. And then involuntarily I would start wondering why my mother became so different.

***

I want to return to my distant childhood, where everything is so sunny, and there is still no misfortune. One should not think that I was a spoiled child; I was punished like any other child.

I was five years old. My parents already had two children. My sister Olga was born in January 1960, a healthy, calm child, not causing any problems. It was a pleasant afternoon in August. My mother was with Olga, having a promenade in the yard; I was there too. My sister fell asleep in my mother's arms; then my mother took her to the house to put her to bed, telling me to stay where I was and not to go anywhere.

Using my walker, I walked aimlessly around the yard for ten minutes, then I thought I should go inside too.

I was thinking: I climbed over the threshold myself, and I did it very well.

However, this time, I climbed up onto the earthen slope, covered with uneven wooden boards — this construction served as a porch. I safely passed the first room — we call it сени in Russian — an entryway which is located at the front entrance of the house. I opened the door to the house. I put the front wheels of my walker by the threshold, which was very high on the side of the entrance, and I grabbed the latch hanging on the side of the jamb. However, being focused on my physical maneuvers, I did not notice that I did not put my feet on the threshold. Pulling the latch with force to make my walker cross the threshold, I hung helplessly on the bar of my walker. The wheels rolled out from the threshold, and then in a full blow I fell down and slammed my little face over the threshold, feeling its hardness with all my senses.

At first, I did not feel any pain; my first thought was, if anyone should come and see that I knocked over my walker, I would be scolded. But when I raised my head and saw a puddle of blood on the threshold, I realized it was my own blood, and I cried loudly.

And then I cannot remember what happened next, and I do not know if my memory conveniently hides unpleasant moments, or if I lost consciousness. I remember myself in later episodes: I was lying in my grandparents' bed, and I heard my family members arguing loudly from the kitchen.

***

No one could imagine how far away I was flying in my dreams. In my dreams, which were certainly not dreams of a child, I would constantly experience someone's (certainly not mine!) terrible past in wartime.

Some people will not believe me; they could think I made it up to make my book more interesting. But I want to assure you, I did not invent this.

I do not remember when this dream started to haunt me. I think it was with me from the day I was born, and it was just when I grew up I started analyzing it. It was a dream of an adult person. In my dream I always ran away from a tank. Although I have never seen a tank in my life, I had it in my dream. It is a dream in which I am running through the house, and I am looking for a place where I could hide from a terrible tank gun barrel, and this gun barrel will find me any place I hide.

Another version of this dream is as follows: I am running through a field which is shell pocked, and the wheat on my right is burning, and on my left there is a railroad or some abyss. But any version of my dream ends up the same way; I am staring at the gun barrel. I feel like I am about to be shot… and I wake up.

And the strange thing is, when I woke up, a sort of protective shield was triggered; I was not afraid at all, and I knew very well that it would never happen in my life. I still ask myself this question: how come a little child had this nightmare? Well, if I had seen some movies about the war, they would influence my dreams. But we did not have a television at that time, and I had never been taken to the movies. Where did this dream come from? It is a mystery… Was it a premonition of my life? The premonition of that which would happen later?

The Hat

My sister Olga turned one; my mother was making her a bonnet for promenades outside. My mother did not have lace for the decoration, and she decided to disconnect the lace from my old little hat. The fabric of this hat was tattered, but the lace was still in good condition. I used to wear this hat all the time; it was very comfortable and had strips of ribbon which I tied up. In spite of my love for my little old hat, my mother decided to deconstruct it, and while I was crying, repeating that it was my hat, she took it apart.

Then she dressed me up to go outside and put the hat she just made on my head. The new hat was white in color; it was well designed and tied up with one button. I went outside, and three minutes later, my family members heard me crying. They all were puzzled and immediately ran from the house to the courtyard.

"Nemka, why are you crying?" My mother was bemused.

"My hat!" I screamed, choking in sobs.

My family members thought someone had taken my new hat from my head, but it turned out that as soon as I went outside, my new hat had fallen off and ended up on the ground.

The hat was found and put on my head. But this episode repeated, as if the new hat had a full freedom without strings, and it did not want to rest on an excessively mobile head! After three flights to the ground, the hat turned into a dirty rag. Then my family left me alone, and I had my promenades without a hat.

Papa Sasha

"Father, let's go to Aunt Valentina; you promised… Well, Papa Sasha, let's go…" I repeated this, every five minutes, reminding my father that he had promised to take me there. I can imagine my behavior was very annoying to my father.

"Didn't you hear what I said? I'll finish my study, then we'll go," my father answered.

There were just the two of us at home; the others had left the house to do some chores. My father was sitting on the logs, which were brought by my grandfather for some domestic purpose, immersed in his textbook — he was preparing for his evening classes. But because of me, who continued bothering him, I assume he did not understand anything in his textbook.

I was about to bring my nose to the open page of his textbook, whining, "When are we going to see Aunt Valentina?"

"Wait here, I'll take the book to the house, and we'll go to Aunt Valentina." My father had surrendered.

But I knew my father's character — when he did not feel like doing some things, he could get rid of them by many means. He went inside the house and did not come out. I waited for him, but when I realized my father's deception, I decided to go to Aunt Valentina by myself. I went to the gate, I pulled the latch, I went to the road and started thinking about which way I should take to go to the house of Aunt Valentina. Aunt Valentina was my father's stepsister on my grandmother's side; she lived in the beginning of the street; our house was located in the middle of the street.

I was afraid to go down the road. I knew if a car came, I had nowhere to turn. There was a trampled path by the fence, so I jumped there, using my walker and started running. Of course, it was not real running, but I wanted so much to imitate running and I acted as if I were running. I chased my walker down the path and tried to stomp my little sandals as loud as possible. I am sure I looked hilarious. I noticed our neighbors were looking at me and smiling. I had already passed three houses when my father caught me up; he grabbed my walker with such force that my teeth clicked. Now it was a performance by the two of us — my father dragged me home impertinently.

"Sasha, are you playing with your daughter?" our neighbors were joking.

Later I was lying in bed, covered with tears until the evening. When all family members returned home, my father told them about my escape. Everyone laughed, and I continuously repeated in my mind, 'I will run away anyway.'

***

When my father was in a good mood, he would put me on his shoulders, and in this fashion, he would take me to the circus and to the zoo. At that time, I did not have the slightest idea that my father would take me to the orphanage, and he would leave the family. Up until this time I try to find a justification for my father, but I cannot find anything except man's egotism.

No, there is an explanation: no one wants to look inferior. When perfectly healthy parents give birth to a disabled child, it may appear as an indication of their inner illness, revealing hidden diseases and invisible defects that manifested in their disabled child. Very often the man blames the woman and ruthlessly abandons her and the child.

But the causes of congenital disability can be different: genetic mutation, birth trauma, fetal infection and bad environment. It seems the latter does not bring visible harm to either adults or children, but it will affect the intrauterine being…

Or perhaps our Mother Nature does not want all human beings to be the same, demonstrating that they can be of different kinds, saying just give them a chance to live, to grow, to develop, to improve.

And indeed, very often powerful, gifted individuals are formed from invalids. So do not be afraid if you have an unusual child in your family. Just help this little unusual person to make their life extraordinary and interesting.

My Parents Visit Me

One day, during the period of my adaptation to the orphanage, I had a dream that my mother was coming, and I almost screamed loudly. I did not know that I sensed her visit, and later each time before she came to visit me, I would feel something. That day she suddenly appeared in the ward. She dropped her bag by my bunk; she was crying, and then in tears ran to my teachers. I had a lump in my throat, and I did not know whether to be happy that my mother had arrived, or whether I should share her sadness. I heard from my ward my mother crying, telling something anxiously to Zinaida Stepanovna.

My mother was absent for thirty minutes. I waited for her and felt abandoned. Finally, she came back, and sat on my bed with her eyes full of tears, staring out the window.

"Mother, when am I going home?" I asked the most important question, realizing it was not very tactful.

"Never!" she bluntly answered, staring out the window.

I cried vociferously. "I want to go home! I don't want to live here any more! When will you take me home?"

"Your father left us. Now I live with Olga at Aunt Masha's," she said in a cold voice, leaning to the floor and searching for something in her bag.

Then my mother took the tomato out of her bag, put it on the windowsill, and prepared to leave. For a long time, I did not fully understand the meaning of the word 'to throw'. There is an expression in Russian, 'to throw', which means to leave, to abandon. In my understanding it meant throwing an object or something which one does not need any more. But after a moment of silence, I suddenly understood the meaning of 'throw', and I started howling with such grief, not like a child, but the way women lament.

"If you keep yelling like that, I won't come to you again," scolded my mother and ran away.

At night, I had a fever again, bouncing around the bunk. In the morning the nanny came to feed me, but seeing that I could barely open my eyes, she just waved her hand and left.

***

Two weeks had passed, and I started rejuvenating again. The girls, who heard my parents were getting divorced, started asking questions.

"Did your parents fight at home?"

What a stupid question! I had never experienced a parental quarrel at home, but for many girls it was not unusual to see their parents fighting. And when I said my father never beat my mother, no one believed me.

But why had they divorced? The girls could not comprehend; they looked agitated and continued asking questions.

They bothered me with questions so much, that one day I could not stand it any more and I lied to them that my father was throwing dishes at my mother. After that confession, the girls left me alone.

***

In August, my nanny came to see me — it was my Aunt Tamara. We had a dead hour — this is what they called siesta. I was sleeping when the orphanage nanny walked in the ward; she woke me up. "Toma, wake up; you have a visitor."

I hesitated, not knowing what to do — should I rejoice or cry again? But the nanny started dressing me up in order to take me outside, so I would not wake up the sleeping girls with my crying. She found my own dress too shabby and dressed me in a garment of one of the girls, so I would look presentable.

"What if she wakes up and becomes angry that I took her dress?" I lamented.

"She won't be angry," the nanny assured me. "I'll say I took it."

The orphanage nanny took me to the meadow, and then I saw my lovely Aunt Tamara. I sniffed my nose, and I was ready to cry, but Aunt

Tamara beat me to it. "If you cry, I won't show you what I brought." She fixed my collar and asked me, "Why are you crying?"

"I want to go home…" I squeaked, barely holding my tears.

"Don't cry. I'll tell your father and grandfather to come here and take you home. We have to repair your stroller; you need something to sit in."

Of course, I believed it. But then the orphanage nanny appeared and said, "We don't have any clothes in her size. Could you bring her some dresses?"

"Okay, I'll look at home. If there's anything left, I'll send it here," my aunt promised.

After Aunt Tamara left, I did not cry so desperately any more. Aunt Tamara often visited me in the orphanage; later she visited me in the psycho-neurological boarding school. Twice she brought her son Sergei — the first time when he was a little boy and the second time before he was summoned to the army.

I still wonder why Aunt Tamara had more compassion for me than my father and mother at that time. Did she love me because I was her niece? Or did she show her tenderness and better understanding because she had her own injury?

But why did Aunt Tamara become so cold to me later? Many years later, when she and I happened to be in the same invalids' house in Novokuznetsk, she refused to feed me. And in response to the request to come sometimes to feed me, she cut me off sharply — "And who will feed me?" I tend to forgive her crudeness — she was not very happy with her son. My cousin Sergei started drinking heavily; his wife left him and his adult daughter had little respect for her father. I feel pain in my heart when I hear people say that Sergei became a drunkard and hit bottom; he was my playmate… Sergei and I had such a serene childhood, and later we had such different life paths…

Then later at the invalids' house, Aunt Tamara met a man, who became her life companion; they found happiness together. And I am very happy for her. I only regret my tears and bitter suspicion that her attention to me was not sincere; it was indeed sincere…

***

At the end of August, my father and grandfather arrived at the orphanage; they brought a stroller, which my father had built. My father had not finished attaching the wheels to the stroller when three nannies, led by Livshina, burst into the room, and here it started…

"Shame on you! How dare you look with your shameless eyes at your crippled child? How dare you leave such a beautiful wife with two daughters!" This was Livshina, yelling at my father, putting her hands on her hips.

It seemed to me absurd, as if my mother and father had never left me in an orphanage.

I was sitting in my grandfather's arms, eating candies. When Livshina yelled at my father, he stood up and went to the hallway, still holding me in his arms. So we sat in the hallway until my father had finished his work with the stroller. I was scared like a little rabbit, and tried to press my body closer to my grandfather, each time shuddering when I heard the loud chastising of Livshina.

I felt my grandfather's hands shaking; I realized something really awful had happened, and I did not dare to tell my grandfather that I wanted to go home. When the stroller was ready, my grandfather put me in it, rolled me to the ward, and then he and my father left without saying goodbye.

The Orphanage School

The autumn of 1963 brought radical changes to our orphanage.

In September, they provided us with flannel dresses: not new, but the correct size, and they started changing my clothes more often. But still, often I had to sit in a wet dress, soaked in soup or tea, and often drying up before my clothes were changed.

One day, when we were sitting in the playroom, we were solemnly informed that school would begin next week. We were in agreement with the world: for normal children, school starts in autumn, and we were included in this tradition.

It was still spring when Anna Ivanovna Sutiagina came to the orphanage to work as a teacher. Prior to this she was teacher at the village school, but health and age determined she could no longer work there. She was quite old. During her six months of work at the orphanage, she had been observing us, making plans for our development and coordinating them with her superiors. In fact, with her arrival, life in the orphanage began to change considerably. In our building, which consisted of five rooms where we slept, there were three playrooms designated for our school.

According to our age, we were divided into three groups — each consisted of about twenty-five children. However, because the children were different in their development, they decided to divide us in groups according to intelligence, but not to age. I was immediately accepted into the most advanced group, even though I did not know any letters. Four students from my group had attended high school before.

Two students, Varia and Sasha, were both fifteen years old; both were deaf and mute, and they could read the alphabet designed for their disability. Our teacher Zinaida Stepanovna learned this simple alphabet without difficulty as well as I, even acting as a sign language interpreter. I do not know which winds brought these two infelicitous individuals to our orphanage. Varia was perfectly healthy physically, and had successfully completed eighth grade. When she was asked why she had come here, she explained that at the school for the deaf and mute she had an argument with the head teacher who sent her here for revenge. But how Sasha came to the orphanage remained a mystery.

Two other students had completed the auxiliary school: one was Nadia with the 'sheep haircut'; the other girl had a common handicap — her arm and leg were disabled and she had a drooping head.

Oh, how reluctant other teachers were to work with students like us! Half of our teachers had no training. They preferred to put us in the same room and just to sit by the entrance doing their own things, and assisting us one at a time if we needed to go to the toilet. They worked in this fashion until the end of their shift.

But Anna Ivanovna came and broke the teachers' routine, forcing them to work in the field of education. Tables and chairs were brought; a blackboard was placed on the wall. The playroom started looking like a regular classroom. In the beginning, they did not give us notebooks; they just distributed to each student a sheet taken from the notebook. We learned how to draw curves and other symbols on these sheets. This exercise was new to many students, though most of them were teenagers.

For me, the most interesting thing was to study letters. Anna Ivanovna had letters drawn on square cardboard cards; she taught us which letter was represented on the card and the way it sounded. She would walk around the room, demonstrating letters first to the students who were sitting at the tables, then to those who were sitting in their strollers.

There were three of us sitting in strollers: Igor, Vaska and I. Vaska's father worked as the head of the accountant department; Igor's parents worked in the Kemerovo social welfare office. Because of the prestigious positions of their parents, both boys were given special attention. Then these boys, because of their parent's connections, would go to good homes for the disabled. Not I, doomed to institutions for individuals with chronic psychological deficiencies.

The teachers individually approached Igor and Vaska, showing them letters, asking whether they had memorized them or not. I was not privileged to have such attention, and if I could not view from my place a demonstrated letter, I would let them know, saying in a high-pitched voice, "I cannot see!" The teachers would turn around and show me the letter I missed.

So at the same time, I learned to be literate, and I expressed my assertiveness and ability to stand up for myself. Because I had a great memory — at least one gift of nature — by the new year I had learned the alphabet. I was so proud of my achievement — I met the year 1964 as a literate person.

***

During the winter, I finally mastered the precepts of reading, but there were no books in the orphanage; they would certainly have accelerated my progress in reading. But as it was not possible to read a book on our own, Anna Ivanovna Sutiagina gave us perhaps an even more important reading.

Usually, after dinner, between seven and eight o'clock in the evening, our teachers were still on their duties; their shift ended at eight o'clock, and they could not find any occupation for us. In the summer, we could go outside; in the winter, it would take an hour to get dressed and undressed, and there would be no time to go outside. Therefore, the teachers used this hour as they pleased. Most of them would put all the groups in the same playroom, and they themselves would sit like guards by the entrance and lead their personal conversations, while the students would 'stay on their ears', being on their own.

But Anna Ivanovna, whom her colleagues called 'the white raven' behind her back, as well as applying to her the contemptuous word 'intelligentsia', invited us to the playroom where she read books to us. Thanks to Anna Ivanovna, at the age of seven, I became familiar with my first literary works — there were excerpts from 'The Prisoner of the Caucasus' by Leo Tolstoy and 'Kids of the Dungeon' by Vladimir Korolenko. I was so impressed by the fate of the children of the dungeon, I could not sleep all night; perhaps it was my first lesson in nobility and compassion. The story of Zhilin and Kostylin, the protagonists of Tolstoy's 'The Prisoner of the Caucasus' taught me resilience — in any situation, a lot of things depend on the individual.

I Learned How to Sit Down

Spring, 1964. We had our elementary school classes from January to April. I enjoyed studying so much! It was a pity I had fewer classes than I wanted. All teachers, except the heroic Sutiagina, instead of helping us to strengthen our skills in learning letters and syllables, preferred something easy: "Play, children, but do not disturb us."

Once, after dinner, I was already in bed, but I did not want to be there. I had spent all day sitting in my motionless stroller. At first, the boys rolled the stroller back and forth for me — such an entertainment for them and myself. Three teachers and two nannies, after they had gathered all the groups in one of the playrooms, sat by the entrance, conducting endless conversations about 'life'. One of them, Vera Aleksandrovna, was terribly nervous about my stroller being moved by the boys. It was unlikely that she was bothered by the noise generated by the stroller; the children's voices were much louder. But Vera Aleksandrovna initially treated me with antipathy, which no one could understand and explain, including her.

"Put Cheremnova near the wall! Do not move her stroller any more!" she screamed in distress.

The boys obeyed in fright, drove the carriage to the wall and walked away, fearing inflaming Vera Aleksandrovna's anger. It turned out that I was facing the wall. Why the teachers did not turn me around to face society is incomprehensible. Either they did not pay attention to such a trifle that a girl sat facing the wall, or they were too lazy. So I sat until lunchtime, listening to the children, who had a lot of fun behind my back, and to the employees who chatted animatedly, discussing family troubles and everyday ups and downs. And here I was in complete isolation; in front of me is a dead wall...

I will remember this cul-de-sac wall for the rest of my life. At first, the wall was just a child's grudge, and then it turned into a symbol; the wall became an implacable enemy that I had to defeat. Later in my life I would have to break down so many such cul-de-sac walls!

And when the last wall collapses, I would be astonished by a huge, empty space. And it would take a long time before I came to terms with a new obstacle for me and a new enemy — emptiness. And I still do not know which is worse — a wall or a void?

Oh, if only all, all disabled people like me, with paralyzed legs and arms, had a normal life; if only we could see, hear, feel, touch the world around us and merge into its ebullient life! And, most importantly, so as not to be tormented by the question: will they provide us with the necessary empirical help, or not?

What will await me tomorrow? For I am physically helpless, if, God forbid, my assistant Olga, a deaf-mute roommate in my current Novokuznetsk invalids' home, gets sick. Yes, without Olga, I will literally be left without hands! No matter how famous I become, I will always and everywhere be haunted by my infirmity — a cross that I am destined to bear to the end of my days. And it is so humiliating to live in complete physical dependence on others...

People! Healthy, normal, not crippled, not invalids, able to move on your feet and control your own hands! Breathe freely and rejoice that you are gifted with unthinkable wealth — the ability for independent and controlled movement! Consider yourself happy as long as you do not depend on anyone! Don't you think that a healthy self-governing body means happiness? Then at least agree that this is the basis for happiness.

But let us go back to that memorable evening. After spending the whole day in the motionless stroller (after lunch they did not stroll me either), I crawled onto the bed, desperately demonstrating a protest against the boring immobility and tedious helplessness... And suddenly, without even realizing it, I jerked, and lo and behold! I sat down on my butt, clutching the metal bed structure with my fingers in order not to fall! Well, no matter how much I tried to learn how to sit at home, I could not, but in the orphanage, where no one was involved in my physical development, everything worked out!

The nanny entered the room; she did not immediately notice me sitting, but when she saw, she was surprised. "Toma, you're sitting! Did you sit down by yourself?"

I confirmed with a nod of my head. I could not speak, because I was so happy that a lump rose in my chest with joy, and it was difficult for me to breathe or to say anything. The nanny, clicking her tongue, praised me and left. I turned my head to the window, and I saw a passenger train and rails. In the distance, beyond the railway line, I saw a forest. I sobbed with joy and fell down exhausted on my pillow — my first independent sitting took so much energy from me. Now I can reach out to the window, and I can see the forest, the train, and the people in the lighted windows!

No one would envy my life, of course, but that spring evening I was jubilant.

I Envy the Poplar and Ants

I learned how to sit on the floor in the ward, corridor, and playroom, although I did not keep my balance well and often fell. Sometimes I would fall and hit my little head on the floor so hard that I saw stars. It was much more comfortable to sit on the floor than in the stroller, although very often the nannies scolded me because I displaced the rug. There was a rug in the middle of the corridor, and I involuntarily shifted it to the side with my naughty legs.

Despite the nannies' displeasure, I asked them to put me on the floor in the corridor, where there was more space. The adults were perplexed, they grumbled, but anyway they would put me on the rug and straightened it when I disarranged it involuntarily. Apparently, they realized how ridiculous this miserable rug looked against the background of shabby walls and windows without curtains.

***

When the spring of 1964 had just begun rumbling with its streams, considerable changes happened in the orphanage. They started a new construction, using large-panel blocks, not for children, but administrative offices — it consisted of the director's office, the accounting office and the dining room. Inside our wooden-barrack housing they decided to install steam heating, and as soon as the snow melted, they started installing radiators.

And with the arrival of summer, they began taking us to the bathhouse. We traveled there in a cart pulled by a horse. And, finally, they began to wash me thoroughly with soap and a washcloth! Also, to change my clothes more often. At the beginning of spring, the girls were dressed in light dresses, but in the summer, they changed their minds and decided to dress all of us 'comme des garcons' — they gave us T-shirts and another article — something between underwear and shorts.

Sometimes they would carry us, stroller restricted, outside and place us in the shade of the large poplar, which was near our building. Sitting in the close vicinity of the tree, I observed with curiosity how ants, bugs and spiders crawled on the wrinkled skin of the poplar trunk… By this time my long-suffering stroller was completely without wheels, so they could not transport me inside it. First, they would place the stroller on two chairs or on the land; after that I was reintroduced into the stroller.

What do you think — what can an eight-year-old child think about at such moments, sitting in a broken stroller? Well, I will tell you. I envied the tree. Because it constantly lived outside, in the air, under the sun, moon, breeze, rain and snow. Because the tree did not need to return to the building, where it would surely be scolded, and at night the melancholy would flood. The poplar branches swayed high above the ground, and they seemed to brush against the clouds. How wonderful for the poplar to be here; no one can offend him… I thought enviously and sighed quietly.

Then I became interested in all moving creatures: animals, birds and insects. Especially I was interested in insects — they were very close to me. It was so pleasant to watch small bugs and spiders, scurrying here and there. I enjoyed observing ladybugs crawl — they were red, orange and yellow, with black polka-dot spots on their backs — and how they suddenly took off, tucking their legs and releasing translucent lower ones from under the dense upper wings. I loved to see how moths soared up, spreading their wings. I admired how gracefully multicolored butterflies fluttered and landed on a leaf or blade of grass. I observed a briskly marching ant and imagined that it was me running. I perceived this ant as if it was me, and with my own eyes I experienced objects which this running ant was passing by. And I envied them all — they were capable of moving independently on their feet…

"Lagging Behind in Mental Development…"

The short Siberian summer passed so fast. It seemed that not long ago everything was green, but now the cautious tread of autumn was already visible. The poplar acquired more and more gold in the foliage every day.

At the end of August 1964, an important regional medical revision committee came to us to examine the orphanage. They checked us stroller users especially meticulously. Several persons with normal hands were immediately sent to another orphanage. It was my turn. They took off my dress right in the stroller, and I was left in a hefty, oversized T-shirt and no panties. For some reason they did not put them on me that day.

"Why aren't you wearing panties?" asked Nina Stepanovna sternly, taking me in her arms — she was the sister of the malevolent Anna Stepanovna Livshina — as if I dressed and undressed myself.

"They didn't put them on for me…" I sniffed, and I was embarrassed to appear this way.

Putting me on the table, the members of the committee examined my feeble little body for a long time and talked with each other in low voices. I could hear some of their conversation, and I had another source of information reading their faces.

"She does not use panties? Can she understand that it's a shame to be like that? Is she able to take care of herself?"

"No, she doesn't take care of herself," answered Nina Stepanovna. "She is taken care of by nannies; they feed her from a spoon. The girl is very weak; she cries constantly. She lags behind in mental development."

This phrase was like a death sentence. She declared my mental retardation without even asking how my education was going! Meanwhile, I was successfully learning all the letters and could read words and sentences. Studying was easy for me; it was the best entertainment. I already dreamed that, in addition to reading and writing, I would be taught other interesting subjects. But Nina Stepanovna, with her strange categorical statement, crossed out my entire future, depriving me of the right to education. The commission did not require more proof; the estimation of my condition by the chief nurse was sufficient.

***

In October, the heating system was installed in our building; then they started painting the wards and playrooms, transferring us from one room to another. Naturally there were no classes — they could not be carried out during the renovation.

Classes began only after the new year, in January 1965. It turned out that none of the children remembered anything from what they had studied; only I could name the letters I had learned, and those who had finished auxiliary schools.

My Mother's Disgust

I recall with bitterness the episode connected with the visit of my mother which finally determined our relationship. It happened in October 1964, when repairs in the building were in full swing, reading lessons were postponed, the weather was gloomy and the mood was somber… I was waiting for my mother's visit with special apprehension.

However, mother behaved very strangely that day. When I asked her to take me in her arms, she pulled me out of the stroller and began to drag me under my arms, as she used to do at home, but this time she tried to move away and not touch me. And when I tried to snuggle up to her, she sharply pushed me aside and reproachfully asked, "Toma, why are you pooping in your pants?"

"I don't poop in my pants! Don't scold me for this" I began to make excuses, taken aback by the unfair accusation.

"Then why are all your pants covered in poop?" She grimaced in disgust.

"We have no toilet paper," I snuffled guiltily, looking at my pants, which were for adult women, so large that they hung below my knees, serving as leggings.

An unpleasant picture — an unkempt disabled girl in a short dress, from under which underwear-leggings hang almost to my feet, and with slipped stockings dragging along the floor. I can imagine I looked like a caricature! Moreover, my mother was informed about my mental retardation and the decision of the committee…

I am unable to understand my mother, Ekaterina Ivanovna. She loved me in the beginning! There are touching photographs where I am in her arms — an attractive woman and a cute baby with not yet visible signs of the disease. When I lived at home, she was affectionate with me and accepted me as I was, with a fair number of disabilities in physical development and believed in my recovery. Is it really possible to stop loving your child because of illness? And she agreed so easily with the mental retardation invented by a nurse — not a doctor, not a teacher — and approved by a careless commission. After all, I lived at home for almost seven years, and my mother could objectively assess my mental development as a *mother*!

Why, during her infrequent visits to the orphanage, seeing her own child in mud and scabs, did this woman never ask for warm water in order to wash her at least a little bit? After all, one could always take warm water in the dining room and wash the girl over the basin.

But it gave her some satisfaction to tell me that when she returned home from the orphanage, she had scabies on her arms and took sick leave for two weeks. I infected her with scabies — that was the main thing, but not that her invalid child who could not even scratch herself suffered from this.

In her eyes there was only disgust for the neglected orphanage person whom her daughter had become, and a secret desire that this unfortunate daughter would not exist in this world any more. It turned out that it would be better for her if I died as soon as possible, so that the absurdity would finally disappear — that such a beauty has such a freak child. And she was forced to visit regularly this freak in the orphanage — otherwise people would criticize her, they would say that she abandoned and forgot her child. And she regularly visited me — this was once every three to four months. Then it turned out that she visited me precisely when she felt miserable, when she quarreled with her former relatives: her mother-in-law or sister-in-law.

My poor mother, Ekaterina Ivanovna! I do not despise her; I do not blame her; I rather feel sorry for her. After all, it was probably not easy to make these visits to the orphanage 'out of the way' and trifle with the invalid daughter by whom she was repulsed, even four times a year.

I think not to love the little person to whom she gave life, to disdain her and be weary of her is one of the most terrible sins. Because it is impossible to measure the depth of this little person's suffering.

The other inhabitants of the orphanage, who like me were not orphans, also had visitors. But these visitors were not like my visitor that was my mother, who paid these visits reluctantly and formally, as if performing the duty; these visitors expressed guilt, love and care. First of all, they would check if their child was clean. And they would never forget to caress and cuddle their child. How I missed this, even if it was not permanent but episodic: love, affection, tenderness and care! Then, later, in clinics for adult invalids, I observed how parents visited their disabled adult children whom they had thrown into the care of the state in order to isolate themselves from the wretched child, or because they were not able to take care of this individual. Nevertheless, they visited their invalid relative not for show, but came to take care, to feed, to support, to entertain, to cuddle…

When, after many years of wandering around the Kuzbass shelters for invalids with chronic psychological diseases, I finally succeeded in transferring to the Novokuznetsk Home No. 2 for disabled people of general type, Ekaterina Ivanovna appeared again. Many people thought that she was attracted by the fact that I became a Kemerovo celebrity. However, she never once mentioned my writing success.

These years have changed many things. My mother became old and did not look attractive any more, but I, on the contrary, stopped considering myself ugly, unworthy of existence, and accepted myself as I am. But she still hints at dissonance — a beautiful mother and a freak daughter. And now she regularly visits me in the same bleak mood — cold, formal, humiliating and instructive. I would like to tell her: please, do not come here any more. But something prevents me saying this; perhaps I feel compassion for her…

Whom to Complain to? To the Sun!

In December 1964, our ward was reformatted. The grown-up girls remained, young children were transferred to the neighboring ward and my bed was moved to the door.

From now, the big girls who were capable of walking were forced to do the nannies' job of cleaning the floors in the playrooms and in the hallways in the evenings. For this they were given extra food — leftovers from dinner and the homemade food, which the nannies brought for themselves and for refreshments. The girls would always share the food with me, giving me a tiny piece of lard on a slice of bread, or a ring of pickled cucumber.

None of the nannies were against it, because I could hold and eat a sandwich and a pickled cucumber on my own, without burdening anyone. And when I was very hungry, I just asked them for bread.

"Just don't litter the floor," they would say, handing me a piece.

And, so as not to mess with crumbs, I put the bread on a towel and began to gnaw, holding it with my hand, then I just had to gently shake out the towel into a bucket with waste, and everything was clean. Only the spiteful Anna Stepanovna Livshina could not accept this. If she noticed that one of the girls was carrying a piece of bread to my bed, she would start screaming hysterically, "Are you going to give bread to Cheremnova again? Put it back on the table immediately!"

Now, many years later, I think: was Livshina normal? Such a pronounced aggressiveness towards a helpless child indicates obvious deviations in the psyche. Such an unbalanced woman, of course, should not be allowed to work with children, especially as a nanny on duty, who is obliged to look after the children constantly and without any control.

When Livshina started screaming, I shuddered and instinctively tucked in my legs. This habit, alas, would take hold and would remain until now; subsequently I would never be able to overcome the involuntary cramping my legs when I was excited.

One day my patience ran out. On the night when Livshina worked, the girls, as usual, went to clean the floors. I, lying in bed, heard her telling the girls in the corridor not to take Cheremnova bread, otherwise she would not give them delicious smoked bacon. I felt a kind of viscous fear inside me; my eyes burned, and the next second, rage boiled within me.

I had an enamel little mug filled with water on the chair near my bed, and I, mad with resentment, threw this mug on the floor. The girl who was walking by picked up the mug and put it back, and I threw it again. When Livshina heard strange sounds, she asked the girl what was going on. The girl had to confess that it was me who was throwing the mug. I did not hear Livshina's reaction for several minutes; apparently, she comprehended my protest and provided her own emotions, then she yelled, with squalling tones, "Cheremnova, if you throw the mug again, tomorrow I will complain about you to the teachers!"

"Go, complain even to Santa Claus..." I whispered, choking with tears. "And I will complain to the sun!"

There was no one else to complain to, but this saving thought gave me some relief.

The TV Set

In February 1965, the administrative building, which had been built for almost a year, was finally opened. In addition to the director's office, accounting, a canteen for those who could walk, the club room was established — it was equipped with the television set, the only one for the entire orphanage.

In March, the children were summoned to this room to watch the newly purchased television and to celebrate Women's Day. We were in the playroom, which was filled with a cheerful hubbub. There were discussions about how the children who could walk would help those who were not able to walk, how they could bring them, and which films should be in the program.

When I found out that they were not taking me, I burst into tears. I was really, really interested in this TV set. We didn't have television at home. I was in tears, grunting exhaustedly when the teacher Nelia Semenovna entered the playroom.

"Toma, why are you crying?" she asked me with surprise.

"I also want to watch TV… I want to watch a movie…" I confessed to her and stopped crying the blues for a moment.

"We would like to bring all of you on strollers, but it's still cold outside. And if someone wants to go to the toilet, then what?" she said.

"No, I will not want to go the toilet; I can resist, I can wait until I get to my room, I promise," I squeaked in a high-pitched voice and a hope entered my soul.

"All right, we'll figure something out," promised Nelia Semenovna, patting my head. "I'll ask the nannies and boys to bring you to the club."

The nannies wrapped me in a blanket, put on my head someone's winter hat, and two grown-up boys grabbed my stroller without wheels and carried me to the club.

I will not describe how much I was impressed by the television — the twentieth-century technology miracle. I could not take my eyes off the screen with images flashing on it, and for the first time in my life I urinated on the blanket. It turned out that I was not the only one who did it. Many children came back to the room after watching the movie wet. But we were not scolded for it, and since the nanny Livshina did not work that night — she would certainly create a scandal — we had a peaceful evening, without screams.

Today, when the TV has become part of everyday life and color models have replaced the black and white models, I remember with a smile my first television viewing in my life — with the gratitude to those who made it possible for me to have this visual feast.

Then on the weekends we were regularly carried to watch cartoons on TV. What a pleasure it was for us, the children in strollers!

My Sister Olga

My relatives chose a convenient way of life in which there was no place for my interests and desires; nevertheless, they kept up appearances from time to time. It made me feel worse than anyone who did not have any parents. Today those with a status similar to mine receive the name 'social orphan' — when parents are present and even from time to time appear, but this does not change anything in the bitter orphan life. It appeared to be ridiculous and embarrassing — the healthy, beautiful woman would come, rush out of the bag something wrapped in a piece of paper, put it on a nightstand, tell me something instructive, then she would go to chat with teachers about women's sensitive problems, then she would leave, sometimes without even saying goodbye.

She did not care that I suffered. I did not even dare to complain to her. Ekaterina Ivanovna — like a bright butterfly — flew in, fluttered her wings and flew away. She did not have time for me! She would not spend with me even an extra second! And this looked so foolish — to make such a long way from Novokuznetsk to the Bochata station — it takes two hours by train, and to spend with me just a few minutes.

It was like the same episode from a movie, which was repeated so many times: my mother would pick me up and hold me like a doll, and without paying the slightest attention to my awkward body movements and desperate attempts to talk to her, she would talk to the employees of the orphanage. And if I complained that I was tired of standing like that, she would immediately put me in my stroller without listening to me or trying to make me comfortable.

Her sympathy for the sadistic Anna Stepanovna Livshina was completely incomprehensible to me. Obviously, she did not tell my mother how she humiliated me, but I tried to complain about her. It was later revealed that the employees had told Ekaterina Ivanovna about Livshina's angry attacks against her daughter Toma Cheremnova, but my mother listened without interest. Unlike other relatives, she never asked the staff about her daughter's life and health; she simply did not care.

And I was torn apart by the resentment, the pain and the jealousy of those to whom my mother was attentive, to my detriment.

***

After much persuasion from my side, my mother finally agreed to bring my little sister Olga to visit me. Three came — my mother, her younger sister Valentina and four-year-old Olga. I missed my little sister terribly because she was part of my happy life when I lived at home.

On the day they arrived, and with the intention of staying overnight, I squealed joyfully, overwhelmed with feelings, and when the nannies or teachers came into the room, I bragged: this is my sister Olechka! Olga stared at me incomprehensibly — she did not recognize me; the little one had forgotten me.

Later in the evening, everyone was commanded to go to bed; that night Anna Stepanovna Livshina was on duty. My mother went to her to chat and to show her younger daughter. Aunt Valentina also rushed after them. The children had started to fall asleep when they returned to the room. My mother held Olga in her arms, pressing to her breast, kissing her, talking to her like a little doll. "You're my little darling! You're my sweet little girl!"

I opened my eyes in wonder — I had never seen my mother like this. At least, she had never been so gentle with me.

"Katia, you and the baby lie down on the free bed, and Valentina will sleep with Tomka," commanded Anna Stepanovna, entering the room.

"No, my mother will sleep with me!" I exclaimed bravely.

"Don't shout, you'll wake up the children!" Livshina barked.

"My mother will sleep with me," I repeated in a trembling voice.

"Toma, when Olga falls asleep, I'll come to you. Your mother will come to you, Tomochka!" My mother and aunt tried to comfort me.

But I was stubborn as a mule, marveling at my own courage, and then Olga and I cried a duet, and indeed, we woke up all the children. I felt right, because Olga lived with my mother at home and I was here. Besides, my mother provoked my crying, lavishing care on Olga in front of me.

After that, Ekaterina Ivanovna no longer brought my sister to me. I saw Olga when I was eighteen years old; at that time, we had nothing in common — we became strangers…

Many years passed. My sister Olga married a young man from Biysk; they have a son whose name is Dmitri. Sometimes Olga visits me, but when she comes, she keeps her distance, as if she is afraid to touch me, as if I am contagious. But concerning infection, she was seriously infected by her mother's cold and squeamish attitude towards me. And, as punishment, the disability once again touched the family — after fourteen years of marriage, Olga's husband became an invalid. He worked as a gas welder on the top of some construction; the podium on which he stood collapsed, and he fell from a height of thirteen meters. Thank God he did not end up in a wheelchair and he could continue walking.

Olga and I have our age difference of four years; we could be friends. I loved her, and in time she could have loved me. But we did not become close, thanks to the efforts of Ekaterina Ivanovna, who built between Olga and me a stone wall, and designated us as an ugly burden and a beloved daughter. Biysk is not so far from Novokuznetsk; Olga and I could have had a warm relationship; we could correspond. Especially now when we could communicate by email. Oh, we are sisters, and we could be close! But it did not work out…

In a few years after the divorce, my mother married for the second time. The new husband adopted Olga, and my mother did not tell him about me, as if I did not exist. She was embarrassed to tell him that in addition to a healthy, beautiful daughter, she had a defective, ugly one. Of course, the truth eventually came out. Fortunately, the fact that I existed did not affect my mother's family life, but her vile cover-up to hide my existence takes my soul away to this day.

The Fire

The terrible year of 1965... The first six months of the year went well. Our school lessons started with an initial repetition, so everything had to be repeated. In my first year of school, sometimes I confused the soft sign 'ь' with the hard sign 'ъ', the two letters of the Cyrillic script which look so similar, but in my second year I learned them very well.

In May, the classes were over and it became warm. The teachers felt relieved; now we could all go outside and enjoy fresh air. Children who were able to walk would go to swim in the Bachatka River; those in strollers would be assisted and sit either under the poplar or in the cool hall.

Midsummer was dry, with no rain. In the morning, we were already outside, and on that ordinary day, I was taken for a walk by a girl; now I do not remember her name. She took me under my arms and dragged me behind the building, where the grass was not trampled, and I could sit on a woodpile. First, we sat together, and she told me some stories, but I listened to her half-heartedly, being immersed in my unhappy thoughts, though consenting cheerfully. Then the boys joined us and started talking. I did not listen at first and only when the word 'fire' came to my ears did I turn my head to them. There was this harmless boy named Sanka Smolichenko, and it was he who was talking about a fire.

"Sanka, where is the fire?" I asked.

He spoke indistinctly, pointing to the toilet window.

"What are you talking about?" I moved erratically, staring at the window. "How is it going to burn? They will see it right away."

"It's going to burn!" he said, then he left.

I immediately forgot about this senseless conversation, and the next afternoon, when we were sitting in the hall, trying to escape the heat, I heard a commotion in the building.

"Ooh, fire! Fire! Girls, fire!" the nannies and teachers were screaming, running in the hall.

We were pulled out of the strollers and taken to the large porch of the new stone building, but even after that, I did not think about Sanka predicting the fire.

We spent some time on the porch, then we were taken to our places for dinner. The nanny who fed me told me that the corner of the windowsill was smoking in the toilet, but she quickly extinguished it. And again, I did not remember Sanka's prediction! It was like someone erased my memory about the impending fire.

In the evening Livshina and Anna Fudina, in whose arms I literally grew up, came for the night shift. I even called Anna Fudina grandmother, though she was too young to be a grandmother. We started exchanging our versions of the toilet fire.

At about ten o'clock, we were commanded to go to bed; the building became quiet. At two o'clock at night, a girl from the room where older girls lived — it was next to our room — went to the toilet, located at the end of the hall. She opened the door and screamed in an inhuman voice. The toilet and the playroom were on fire.

Alarmed by the girl's cry, Livshina came immediately. She realized that it was a serious matter; she sent the girl to wake up everyone in the room and tell them they had to run outside. The second nanny, Aunt Anya, ran to the 'weak quarter' where feeble children lived, and she called the fire department. Livshina tried to transport everyone outside.

Can you imagine what it is like to move the sleeping handicapped at two in the morning? It became more complicated because there were two exits to outside, and when the children were forced to go outside through the door, they would return to the room through the other door. Poor, scared children, they were totally confused.

I was immersed in a sweet sleep, and suddenly, like someone pushed me, I felt like there was something wrong in the room. I opened my eyes and I saw the light was on. I listened to sounds; I heard screams in the corridor. In a minute, Livshina came into the room and commanded everyone to run outside.

"The house is on fire! Everybody outside!" she screamed.

"Anna Stepanovna, take me out, please!" I asked her meekly.

Livshina looked at me without expressing any emotions, then she turned around and disappeared into the corridor. The girls ran outside, and there was only one grown girl; she was trying to find something. By the way, her name was also Toma. I realized that Toma was about to leave the room, and I was going to be completely alone, and I was going to burn. I realized that Livshina had left me to die...

"Tom! Take me, please," I whispered in a pleading voice.

It was a very scary moment — because Toma could not be always persuaded to help. But she just took me in her arms and carried me outside.

We were assembled in the meadow by the office. We were all wearing underwear and T-shirts. It was July, but at night it was cool. I do not know what made my teeth chatter, and I trembled because of fear or cold. It became really cold in the morning. I was sitting, looking at the flames on the roof of our building. And the meadow illuminated by fire was lit up like daytime.

The nearest settlement from our orphanage was the Mordovian village. I do not know how the Mordovians came to Kuzbass. Perhaps they were exiled in Stalin times, or maybe they came willingly for work. The village existed for a long time; several people from this village worked in our orphanage. And in spite of the night, as soon as they saw the flames and heard the screams, they ran to us. The flames were visible from far away. Soon two fire trucks arrived; then the third one was requested.

At eight o'clock in the morning, we were summoned into the club room of the administrative building. They organized the accounting materials in a hurry and vacated the director's office to accommodate the children. From the warehouse, the mattresses were brought in, thrown on the floor and we, anxious and exhausted, fell on them.

But I could not sleep; I would close my eyes and then I would jump up. I felt like my mattress was smoldering. When I jumped again and opened my eyes, I saw the teacher standing in front of me.

"Toma, why don't you sleep?" she asked.

"My mattress is on fire," I said.

"Where?" The teacher was scared. After a careful look at the mattress, she understood I had had a nightmare because of the shock. "Sleep. There's nothing burning anywhere," she said, then she left.

I lay for a long time with my eyes open, and suddenly I recalled Sanka's prophetic words. Flames were flashing in the windows; I heard sirens of fire trucks, and I was lying in my bed thinking about Sanka's words. He was definitely pointing at the toilet window! How did he know about the fire? If he were a clairvoyant, he could have predicted other things, but he never showed his talent. Most likely, the boys had a plan to set the building on fire. At that time, the position of the director of the orphanage was vacant; it was held by two men who had been dismissed. And the last one was six months before the fire.

The position of director was temporarily occupied by the manager, and the new director was supposed to arrive very soon. But no matter how much I strained my childish brain, I could not complete my detective analysis.

In the morning, the voices woke me up. I opened my eyes and saw that the children gathered by the window, which faced the site of the fire, were having a heated discussion. We, the stroller-restricted, were given breakfast, and those who were able to walk were taken to the dining room, which was quickly arranged across from us. I could not eat; I just had some tea. After a few minutes, the girls came back from the dining room. I asked one of them, Valentina, to lift me up to look out the window. I saw the burning barrack; black smoke was coming out of the windows. There were fire trucks in front of it, ambulances, and there was something, covered with white sheets, on the ground near the road.

I said, "What's that under the sheets?"

"There are burned boys," Valia responded with agitation, holding me tightly.

"Who?" I was frozen in terror.

Vadim, who made sabers from sticks and golden candy papers. And the others… there were tears in Valia's eyes. All the boys were burned in their room.

"But I saw Vovka and Vitka in their room. And Vadik was with them…" I said, though I was not sure. "Yesterday in the meadow I am sure I saw Vovka; he had so much fun dancing on the grass. He shouted, 'Hurrah for fire'!"

Valia shrugged her shoulders. And how could she know for sure who died and who survived?

Vadim, Vadim. He was new; he was brought recently. This boy did not look like any of us; he looked absolutely healthy, his arms and legs were normal and he spoke clearly; only he was silent most of the time. Why was he brought to the orphanage, and even to the specialized one? We knew he had no mother. And, apparently, the stepmother tried to get rid of her stepson; she sent him far away. It turned out that she sent him too far, so far away from where one never returns.

***

After breakfast, they started bringing in new beds from the warehouse, and I tried not to disturb and bother anyone with questions. But when the new bedrooms were already equipped, I chose the moment and told the teacher Nina Pavlovna Kamaeva about Sanka's predictions.

"Don't talk nonsense, otherwise we'll send you to the weak quarter," Nina Pavlovna whispered angrily.

On the third day after the fire, still-smoking logs from the burned building were bulldozed to avoid smoldering. As soon as the fire department left, the boys rushed into the ashes and dragged my burned stroller out of there.

A week later, the workers crew arrived, and they began constructing a new building for us. And Sanka, who was still talking about the fire, was rushed to an adult male psycho-neurological boarding school in Chugunash. So one should not be afraid of Sanka's revelations from the other side of the Kemerovo region.

There were six burned boys, all from the same room. They were the oldest and strongest — Vovka and Vitka escaped. There was a boy in that room who, despite the prohibition, smoked. They blamed him. Could it be possible that the young smoker set the window of the toilet on fire and went to bed to die in the fire?

In the report of the investigation team, it was said that the fire was caused by the negligence of an insane teenager who did not extinguish his cigarette. The case was quickly dropped, and the nannies were acquitted because there were only two of them during the night shift in the orphanage, and it was impossible to save all the children. And then after, never was there a word about the fire. As if it was not the orphanage which burned down, but a derelict tent perished in flames, and it was not six children who died, but it was just the inventory.

***

As for Livshina, who intentionally left me to die in the fire, in her understanding I was a useless ballast — not working, not washing floors, and also in need of care. Why would she save me?

Another heartbreaking episode came to my mind. One day we were sitting in the playroom. There was no teacher, only Livshina. At one point, listening to jokes intended to make me laugh, I burst out laughing. And then Livshina hit me with the phrase, "When Cheremnova grows up, she will be sent to Kedrovka, and she will live there until her death!"

There was a psycho-neurological boarding school in Kedrovka, and everyone knew it was the dead end. Shocked by this bleak prospect, I became silent for a long time. And the only thought in my head was, would my mother, Katherine Ivanovna, allow them to send me to Kedrovka forever as incurable?

After the Fire

Day after day we had been recovering from the shock of the fire and the death of the boys, but our life has taken its course. In the morning, the nannies would enter and open the doors to ventilate the room. The stuffiness in the small, overcrowded room was understandable. But when you sleep under a sheet instead of a blanket, which the warehouse did not have in its stocks, your teeth are chattering from the cold. And when the doors are open, the cold air rushes from the corridor... These sensations will remain forever in my body, and the trembling and humiliation will come as soon as I recall these moments.

After the firefighters pulled out the dead bodies of the burned boys from the burning building, the relatives were sent sorrowful invitations to come to say goodbye to the dead. Relatives arrived but only for two deceased boys; the other four had no relatives. Surprisingly, the stepmother took Vadik's body home to bury her stepson in a proper way, although the administration of the orphanage did not insist on this. The other boys were buried at public expense at the orphanage cemetery.

My mother was notified about the fire and asked to bring a typical winter cover — thick, filled with cotton — to use as the upholstery for my burned stroller. She arrived only a month and a half after the notification; she came in September. She handed me a box of lollipops and a magazine, 'Merry Pictures' which she subscribed to for Olga. As usual, she went to chat with the nannies who were anxious to share with her their stories about the fire. Years later, one of those nannies was kind enough to convey to me my mother's words: "I wish she had burned in this fire!"

I'm not angry at my mother for that phrase. First of all, an emotionally frustrated woman can say anything; then the hidden meaning of this phrase would be "I wish she would not suffer any more; death would be a solution." And when I became older, I used to reflect on this idea: would it be better if I had burned? Why should I continue living when all my life will be miserable, useless, and I will be a burden to everyone? The girls who shared the room with me still had a chance to be better; physically they were more or less healthy. And me? Do I have any hope?

Long before my mother pronounced her phrase "I wish she had burned in this fire!" I had realized that my relatives did not care about me, even my mother. But I understood it much better after my mother stayed overnight in my room.

During my mother's visits, this Ritka girl, who did not have any parents, always made circles around us. My mother was already in bed when I needed to use the toilet. My mother asked Ritka to help me with the toilet. Ritka agreed; she looked for the chamber pot and not finding it, she took me outside — I was very light to carry.

"Tom, does your mother have a husband now?" she asked me on our way to the toilet. Ritka liked so much to talk about men.

"I don't know…" I said. This was the first time my mother's private life entered my universe. In fact, after my mother divorced from my father, she had a good chance to marry someone else.

"Ask your mother if she's going dancing with her husband!" Ritka could not overcome her curiosity.

After putting me in bed, Ritka stood by the bunk and waited for when she could talk to my mother about her husband. I was embarrassed to ask my mother about her personal life, but under Ritka's invisible pressure, I asked, "Mother, do you have a husband?"

"Yes!" she answered, after a pause, without opening her eyes.

"Do you go dancing with him?" Ritka shamelessly entered our conversation.

"Sure. Of course, we go dancing," my mother said.

I felt like my soul was pressed by a heavy stone. After my mother left, I started crying from time to time with no reason. I could be all right, no one would say to me anything bad, and then suddenly I would start crying. Even the teachers mentioned that Tomochka cried a lot. Thank God they did not ask me for an explanation. I did not want to reveal the reason for my tears — I am so unhappy here, and my mother has a new husband with whom she frivolously goes dancing!

***

The new director, Vil Mikhailovich Bikmaev, had arrived at the orphanage. He would be director until I left. With his arrival, the life in the orphanage improved little by little. They cooked better meals, dressed us in more elegant outfits and even set up a mobile library.

Thanks to the director, our orphanage became a model for other places; it achieved some excellence and was evaluated as the second-best orphanage in the Kemerovo region. And they even bought school uniforms for us. But this was funny — school uniforms without a school education!

My First Books

In November 1965, with the arrival of winter, the teachers were able to resume the interrupted classes, despite the inadequate conditions — the playrooms had burned down. We sat in the aisle between the bunks. The teachers improvised with visual aids, pieces of paper with written numbers and letters, and with the help of such simple visuals, we relearned how to count and write. "The more crowded, the merrier," our teachers joked. All, would be just all right, but I did not enjoy the repetition!

There was reason that the children were dispersed to different locations after the fire. The older students were sent to the psycho-neurological boarding school for adults; girls were sent to Kedrovka, boys to Chugunash. Oh, these places were not fun, especially Kedrovka, but the students were sent with kind words and best wishes. And new children arrived from the other Kemerovo orphanage, with mixed backgrounds — they were my age but with zero training. It was hard without the grown-up girls who always helped me, but I was glad to see the new children. But I was disappointed that these newcomers were illiterate and innumerate.

I once caught myself not remembering the numbers after fifteen, although at the age of six, living at home, I had been able to count up to twenty. I was horrified with the thought that I was becoming forgetful and dumb.

But I had a great literary memory. When the teacher read children's book written in rhymes, I could repeat the text from the beginning to end, even without glimpsing the book. Everyone was surprised; they praised me and called me very intelligent. I enjoyed success so much, I was ready for new remarkable achievements, but nobody asked me for them.

One day after school, when the students ran away, and I was alone in my room, I noticed a ragged book, which someone had left on my bed. My eyes were attracted to the red letters printed on the cover. I took the book, read the title, syllable after syllable: 'On One Front After Another'. I read below: A.M. Sadilenko. I understood it was the author's name. Out of boredom I opened the book and started reading, one syllable after another, making words, then I came to the dialogue of characters, and I thought it was amazing — it was like two people were talking, and it was all written on one page, and it was so clear. No one had ever explained to us that one could write dialogues, monologues, describe nature, and so on, on a piece of paper. This was the first time in my life when I read; I covered five pages without interruption. And then I looked up and I was amazed how quickly time had flown by; it was already lunch time. And the boredom which I had just flew away! This experience changed my life.

But I was not able to finish this book. I was so excited, and I started bragging that I read a very interesting book about the war. Vaska, the stuttering boy in the stroller, took the book away from me.

"Let me l-l-look at the b-b-book!" Vaska asked me.

I did not suspect anything bad, so I asked a girl to give him the book. In the evening, I sent the same girl to retrieve the book, but Vaska refused to return it. "I am g-g-going to r-r-read it m-m-myself!" He made his eyes frightening and words shot out like bullets from his fractured speech.

I was close to tears. I wanted to know so much about what else was written in this book. The teacher was passing by. "Nina Pavlovna, Vaska took from me the book about the war, and he does not want to give it back!" I complained.

"Vaska is a boy; he needs to read books about the war," Nina Pavlovna answered in an instructive tone. "Let him read it first, and then he will give it to you."

Vaska smiled maliciously behind the teacher's back. But when, three days later, I asked Vaska about the book, he brazenly declared, "I gave it away; I don't remember to whom. It's a bad book."

"But it's so interestingly written." I was indignant. "How could you do this? You didn't read it and didn't let me read it!"

"You are too little to read such books," Vaska said impudently, stretching out in his stroller.

At night I could not sleep, thinking of this mystery book and I sighed quietly. I would be able to find this book searching in the wards if I could move on my own, if I could walk…

In a few years, one of the boys brought this book to me. It was shabbier than before, completely dilapidated, but fortunately all the pages were intact. At that time, I could read very well, and I swallowed 'On One Front After Another' in one gulp, from beginning to end.

I see it in a symbolic way that the first book I took in my hands was 'On One Front After Another'. After all, my life has been a front line, an eternal arena of warfare, defense and offensive, repelling attacks and the reinforcement for the rear, a war for my full existence, with the utmost difficulty, being diagnosed with CP.

***

Three months later, after my encounter with my first book, my mother brought me a completely dilapidated textbook, 'Native Speech'. A relative had finished fourth grade, the textbook was not needed any more, and it would be embarrassing to pass it to the younger generation, as the book was in awful condition. All the pages existed separately, and the hard cover was so shabby that the illustration of Vasnetsov's painting 'Three Bogatyrs' was barely visible. But for the handicapped girl this tattered book would be just right. After my mother left, I opened the book at random and read it:

> The sunset already became pale
> Above the sleeping ground,
> Blue mists are smoking
> And the new moon icon rises.

And the beautiful music of words sang in my ears. It seemed they were ordinary words, but how beautiful and mysterious they sounded! I continued reading. Thanks to my insatiable imagination, what I was reading was flowing in my little head, shining with divine colors. Sitting in my bed, I bent over this textbook in the most incredible position, making a curve, just to be able to read another line in the twilight.

"Toma! Are you sick?" the nanny asked, entering the room.

It took me a while to understand her question. I was far away in a different reality.

"Toma, lift your head." She became angry.

I raised my head; I saw the twilight in the room and the nanny in front of me. "No, Aunt Polina, I'm not sick at all," I said.

"Then why are you sitting bent?" she asked. "Can I help you to lie down?"

"I was reading," I said proudly.

"Lie down, reader! Tomorrow will be light, and you can read your book all day long," she grumbled, trying to make me comfortable in bed."

"Put the book under my pillow, please," I asked.

"Calm down, it's under the pillow, sleep." Aunt Polina covered me with a blanket and left.

On that unforgettable evening I fell asleep feeling happy — I had a magic book under my pillow, and that book was my own, and I didn't have to give it to anyone.

Years later I was retrospectively exuberant that the first lines of poetry that came to me were the lines from Pushkin's 'Ruslan and Ludmila'.

***

Timidly, but confidently, I began to get acquainted with the world's literature, which in fact began to shape my personality. It was literature that would help me withstand, not bend, not lose human dignity. It was the books that would give me the meaning of life.

And in time, I learned to count first to one hundred, then to hundreds, just looking at page numbers. And in my mind, I counted to a million. This is how I used books to recover my lost ability to count numbers and to improve my mathematical skills. I lost this ability due to the lack of practice, but now my talent has come back to me.

Calling Clouds

The former cotton cover, upholstering my burned stroller, had exceeded its life expectancy — very soon it fell off the iron skeleton, which was also completely destroyed, so the wretched means of transport was unusable. The caring boys brought me a baby stroller, which apparently was borrowed without asking permission, because three days later its owner came and the baby stroller had to be returned. And I would remain without a stroller for a long time, which meant with much less comfort, as the stroller provided support for my back. Now I was being fed in a horizontal position; I did not have a sufficient support for my back for a vertical position. I was not able to sit straight on my own. And to make me more comfortable was too much trouble for the nannies. During the feeding procedure in a horizontal position, the liquid food dripped on my pillow, clothes, even under my back, which gave me disgusting sensations. However, this happened quite often when the nannies carelessly held the plate or brought the spoon to miss my mouth.

When I told them later about this period of my unhappy life, people asked me questions:

Why were you fed lying down? Why couldn't you sit down and be fed? Especially since you could sit down on your own.

Let me explain. I needed three or four solid pillows under my back to sit steadily in my bed, and we had very feeble flat pillows. And where could I get extra pillows? There were no extra ones. I could ask the girls from my room if I could use their pillows, but they would not be willing to lend me them even for a short time. First of all, the liquids could spill and the girls would not be happy with soiled pillows. And putting pillows under my back for every breakfast, lunch and dinner, then cleaning and returning them to the owners, would take a lot of work, and the nannies did not want to get involved with such a complicated procedure of feeding.

However, they continued asking me questions:

Why couldn't your mother find for you a stroller, a used one? There should be grown-up children whose strollers would be available? You weren't in a special wheelchair; was it a regular baby stroller? Couldn't she buy a used stroller? It's not expensive! Or could she ask people if they have a stroller which they don't need any more? The fact that the boys brought you a baby stroller is touching, but why didn't the adults do it? Why didn't the staff get you a used stroller? Or was there a stroller deficit in Kuzbass?

I find it difficult to answer these questions. Apparently, they were tired of me; they just did not care about this useless crippled freak, who required individual care…

To be fair, the employees of the orphanage had been asking my mother to provide a stroller. But she replied, "Why doesn't Cheremnov make her a stroller?" And she sent them to my father.

My 'lying existence' continued for a long, long time: more than a year and a half. And they stopped teaching us — they would teach us a month, then they would abandon us. So all I had to do was read and think.

Often, lying still in my bed, I looked longingly out the window. From my bed I could only see the sky and floating clouds. Watching them constantly, I became jealous of them. The clouds were floating indifferently behind the window, free in their movement…

How I wanted to travel on the cloud of liberty and get away from the orphanage! But where would I go? Anywhere, just not to see any more these hateful walls. And the clouds from their height above of course did not notice the little place called Bachata Orphanage, filled with miserable disabled children. They sailed as they pleased, not knowing how much they filled my soul with longing, calling me and calling to follow them…

The Epidemic of Dysentery

September 1967. The unhygienic and confined environment gave its bitter fruit — dysentery broke out in the orphanage. At night I had a terrible stomach ache. Luckily, the nanny Anya Fudina whom I called 'aunt', was on duty that night. If it had been Livshina, I would have been in trouble. I was not the only one who suffered; a boy and a girl who was able to walk had the same problem. In the morning, the three of us were isolated — we were moved to the little house standing by the orphanage fence. The nannies would bring us food, help us with the toilet, fix our beds and then go back to the building.

I lay in bed all day. Sometimes Nadia, who was able to walk, would take me to the wooden porch and run away. But I was not afraid to be alone; on the contrary, I felt like with this change I had a new, interesting life.

In the first days of isolation, we were checked by doctors who came from the village hospital; they prescribed a medicine. But they left quickly; they must have been afraid of infection. Every week they took samples, but could not stop the epidemic. Soon, half of the orphanage inhabitants had dysentery, and several quarantine rooms had to be established. By this time, a new building had been built to replace the one destroyed by fire, but not all were immediately transferred there; the inmates remained in solitary confinement.

My treatment was coming to an end, but there was a new infection — scabies again. But thank God, itchy spots only appeared on my stomach. What kind of infection was it? I saw something similar in the Prokopyevsk PNBS (psycho-neurological boarding school) when I was transferred there — it could be from lack of vitamins and the general weakening of the body. So those girls in the Prokopyevsk PNBS with similar symptoms were oiled with ointment, treated with ultraviolet light and given pills — all these remedies were not available in the supply of our orphanage.

What kind of orphanage did we have? No amenities, no facilities, no hygiene, no proper food, no timely medical care, no proper treatment, no fire safety! Not to mention callousness and indifference, which we had in abundance…

Two weeks later, patients with dysentery were combined into one solitary confinement. So those who were not sick were put in a new unit, and we were left to recover in the old one. In the evening, the lights went on in the windows of the new building, and I could clearly see the girls jumping on their beds. It looked like they had a lot of fun there, but they were actually being chased by the nannies who were commanding them to go to bed.

Aunt Anya Fudina ran into our solitary confinement. "Oh, Toma! It is not a regular building, but a palace! Light, spacious, clean, there is a shower. We will now bathe you often, and you will not itch any more."

The New Wonderland Building

When we finally recovered from dysentery, we were transferred to a new Wonderland building. We just could not wait for this wonderful moment. And the most vivid memory I still have is how I was put in the shower — I had such great fun — it gave me the feeling of being in the rain and the water was dripping down from head to toe.

I did not like only one thing: we were placed on the second floor, as the first floor was occupied by children who were transferred from the 'weak quarter'. There were also new children with severe abnormalities and mental retardation who just entered the orphanage. I had to be dragged from the second floor to the street; then after spending some time outside, I had to be helped up the stairs. And so in this fashion they transported me all day long until the day when I left the orphanage — the boys carried me in their arms up and down; the girls also scooted me down the stairs.

Aunt Anya Fudina was transferred from us to the 'weak quarter'. And I cried because I missed her.

***

As soon as the new building was opened, another visiting team of doctors arrived. The previous medical team had examined me when I was still in the old burned barracks (when I was taken to them without my underwear). And this second team came when I was twelve, and I was dressed properly. There was a therapist, a surgeon and a dermatologist in the crew. Unfortunately, there were no eye doctors, no neurologists, no psychiatrists — doctors whose participation was extremely important for the patients of our kind.

The therapist examined me, and wrote some prescriptions, and I was so happy that she spoke to me as with a friend and an adult. Before that, doctors never talked to us — they talked only to the staff.

"I'll give you vitamin injections, and you will feel better," she said.

After the doctors left, I waited three days for these vitamins, and on the fourth day I asked the nurse if I should have my vitamin injections.

"What vitamin injections?" She rounded her eyes. "You get your vitamins for lunch, and that's enough."

A few years later, I would be able to see my medical history; I would read the entry of that year — 'The girl is healthy, feels better, she receives… vitamin B shots', which I never had.

***

The joy of living in the Wonderland building was overshadowed by another incident with Livshina. In the evening after they finished cleaning, I was approached by Ludka, a grown-up girl from our room. She volunteered to take care of me, and that afternoon she promised to give me a shower.

"Annushka allowed me to take a shower," Ludka said. She called Livshina Annushka.

"I don't think she will allow me to have a shower." I said, starting to doubt.

"I am going to talk to her, maybe she will allow it," Ludka said and went to the corridor. And I started listening to her conversation with Livshina. "Annushka, Tomka asked to shower her; I promised I would." I heard Ludka's voice.

"Did she work in the mine today that she needs a shower?" Livshina said sarcastically.

She did not allow me to take a shower.

I was lying in bed wondering, why can't I shower now? I have very few simple domestic pleasures in my life! According to the hygienic point of view, one has to take a shower daily, and I had so many skin diseases, because I was not washed for a long time. And unfortunately, Livshina was not the only one who had such strange views on sanitation…

***

Two months later, the new nurse, Elena Petrovna, came to work for us after graduating from a medical school. One day, she substituted teachers who just finished their day shift and went home. She fed us lunch, and graciously allowed the senior group to watch TV during the 'dead hour'. It was New Year's Eve of 1968. It was supposed to be a TV music show, which I loved. So, I was sitting on the floor, waiting patiently to be delivered to the TV room; the girls were whispering some secrets to each other, and I did not want to rush them. Our benefactor walked in and, pointing her finger at me quite rudely, commanded, "Take this one to bed!"

The girls stood up for me. "It's Toma, she understands everything; let her watch TV."

But Elena Petrovna grabbed me behind my arms, causing pain; she ordered the girls to hold my legs, so in this barbaric way they dragged me together to my bed, and threw me face down. After that, Elena Petrovna left. With some efforts, I rolled on my back. I did not even feel like crying. I was just trying to digest what I had done and looking for words to explain it. But is there any explanation at all? The only thing I realized was that I had another enemy.

By the spring of 1968, my hair had grown and the girls started tying my hair with bows. Seeing this innocent occupation, Elena Petrovna for some reason developed a keen desire to cut my hair as short as possible. One day, when she saw me in the hallway with bows, she said out of the blue, "We have to cut her hair off!"

All who were in the hallway turned their heads in my direction with a great surprise. I felt embarrassed and lowered my gaze, thinking: Why do they want to do this? I just started to grow my hair. I want to look like a girl, not a boy… Fortunately, Elena Petrovna was not supported in her irrational desire to cut my hair; after that she did not take her proposition to the staff.

I tried to avoid her; however, when it was her shift, I always heard her brazen voice, resounding like a moral imperative: "We have to cut off Cheremnova's hair!" I could not stand it any more and told the teacher Sukhodoltseva about the bizarre obsession of the teacher Petrovna. A staff meeting was scheduled that day; among other items to be discussed was my hair, also included in the agenda. When they came to the point, Ludmila Vasilevna posed the question to the meeting not without sarcasm.

"Should we cut Cheremnova's hair?"

Everyone laughed — the posed question sounded like a mockery of the famous Hamlet phrase: 'to be, or not to be, that is the question'; and if Hamlet's question was elevated, the question 'to cut, or not to cut' was simply absurd. But here, taking away his smile, director Vil Mikhailovich stood up. "Tamara is a big girl and she will decide which hair style she wants to have. Leave Cheremnova alone, her hair is her only joy…"

The staff members were delighted to tell me about that meeting in detail, and not without gloating — many disliked Elena Petrovna. After the director's intercession, the disgraced Elena Petrovna did not repeat her attacks.

But then, when she went to accompany us to the Prokopyevsk psycho-neurological boarding school, she could not resist one last affront. When we were transferred from the car to the emergency room, Elena Petrovna said, "This one, writes poetry, but her poems are so miserable and make no sense!"

***

I tried to find an answer — why was I treated this way by some of the staff? I did not do anything wrong and I tried to be quiet. Oh, well, I could annoy them with so many things — they had to help me with dressing, washing, toilet, feeding. But I was not the only one who needed help. And everything that I could I did myself! I called for help only when I could not do it myself. Was I disgusting? Yes, I was often shaking; spasticity and hyperkinesia make a depressing impression on others. And I was cross-eyed — it is not pleasant when a person does not look directly into your eyes, but looks away from you. But it was not my fault, it was just my tragedy! Why did they not express compassion, but disgust? I have been speculating on these questions for a long time, but I never found a precise and satisfactory answer…

***

The negative attitude of the staff was not my greatest grief. The absence of the stroller caused me much more distress. And I needed a stroller like air! I spent most of my time in bed.

After I had been without the stroller for more than a year and a half, Zinaida Stepanovna, a very kind teacher, found a more or less tolerable stroller's skeleton in a local garbage dump. It was only a skeleton; the wheels were missing as well as other essential parts. In order to substitute the missing seat, she attached a wooden plank and a pillow to the remains of the stroller back. So I was sitting in the ex-dumpster stroller like a little princess, but this structure was so uncomfortable — it was so hard on my back, and my legs were uncomfortable. They would fall asleep; in other words, they would become numb; the medical term is transient paresthesia— the reason I chose to spend most time in bed.

In 1968, the first factory-made strollers with an elegant design appeared in our orphanage. I received a yellow one, with a red soft seat, with similar back and armrests. I was happy and almost jumped for joy. The stroller was mechanical, designed for manual control — rims for hands were attached to large wheels. But I, with my one slightly working hand, did not operate it well. Inside the building I was able to move back and forth, but on the street, my friends/comrades drove me; it was not the responsibility of the staff.

Sitting in the stroller was comfortable and aesthetically pleasing; I had a feeling I had a new luxurious dress. But the luxury did not last long. Three days later, the group of boys went to the river and took me with them. As soon as they reached the road leading to the river, my magnificent carriage broke — the left wheel together with the axle fell apart. The boys had difficulties carrying me and the stroller back. The stroller was repaired, but I did not dare to leave the gate.

Later, in 1970, my father brought me a homemade stroller — not so elegant, but reliable. And in the same year I was given a new state-owned stroller, so I became the owner of two strollers. The orphanage children behaved much better and did not break them any more. On the contrary, the grown-up boys pumped up the wheels and changed the valves. And the government substituted the worn-out strollers for new, so that I was no longer left without a vehicle.

The Location Mystery

During my long-suffering childhood and adolescence, I endured so many forms of abuse and mistreatment from different people. I did not expect that these evil but still not mortal flowers, would transform into something more sinister — that very soon the villains' fate would attempt to bend me into a ram's horn.

I remember very well the sunny summer day in 1969. I was fourteen, a teenage girl, and something charming appeared in my face. Local good-hearted people would make comments: "Our Tomka has blossomed; just look at her." Especially they praised my 'turquoise eyes'. They told me as a result of oxidation, turquoise stones could change their color — blue turquoise would transform from light blue into dark green. It was the time when I started accepting my appearance, and examined myself in the mirror with satisfaction, but that was not to last. All the worst things would happen with my mother's participation. And on that day, things happened also with her submission. We were sitting outside; she was about to leave for the station. The nurse came up to us, and they started talking.

"Your girl is so intelligent; she can read. If she were healthy, she could be a great help at home. And she is beautiful like you are; she looks like you." The nurse could not stop paying me compliments. "I think she has polio? I don't remember what's written in her medical history."

"No, she has mental retardation," my mother said, not at all embarrassed that I was sitting next to her. "It's written in her records."

"Oh, I see…" The nurse was disappointed.

The sun was still shining, but I felt I was covered with darkness. I did not even hear what my mother said.

I had been not very open to social communications and conversations, always preferring reading, but from that moment on I closed myself completely and began to cling and feel paralyzed at the sight of the teachers. Why teachers? Because they prepared our evaluations and always included diagnoses registered in the medical history. I decided to find out what kind of evaluation the teachers wrote about me.

I am an alarmist. If something is wrong, I start to panic, feel threatened, and fall into inner hysteria, but here I was calm; I just wanted to check my medical history. Of course, I had to do it secretly. It was impossible to ask directly to be shown my medical history; they would refuse. I waited for the day when the teachers updated our evaluations. I had never thought about my evaluation until I heard this unpleasant conversation between my mother and the nurse.

When our group was in the playroom, the teacher gave us pencils and drawing paper, and I made myself comfortable to do my writing. I whispered to Luba Labysheva, the girl who assisted me until my very last day in the orphanage, asking her to sneak my medical history. While the teacher was working on someone's evaluation, Luba secretly brought me a file with my medical history.

When I opened it, I was surprised. Besides the notorious 'irreversible damage of CNS (central nervous system), there was the diagnosis of 'oligophrenia at the stage of debility' with the teacher's additional note, 'primitive thinking'. Of course, I was impressed with the words 'oligophrenia' and 'idiocy', and the phrase 'primitive thinking' had some impact on me, but most of all I was astonished with another thing, which was my location. I remembered perfectly well that I was six years old when I was brought to this Bachata orphanage, and it was not a dream that I used to have a family, and we lived together in Novokuznetsk. Nevertheless, regardless of my crystal-clear recognition of my whereabouts, there was an absurd location, written in black on white on the first page of my medical history, saying that I live in the Chugunash orphanage. I must be omnipresent if I could reside in the two locations at the same time!

As far as I knew, there was the adult male psycho-neurological boarding school in Chugunash. Even if there was an orphanage, how could I live there and at the same time live in the Bachata orphanage, where I have already spent seven years? It might be assumed that the person who filled out information about my location made a mistake, and I find it natural, because the Chugunash PNBS often appeared in our conversations, and grown-up boys were frequently sent there. But on the other hand, the teachers who regularly reviewed the medical history should notice this discrepancy; they always flip through the first page when they fill in their evaluations. Didn't they care? If they turn a blind eye to the incorrect diagnoses regarding my mental development, then what difference would it make to which orphanage Toma Cheremnova was assigned?

I wanted an explanation: Why, living in Bachata, was I listed in Chugunash? Destiny gave me a chance to be outraged. But I was afraid, scared, frightened…

The readers could wonder: what are you afraid of? The young lady, almost fourteen years old, has the right to know the content of her medical history, particularly the first page. I could go to the teacher and ask her face-to-face, why do I reside in the Chugunash orphanage? And to be more specific, I could ask if there is an orphanage in Chugunash, or is there just the adult male psycho-neurological boarding school? I could also make a witty remark that I was assigned to the men's school in the way similar to the practices for the offspring of nobility, who from their early childhood were enrolled in a military regiment.

Once I had the audacity to mention to the staff my diagnoses and prospects. It was like being interrogated by an inquisition — they tortured me with questions about how I had found out about my diagnoses and their plans regarding my future. If I had betrayed Luba, who secretly brought me the file, she would have been punished. And they punished the girls, even the adults, in the cruellest way — they would strip them down to their underwear, take away the mattress and blanket, leave the girl just a sheet and a pillow — and then the girl had to lie on the bare metal net until they believed she had come to her senses. And Luba would not get away with this punishment. So I kept my mouth shut.

So Toma Cheremnova's official whereabouts remained a mystery.

I am Growing Up

In 1970, another building was added to our orphanage, just like the one which was built after the fire, in two floors, similar in design, but unfortunately with fewer accommodations — toilets, sinks, and showers were only on the ground floor. They put the girls on the second floor where in addition to bedrooms there were playrooms. I had my own pot under my bunk, but my poor roommates had to run to the ground floor to go to the toilet and do hygienic things, and even to get water.

The feminine hygiene conditions were a real nightmare! Especially on these menstrual days, which are delicately called 'periods'. Feminine hygiene products such as pads and tampons were not available at that time. In the 1960s-70s women used cotton pads and gauze. One could take some cotton and cover it with some gauze, creating a sanitary napkin, which later could be thrown away. We were not provided either cotton or gauze, but instead they sent us to the laundry room, where we could get washed cotton rags to use as sanitary napkins. After their use, the teachers and nannies expected us to throw them away, but the launderers screamed at us, "Where are we going to get so many rags for you?"

It was more difficult for me, compared with the other girls, to follow feminine hygiene properly. I could give my used rag to one of the girls to wash it, but more often I had to throw it out and beg for washed rags. God forbid you, dear women, to suffer such humiliation!

***

In the same year, 1970, our group was completely reassembled; only Vaska and I remained from the old-timers. Many children came from auxiliary schools with low grades; they continued to follow the curriculum of their previous schools.

I had an advantage of learning how to count pages of books which I had read in abundance. It was easy for me to solve x and y problems in mathematics — to me it was the same as arithmetic; I just had to find hidden numbers. I could do it easily. The teacher would write a mathematical problem on the board — I would immediately solve it. And when I had the final answer, I pronounced it aloud, being excited by mathematical challenge. The teacher would rebuke me. "Toma, don't give the answers! Solve the problem in your head."

I had difficulties in writing with my hand, but otherwise, I was just as good as the other students.

They once gave a problem, which was not so easy: you had to minus one from ten and then transfer it to another ten, and then to another ten, so you had to deal with a few sequences of ten. I concentrated on thinking and I got it right. I was sitting next to a girl who could not understand it, though she had finished seventh grade. And when I explained to her how I solved the problem, the girl understood. I was praised: "You are like a teacher!" And after that I was often asked to work with those who had problems in mathematics.

My readers may find my story naïve; I am telling about such simple mathematics and I was already fifteen! But it was the kind of math they taught us at the specialized orphanage. If I could have learned math in a normal school! But there was a tall wall between me and the real mathematics, and it was the diagnoses they falsely gave me, as well as their false evaluation of my cognitive development...

***

One day, Vaska and I were sitting in our strollers in the hallway, and he was approached by the new teacher, Valentina Fedorovna, a very young woman, still not married.

"Did you read the book, Vaska?" she asked in a friendly way.

"I read it, thank you," Vaska said smartly.

"Would you like another one?" Valentina Fedorovna asked.

"Okay," Vaska agreed.

"Like the one you read? Love story?" she asked.

And before Vaska was able to answer, I said, "Please bring me something to read."

The next day, she sent me, through the girls, the book of Georgi Egorov, 'You Are Salty, My Land'. It was a great book by a genuine Altai writer, serious and truthful. Going forward, this book has been republished several times, but its continuation, 'To Those Who Live on This Land' was put under the cloth for censorship reasons for many years, and it was only released in the Perestroika era.

***

Valentina Fedorovna and I became friends, though we did not show it openly — why tempt fate? Officially I was not under her guidance; she taught classes with younger students, but she visited me regularly, was interested in my affairs, brought books, and I was happy to have her attention.

Thanks to her, I read a book by the Kuzbass writer Vladimir Voroshilov, 'The Sun Continues to Shine' — it was about the miner Sergei Tomilov. He became blind after an accident in the mine, but found the strength to live on, adapted to his blindness and returned to work. Then he became the director of society for the blind, then he acquired a family. But it was not about my case; no books had been written yet on my topic (cerebral palsy). Such books would appear later, for example, Valery Zavialov's wonderful book 'And the Impossible is Possible', published in 1977. The book 'White on Black' by Ruben Gallego, published in 2003, gained wide popularity and was even transformed into a play and staged.

In my time, the heroic example was Nikolai Ostrovsky, a blind and immobilized man who continued to work as a writer, dictating his books. I saw a film about him, and after watching the last episode I, who seemed to learn to restrain emotions, was crying so bitterly that the teacher Nina Pavlovna had to take me from the hall to the corridor, so I could calm down.

I always had a book in my hands. There was no shortage of fiction in the orphanage. In addition to Valentina Fedorovna, who provided me with books, books were brought by employees and relatives. The director

Bikmaev organized a mobile library — books were delivered to us from the village library. So the orphanage inhabitants, including those who were bedridden, could choose books they liked. Later I learned that books were collected in schools and clubs specifically to donate them to the orphanages. Both adults' and children's books were part of our book collection.

Oh, my passion for reading… I even managed to read at night; my bed was located in front of a glass door through which the light from the corridor came in. After such night readings, I had a severe headache; I was also emotionally affected by the books. In addition, my hyperkinesia worsened, and then during the nap or at night, when I was falling asleep, my head was pulled back and assumed an unnatural position. Now I understand that it was necessary to take urgent measures; it could be stopped and corrected. But then none of the orphanage workers cared about such nuances. And the consequences of my passion for reading were: the spastic torticollis, which had developed during my reading sessions, acute pain in the cervical vertebrae, and my vision also deteriorated.

***

I think after reading about my struggles, people could think: Well, why should she worry so much about the diagnosis of 'oligophrenia at the state of debility'? There are many people with diagnoses that have nothing to do with their real conditions, but they live their lives without such worries! People tried to console me: "The mental retardation is recorded in your medical history, but in reality, you are intelligent. Don't pay attention to it! Just live and use your brilliant mind."

Of course, you could ignore the wrong diagnosis, but after all, I was so dependent on others! Because of this wrong diagnosis, I did not receive any education. I did not even complete elementary school! I did not have any certificate of any education! I did not even have my teachers' evaluations regarding my studies! In addition, I did not have my medical history, with which I was transferred from the orphanage to the psycho-neurological boarding school. And how could one call it education, when during six years we had been taught only how to count from one to ten, and then they had made us jump to studying mathematical problems with x and y? It makes me laugh!

So until this day I am formally considered illiterate, unable to read, write or count. However, today the absence of a certificate and diploma does not bother me any more, and in the questionnaire, in the column 'education', I write 'self-educated'.

But then... then I did not see any prospects for myself, only the pitch darkness looming ahead, in which one could degrade, and be drowned, to go to the bottom... At night, until my teeth started gnashing, I meditated on the same question: why, with my physical illness am I considered mentally disabled? What does it mean: I lag behind other children? Yes, I am different, with disabled arms and legs, but I believe I have a great capacity for logical and critical thinking and problem-solving. I can think abstractly, and I can comprehend complex ideas, which indicates I have intelligence. All I have to do is to try to prove that I have sufficient intellect. And as far as mental illness and debility are concerned, it might relate to someone or something, but not to me. And I started studying all school textbooks I came across. I even begged my mother to buy a physics textbook for sixth grade for me. After her wrangling, my mother bought it; such books were cheap then. I dug into this textbook, reading it like a novel. And I easily understood everything in it: be it Archimedes' law of the body immersed in water, or Newton's law of gravity. I did not even stumble on Einstein's theory of relativity. I just tried to understand it, taking myself as an example: I am sitting in my stroller; I am at rest in relation to the stroller, and relative to the road along which my stroller is being taken. I am in the state of motion. Subsequently, I would write a fairy tale 'Whose Moon Fell into the River', where I would explain the theory of relativity to children, using the example of the moon and a puppy, and a kitten catching up with it.

My readers may be perplexed: What is the problem? Yes, I had acquired some knowledge in various subjects, including in physics, and I did my studies independently. But I had to act and not suffer at the psycho-neurological boarding school, where I was sent later by the social security authorities. My dear readers, the fact is that while studying school disciplines on my own, I was not sure that I understood them correctly, and I did not dare to confirm it.

One day one of the nurses asked me "Do you like the school program?"

And I innocently admitted that I was bored, that I would like to get more in-depth knowledge. And she passed our conversation over to the teachers, and then they tore me to pieces. And they laughed at me for a long time — the mentally challenged Cheremnova is thirsty for in-depth knowledge!

Lubasha

I would like to dedicate this chapter to Lubasha Labysheva, who was my assistant for three years. Like me, Luba was brought to the orphanage from her home. She suffered from epilepsy. She completed four years of elementary school, but was unable to continue her studies, as frequent epileptic episodes disrupted classes and she was released from school.

We became friends. She was a strange girl, but amiable and supportive. She wrote well under my dictation — despite my mother's indifference, I wrote her letters and even sent my poetry. Luba dressed me, put me in the stroller, and sometimes helped me with laundry. However, I was so tired of her habit of telling the same story; she did it not because of lack of memory, but she did it obviously on purpose. One day, when I was reading a book, I could not stand her vapid talking and I lost my temper.

"Luba, shut up and leave me alone! How many times can you repeat the same thing?"

"I won't do it again. But can I sit next to you?" she asked.

"You can sit next to me." I already regretted that I overreacted.

Luba sat on the foot of my stroller, but even a minute did not pass till she started talking incessantly like a magpie. What could you do with her? For a habit of talking which irritated the ear, she was called the magpie. So there was a magpie sitting next to me, talking non-stop, while I was studying a book titled 'Chrestomathy'. The topic of my study required a lot of attention — it was about basic repeating rhythmic units which form verses: iambs, chorees, anapests, amphibrachs and dactyls. But because of Luba's talking, I could not understand anything, and my ear was caught by the repetitious nonsense. I asked her five times to be silent, but it was like talking to the wall. Then I had no patience left, and I grabbed her ponytail which held her gorgeous thick hair, pulled it, and I strictly said, "Don't come near me again!"

Luba resented this and left. She cried, then felt better and came back. She apologized. "Toma, I'm sorry; I won't bother you any more."

"Why are you doing this?"

"Sometimes I like to tease people," she confessed.

The next day, the teacher Nina Stepanovna rebuked me. "Toma! Why did you hurt Luba? She looks after you and how could you act like that?"

"Nina Stepanovna, why does she disturb me when I'm studying?" I defended myself.

"Girls, stay away from Toma. There are many of you, and if everyone bothers her with conversations and ideas, she won't have time for herself," the teacher said.

I described this case in order to express my sincere regret to the girls, whom I rejected not always tactfully, while immersed in my studies as it was my favorite occupation. Self-education became for me like a drug, but nobody wanted to understand it.

Shortly before I was sent to the PNBS, two teachers from a secondary school came to work as educators, having left their previous jobs because of health reasons. I was so happy: I imagined I would show them my knowledge and they would appreciate it, and they would advise me what should I learn next and which books I should study; they would help me, they would give me school programs. But…

One day when we were all in the playroom, the newly arrived teacher started talking to Luba. Their conversation was quite peaceful until Luba, with her usual importunity, began to defend her point of view. There was nothing impolite in her behavior; we freely argued with our teachers on various topics. Suddenly, the new teacher grabbed Luba by the collar like a naughty puppy, dragged her into the ward, and there she stripped off her clothes, threw the mattress off the bed and pushed her into the bare metal carcass, saying, "It should teach you not to argue with superiors!"

When she left, our girl team tried to console Luba, but she was inconsolable. I could understand; she was almost an adult girl, and she experienced such humiliation!

After this execution, my ardor to discuss with the new teachers the topic of education and ask for advice instantly faded away. And they began to put a stick in the wheel to my self-education. If with my previous teachers I could sit alone in the ward and read in silence, then during the shift of this fiasco-teacher I was pushed along with other children into the playroom. When I protested that I preferred to read alone, she angrily hissed that in the playroom I could read too. But how could I read with the noise and shouts of playing teenagers! I did not have enough control of my hands to cover my ears with my fingers, and I could hardly isolate myself from the background, reading the text. Sometimes I would succeed.

What tricks I had to indulge in order to read calmly! For example, I would say I needed to go to the toilet, and I would go in my stroller to the ward and immerse myself in reading. None of the previous teachers blamed me for this: Cheremnova is sitting alone in the ward, reading, so what? It will not bring any harm. It took a lot of time and effort to make the new teachers come to terms with this. Then they would say to each other, how passionate this girl is about books and for studies! And they would add, what a pity that she is crippled; why should she read and study?

My Last Years in the Orphanage

During the last two years they left me free of their previous harassment — the girl has grown up intelligent, serious, well-read, does not require special care, does not cause any trouble, has a personal assistant in the person of her friend Luba and does not bother the staff.

I would have been glad, but my health started rapidly deteriorating, whether this happened because of my hard work on self-education or because of too much stress. And my neck became more problematic, my head buzzed and my back whined. And then one day, sitting on the ground floor, I looked in a mirror hanging on the wall, and at first, I did not understand what was wrong with my face. My eyes looked strange... At one point the teachers observed I was cross-eyed, but nobody took responsibility to request an eye doctor. "Anyway, she will go to the psycho-neurological boarding school, and her life there will be miserable until the day she dies." This is how the orphanage staff would see my future. When I was finally convinced that my eyes were looking in two different directions, I felt down. I was already pinned down by terrible diagnoses, and now I had another one! It was useless to ask for an eye doctor; they would never invite him, and they would never take me to him. And the depression started again; when the night came, I would gnaw the edge of my pillow and cry desperately.

During the last spring of my life at the orphanage, I did not hide my depression. They would take me outside, I would start my reading, then look around and everything would seem normal, but when I saw blooming trees, the sudden realization would come to me that I also have my blossoming season, and then I would start crying so desperately. The teachers would take me away, not saying anything; they did not want me to disturb or annoy anyone. I cried in solitude but with no relief; my soul continued crying without tears. And dark thoughts penetrated me... I realized that I would have nothing in my life, no love, no someone close to me, no home. There would only be a ward and a bed on which I would lie, for how long I did not know, in what condition I did not know either, and by whom I would be surrounded I did not know either. But deep inside there was a tiny seed of hope — a better time would come.

***

There were rumors in the orphanage that I was about to be transferred to the psycho-neurological boarding school. And not only I would have to leave the orphanage, but the rest of our group also would move to the Insk Boarding School.

During the last two years of my life in the orphanage, we stopped our studies: instead, the girls were taught how to knit and sew. And here I took a very active, albeit theoretical part. I could not maneuver my hands, but my intellectual ability never betrayed me. I helped laggards, giving them instructions. I still remember the English-style knitting and how it is similar to the patterns of sport-style knitting, and I can teach anyone to knit socks, mittens, hats and scarves, even though my hands are problematic.

It is a shame that the teachers saw my involvement in knitting, my academic achievements, and that I was so quick in understanding, but they did nothing to prevent me from being sent to the psycho-neurological boarding school, when I could have gone with the other girls to the boarding school of the general type. There was a huge difference between boarding schools for people with chronic psychological maladies and homes of a general type for disabled people! Of course, I could not sew or knit or do anything with my hands. But I could do something else, because regardless of my diagnosis, I was intelligent and well-read. Would I ever use my talents? I did realize that when they made their decisions as to which place to transfer the orphanage inhabitants, the diagnosis written in the medical history was taken into consideration. But there were other indicators!

Two weeks before my departure to the psycho-neurological boarding school, a medical and pedagogical committee arrived. While waiting in the corridor, I imagined that the doctor would open my medical history and detect this horrible mistake. He would say, "Oh, I see a wrong orphanage is indicated here! In which orphanage do you live:

in Bachata or Chugunash?" Then it would give me a chance to discuss the injustice, which I had been enduring, and to show that I was absolutely normal mentally and should not be sent to the madhouse. But, alas, when they took me to the playroom, where the committee had a reception, the chairperson woman read aloud the diagnosis from my medical history, glanced at me briefly, muttered something to the head nurse, and they took me out of there, not letting me say a word.

Thus, the death-threatening diagnosis of mental retardation, created in August 1964 and never revised until I was discharged from the orphanage in 1974, had an adverse effect on my life. This false diagnosis was the result of the negligence of the visiting committees, the disregard of the local staff and the baseness of my mother. And this person, Ekaterina Ivanovna could intervene, protest the diagnosis, and demand an examination. Ekaterina Ivanovna, what have you done?

***

On the eve of my departure to psycho-neurological boarding school, Anna Stepanovna Livshina entered the ward. I was sitting in my bed, reading a book. She sat down on the edge and said, "Tomka, you have been living with us for a long time, almost since the orphanage opened. Your mother is not going to take you home to visit at least once before leaving?"

I silently examined her face, aged and tired, with rough features, without the slightest hint of female charm. A callous, unhappy woman with sadistic inclinations, but it appeared even in her, compassion could awaken.

"No, Aunt Anya, she won't take me home..." I answered, remembering my numerous requests to take me home, even for a while, even for a week, even for a couple of days. Other children were taken home.

I also remembered how one day the teachers started talking about our parents, and one teacher said, "I like Toma's mother, she never demands anything."

Yes, it was a mother who was convenient for the orphanage, who never demanded anything for her child, who never interceded, never insisted on anything, who closed her eyes to everything. Ekaterina Ivanovna would continue to be convenient. Occasionally, with the frequency of three times a year, she would appear at my place, both in the PNBS and in the home for invalids. She would say something, then she would show something. But she was never interested in my problems, and she would never request anything for me; she would never be an advocate for her helpless child in her affairs with the staff, administration and higher authorities.

***

I want to describe another episode. Two girls and two boys, who did not have mothers and fathers, came to our orphanage from the Kemerovo orphanage, known for its mixed population. One of them, Valentina Pozdniakova, apparently hardened in the struggle for existence, was too active and combative. And among other diminutive names, the name 'Valiukha' was the most suitable for her. And about a week later, a Tatar man brought his daughter Natasha to submit her to the orphanage.

The quiet Tatar girl Natasha soon became friends with Valiukha, or rather, Natasha meekly obeyed Valiukha's orders. And it came to the point that the voluntary slave sacrificed pies which she received for lunch in order to pay a tribute to her master. I, swallowing book after book, did not immediately catch the essence of their far-reaching relationship, and once, seeing that Natasha was carrying pies from the dining room into the ward, I left my book and asked, "Natasha — bring me a pie too."

And when she brought me half a pie from dinner, I thanked her, and without thinking why half a pie, and not a whole one, put it in my mouth and, chewing, buried myself in the book.

"Why didn't you bring it to me?" Valiukha asked capriciously.

"They gave me only one pie in the dining room; I ate half, and brought half to Toma." Natasha began to justify herself. "Tomorrow, I will bring you two; I will not eat myself."

"Just remember, don't come to me without pies," said Valiukha, and Natasha walked away looking very sad. "Bring some pies, and then you can be my friend."

I looked up from the book and saw their faces — Valiukha's face was menacingly imperative and Natasha's face was that of a humiliated slave. The pie was stuck in my throat — not only had Natasha been giving her pies to Valiukha, but she brought me her portion as well. I realized that I was no better than this 'slave owner'. I was terribly ashamed.

***

On May 24, 1974, I was sitting in the playroom as usual with a book on my lap. The door opened and the nurse came in. "Tamara is leaving," she said.

"And what, she is already being sent to the madhouse?" The girls were excited.

"Quiet! Do not frighten Toma in vain! Better go and help her change," ordered the teacher who was sitting with us. "Toma, you will go to the boarding school in the city of Prokopyevsk."

The entire ward went to help to change my clothes. Luba and Natasha pulled on my clothes; the others stood in silence. Several girls had tears in their eyes. At that moment I did not feel anything; I felt paralyzed inside. And only when they lifted me into the back of a covered truck, I started crying quietly.

Four more people from the 'weak quarter' were sitting with me in the back of a truck — we were transported to the Prokopyevsk psycho-neurological boarding school. One of them, a boy who was completely unbalanced mentally, screamed shrilly all the way, and this made our voyage even sadder and more painful. I will have to live with such troubled companions all my life, until I die, I thought bitterly, and tears flowed in torrents. And no matter how many great books I read, I would still be under the same bar as these unfortunate people with damaged brains.

"Don't cry, Tomochka; maybe it will be even better there." The nurse from the 'weak quarter', who accompanied us, sitting with us in the back, tried to console me, and carefully dabbed my face with her handkerchief.

Thank God the mean nurse, Elena Petrovna, who also accompanied us, was sitting in the cabin of the truck, next to the driver; otherwise, she would certainly have had a chance to throw her parting words, something caustic and nasty like "This is where you belong — at the madhouse — your place is among the fools."

Part 2
The Prokopyevsk Psycho-Neurological Boarding School

The Crazy Night and the Mad Day

We arrived at Prokopyevsk Psycho-Neurological Boarding School in the evening. The local boys carelessly unloaded the newly arrived disabled to the infirmary; the staff on duty examined us and then locked us inside the isolation room. They did not feed us; they even did not give water. Then, exhausted by crying and feeling thirsty, I asked the visiting employee to give me some water. She examined me for a minute, pursing her lips, and then opened her mouth. "I'll tell the nanny to bring you water."

She went out into the hallway; the isolation door slammed shut and the lock snapped. I waited until dark for water and listened to the steps behind the door, but nobody came.

I will never forget my first night in the madhouse, until my death! They locked me in the company of the mentally challenged, among whom there were real idiots: laughing for no reason, muttering incoherently, shouting nonsense, making obscene sounds. My 'roommates', who were also brought from the 'weak quarter' of the Bachata orphanage, could not move independently. They were recumbent. I was brought to this place without a stroller — government strollers were supposed to be left in the orphanage upon departure. Why lock up the isolation room, whose guests were turned to stone, and we were certainly not rolling stones?

Until the morning, no one came to see us. I lay in bed, licking my dry lips, but then I thought: I should take it as something advantageous. If they gave me water before I fell asleep, I would now want to go to the toilet. And it seemed that there was no vessel or pot here, and who would help me with the toilet? I consoled myself: It's all right, I'll wait, they still have to come and take care of us. But no matter how I strained my ears, the silence reigned outside the door. Then I shouted once, twice, three times. The boy, whose bed was next to mine, and whom I had already recognized as a great screamer, woke up and immediately started making animal sounds.

"Don't shout; they won't come until morning, anyway," said Luba, who was also lying next to me; she was more or less sane.

The night before, as soon as we were dragged into the isolation room, an attendant on duty came. He was completely drunk. He started feeding Luba with chlorpromazine pills. He treated her with such generosity, as if these pills were candies. First, he gave her one pill, then he shoved into her mouth two pills more, and he was about to give her the fourth pill.

"She will die of an overdose!" I could not resist.

My reply frightened the man; he hiccupped, and immediately left.

"How do you feel?" I asked Luba.

"I want to sleep," she said and fell silent.

The screamer boy also became quiet, and I was gradually overcome by sleep.

I woke up, probably at about ten in the morning; it was bright and sunny outside the window. I desperately wanted to go to the toilet. I was taken from the Bachata orphanage somewhere around twelve hours before; since then, they had not asked me if I needed to empty my bladder. During our voyage, I did not use the toilet and endured the entire night here. A bad thought came into my head — maybe we were dumped here on purpose? In a month they will open the room and find corpses! We could not escape; none of us could walk…

Then I heard footsteps. The door was unlocked, and the nurse entered, accompanied by two young men. She said to them, "Load everyone onto the cart and take them to the 'weak quarter'. And then take them to the second floor, to the former red corner."

The name 'red corner' is an interesting Soviet invention. It combines the noun 'corner' which can be read as 'premises for holding classes' and the adjective 'red', which stands for 'related to revolutionary activity'. Red corners originated in the early 1920s for the needs of agitation and political education, literacy classes, and other activities as well. I noticed that here they used the same terminology 'weak quarter' as it was used in my orphanage. And I felt horrified that they were sending me, mentally normal and capable of thinking, to a doomed place for wretched individuals with mental disorders. Here the power of a wrong diagnosis demonstrated itself!

We were put inside a cart led by a tired horse. The cart proceeded to the furthest corner of the territory of the PNBS, where it stopped by a shabby building; and then we were taken to the second floor. It was filled with patients with severe mental disorders and psychic deviations. One of them stood by the window and carefully tore the curtains into small ribbons; another, stripped of his pants and underwear, was running naked through the passage of the corridor. And they were not little boys; they were adult men.

They put me on the couch. The staff left. I listened to distant voices and when I understood that what they were saying — all of us would stay here for the night until they found places for us in the wards, I turned into a screaming beast, probably giving the same impression as screamers from the 'weak quarter'. But at that moment I did not care about what kind of impression I would give.

Ten minutes later, the nurse from the 'weak quarter' entered. She examined me without reaction. She expressed zero reaction to my screams — she had got used to such performances. She was about to leave, and was going to open the door, and here I screamed in full voice, "Please, get me out of here; I'm not mentally retarded, I have a normal brain. I'm afraid to stay here!"

She looked at me still thinking, then she said, "Where am I going to put you? There's no room in the wards. Well, the hostess is coming; we'll figure something out."

She pulled the curtains away from the crazy young man and walked out. I wished she would stay. When I recall what happened next, I feel chilled with horror. As soon as she left, the madman, who was running around naked, screamed and headed towards me. I thought I was going to faint. The only thing I knew was I should not start a conversation with him; I had to act as if I did not notice him. I was silent, but I was frightened, swallowing my tears. The madman made several circles around me, then he lost interest and walked away. I calmed down and even dozed off.

I don't know how long I was alone. I was still half asleep when I heard footsteps approaching the door. The same nurse came in and another woman whose title was 'hostess sister' — she was the manager in charge of supplies. As I learned later, the manager had the intriguing nickname 'The Queen of Spades', by which she was called behind her back. She was majestic, black-haired and, indeed, looked like the queen of spades from the deck of cards.

"This is the girl who needs to get out of here," said the nurse. "She's intelligent, she understands everything, and she's afraid to stay here. Do we have a spare bed?"

The Queen of Spades replied with arrogant indifference, "I think there is a place in ward number seven."

"I'll tell the boys to take her there." The nurse was happy. Then she left, leaving me in the company of the Queen of Spades.

"Are you wearing public underwear?" she asked me without any emotions. "Or is it your personal?"

"No, it's from the orphanage," I said.

"From which one?" The Queen of Spades interrogated me indifferently, in a mechanical voice.

"From Bachata." I sighed, thinking that in the 'native orphanage' I had lived in a room with normal girls, not with madmen.

"Are your shoes state-owned?" The Queen of Spades continued reviewing my wardrobe.

"Yes, state-owned. And the coat that I'm wearing is also state-owned, and the T-shirt, pantaloons, tights." I predicted her next questions. "And I have my own underwear in my suitcase."

"I'll take the boots; you don't need them," the Queen of Spades declared.

"Do you have strollers for people who cannot walk?" I asked her with a trembling voice.

"We don't have strollers," she answered indifferently, and left with my shoes.

The nurse came back with two young men. "Tomorrow, we'll put you in ward number seven, and tomorrow morning I will speak about you at the meeting to transfer you to the women's building," she said.

"What is your name?" I asked her, hoping to continue our friendly dialogue.

"Zinaida Ilinichna," she said.

"And I'm Tamara Cheremnova," I said, introducing myself.

However, there was no further dialogue. Zinaida Ilinichna looked at me attentively, as if she was thinking of how to report on me to her superiors. She ordered the boys to take me down to the ward seven.

I observed the room. It was light and quite clean. There was a round table in the middle. There were five beds; they put me in an empty one. Three beds were occupied by old women — immovable, unresponsive, unemotional, passive... The fourth bed was occupied by a girl about my age; she did not walk well. A nanny came in; I asked about the pot.

"We don't have any pots," she answered. "Do you want a bedpan?"

I said yes. After the simple procedure, the nanny left. I was lying in bed, reviewing my situation. Of course, the barely alive room was a lot better than the red corner with unpredictable lunatics, but spending the rest of my life like this... Sooner or later I would become mad here... and become like the inhabitants of the 'weak quarter'.

When the dinner came, the same nanny came with a bowl of milk soup, and I was not capricious; I finished it and had a cup of tea. Then I fell on the pillow and sank into oblivion... and I was never asked to undress.

They Sent me to Machas

The morning of the new day began with an unusual dead silence. At the orphanage, when I woke up I would hear the cheerful voices of my roommates. Here, the nanny on duty glanced into the room without asking if anyone was in need. After a while, I decided to act; after all, I was not dead yet.

At that time, the girl that did not walk well showed signs of waking up. I lifted my head and said, "Can you go to the nurse? Can you tell her that the new girl, Tamara Cheremnova, is calling her, that she is not well?"

"Sool," the girl said, mispronouncing the word 'sure. She left her bed and went to the corridor. In ten minutes, she came back and said, "Si ill tom." ("She will come.") Then she returned to her bed.

I waited, but no one came. The need to urinate was growing unbearably. If they expected me to pee in my pants, wet the bed, which I have never done in my life, I would never do it. I would rather my bladder burst. I would rather die than lie in bed wet to my ears, which I find disgusting and humiliating.

***

About three years ago, the boys had taken me to bathe in the river. They would take me there often, and I usually sat in shallow water near the shore, where the water was only ankle-deep. So I was sitting in the river, immersed in my thoughts, far away from reality, as it happens to me quite often. In the meantime, someone came up behind me, tickled my neck and ran away. It was such a sudden intrusion in my world that I lost my balance, which had always been problematic, so I fell into the water with my face down. I slapped my face in the water. I do not know how many minutes I was under water with my eyes widely open out of fear. All I remember is the muddy yellow water from the sand, which I swallowed, and it kept flowing to my mouth as if the river invited me to drink it until it became dry. I managed to lift my head; otherwise, I would have choked. Then an unknown force lifted me up and I was sitting on my butt again.

I looked around, still overwhelmed after the shock I just experienced. There was no one around, which means, somehow I got up on my own. And I do not think anyone even noticed that I fell on my face in the water. If they had, they would have helped me. But the boys were happy screaming in the water, and I thought it would be quite foolish to cry now and tell everyone I almost drowned a few minutes ago. And after my confession, the teachers would never let me go to the river. I called to a girl who was enjoying herself in the water nearby, asking her to pull me out of the water and put me in my stroller.

When we were coming back to the orphanage, we met my mother, who was walking along the road towards us! She approached my stroller, looked attentively in my eyes, and for some reason, I thought that she had come to the orphanage and gone to the river, because she felt something was wrong with me. My mother said, "I came to the orphanage, and they told me that you went to the river. They showed me which way to go and I went…"

I do not know if she felt that something threatened my life. A loving mother is always intuitive; she has the sixth sense.

***

So, lying in bed, waiting for the nanny, I asked myself again if my mother felt this very moment when I was about to be drowned in the river. Perhaps she received a message saying that I felt was in danger, and then she appeared almost magically.

Unable to tolerate my overextended bladder, which had been relentlessly putting pressure on my organs, I was prepared for the worst. But apparently, God took pity on me. The door opened and the nurse Zinaida Ilinichna entered the room.

"Please tell the nanny to come here!" I yelled, no longer with good manners. "I need to go to the toilet! I need to use the toilet! I don't want to urinate in bed!"

The nurse said, "We have good news, Tamara. We discussed you at the meeting. We are going to move you to the women's ward."

Two young men entered the room; one grabbed me from the bunk and carried me to the cart with the same tired horse. When we came to the women's ward, the two men carried me together on a stretcher. When we reached the destination, they put the stretcher on the floor. Paramedics Olga Fedorovna, nannies on duty, and the ward residents gathered around me.

"Where should I put her? Is there a bed available?" Olga Fedorovna asked the nanny.

"We don't want her in our room!" screamed an unkempt woman whose head was covered with a dirty scarf. She was sitting on the bench.

I answered her with my thought: our displeasure is mutual. I don't want you to be my roommate.

"Shut up! No one's asking you. If we choose your room, no one is going to ask your permission," said Olga Fedorovna to the unfriendly woman.

"Let's put her in room fifteen," suggested the nanny. "There's Marusia Diborskikh; she can help this girl; there's a free bed in this room."

The men took me to room fifteen, put me on a freshly prepared bed and left. A woman was standing by the window.

"Hello!" I babbled.

"Hello! My name is Aunt Marusia. And they are also Marias," she responded, friendly and pointing out two old women lying in their beds. "This is Aunt Masha and this is Baba Masha. You have to speak loudly to them; they are a little bit deaf."

"My name is Tamara. Aunt Marusia, please call the nanny; I need to go to the toilet!" I was begging, losing my patience.

Marusia went out; a minute later she came back with the nanny on duty.

"I need to go to the toilet," I said to the nanny. "Can you bring me a night pot please?"

"I don't know if we have night pots." The nanny looked surprised. "Masha, look in the toilet; I think there is one left."

"You don't have night pots?" I was surprised — I believed such objects should be in a specialized institution full of paraplegics.

"The residents who lived here before moved to another institution; they took their night pots with them," the nanny explained.

Aunt Marusia returned to the room with a shabby night pot in her hand. "I just found this one," she said. "Old, but without holes. We'll find a better one later."

As I emptied myself, I looked around. There were four identical beds with dressers and a wardrobe along the walls, a round table by the window and a speaker on the wall. Everything looked fine, according to the standards and style established for dormitories. And the neighbors were nice. They had the same name, but each Maria or Masha was called differently: Aunt Marusia, Aunt Masha and Baba Masha. I had calmed down a bit, and my primordial fear had receded slightly.

"He is Good-for-Nothing!"

My roommates participated in my affairs: Aunt Marusia fed me, Aunt Masha helped with toileting, and Baba Masha observed me and my helpers dealing with my physical immobility. From time to time she would exclaim, "He is good-for-nothing!" For some reason, she used the masculine form 'he' instead of 'she'.

"Are you good-for-something?" I answered insolently, with resentment in my voice. I emphasized the informal 'ты' (informal you), though I was supposed to use the formal pronoun 'Вы' (you) to respect our age difference.

"I am also good-for-nothing," she would say, trying without success to stretch her paralyzed arm. And then, desperate to cope with her twisted limb, she would tightly close her lips and become silent for a long time.

At night I waited until my roommates' breathing became smooth, indicating deep sleep. This was when I allowed the misery to dominate me, moving from one bitter passage of my life to another, crying my heart out. Tears were streaming down my face in my silent act of lamentation, as I did not dare to cry aloud. Then I would compose myself and stare at the obscure ceiling, trying to adapt myself to this strange reality…

What else do you want? I would ask myself. With your condition, you deserve this kind of life. You're lying in bed, all crooked and cross-eyed. Nothing is ahead… I would bite my lip and drown in tears without a sound. I was nineteen.

Influenced by books which said that each person has dignity and lives for some purpose, I was thinking that I was born in the image of God too. This kept me from giving up. Why did they send me to *such* a boarding school? How could I be a threat to society? Why did they hide me behind the high fence, separated from those who are considered to be normal, which means they are not deformed, and do not have crossed eyes. There are two worlds: one is the dreadful asylum; the other is the outside world. And why was I privileged to be in prison? Probably, as Baba Masha says, I was 'good-for-nothing'.

The Story of the Three Mashas

All three roommates, the three Mashas, were once healthy and lived with their families in different parts of the country.

Aunt Marusia Diborskikh started working as a babysitter when she was still a child. When she was fifteen and a half years old, she was raped by her master; after that she gave birth to a son. And her mistress, to protect her husband from being sued in a court, sent Marusia to the culinary school to receive the profession of a cook.

After graduating from the culinary school, Marusia moved to Sakhalin, but shortly before leaving, her son was run over by a car and died. In Sakhalin, she got a job at a restaurant, but they found a shortage of money and blamed the young cook. She went to prison, where she became again a victim of violence; this time it was an investigator who raped her. Released early for good behavior, Marusia left the prison with a daughter in her arms.

Finally, fortune smiled on her — she got a job at a port restaurant and met a respectable man. Two happy years together had passed like a dream — good life, job, and a caring husband and daughter.

In the third year the happiness ended — suddenly the legal wife arrived. Marusia swallowed bitterness and stepped aside... And when they celebrated the birthday of the bigamist, the legal wife slapped Marusia in the face in front of guests. The husband did not stand up for her. The competition between the two rivals ended, and the legal wife took her husband to the mainland.

Then Marusia started to drink, ultimately stopping and remarrying. But the new husband beat her relentlessly, cracking her head, resulting in epilepsy. She received medical treatment, which was supposed to improve her condition; however, her epilepsy worsened rapidly. It caused seizures with a sudden loss of consciousness and violent muscle contractions.

After one of her epileptic seizure episodes, she was placed in this asylum, aka Prokopyevsk Psycho-Neurological Boarding School. Some guardianship authorities had expressed concerns about how the condition of Marusia, with a severe form of epilepsy, would affect her daughter. They decided that the mother and her daughter should not have any contact. This is how Marusia became completely alone: her husband left her, her son died in an accident and her daughter just disappeared from her life…

Aunt Masha lived with her husband. They had four daughters, and they wanted to have a boy. And when it seemed like the dream was about to be fulfilled, at the fourth month of her pregnancy, suddenly she started to experience severe schizophrenia. It could not be controlled; her suffering became permanent.

The case of Grandma Masha was less exotic. She worked at a construction company. She did not have children. Her husband died some time ago. She had a stroke and became paralyzed.

This is how these three women ended up in this house of sorrow. And then destiny brought Toma to join the three Mashas in the ward of misery 15, where the sane are locked up for their madness and the cynical serve the state by acquiescing…

***

One afternoon when I was lying in bed — they never gave me a stroller — I noticed Aunt Marusia was going through her papers. I asked, "What are those papers?"

"They are letters — answers from places where I inquired about my daughter," she said sadly.

"Did you find her?"

"They say that there is no such person." Aunt Marusia sighed.

"Where did you send your letters?" I kept asking questions."

"To the Yuzhno-Sakhalinsk Boarding School. She lived and studied there when I was healthy."

"How old is she?"

"She is adult now… so many years have passed…"

When I lived in the orphanage, I had watched a TV show about a woman who found her missing son through the Red Cross. "Write a letter to the International Committee of the Red Cross in Moscow; they will organize a search for your daughter," I assured Aunt Marusia.

I dictated to Aunt Marusia a letter to the Red Cross, thinking that even a faintest hope would be better than doomed despair. I know what it is like to be up to my ears in the gravitational mud of desperation, how it darkens your soul and squeezes your life force until the last drop of your vital fluid evaporates.

Aunt Marusia started counting days and asking if there was mail for Diborskikh. Days and months passed; seasons changed, but there was no answer. Marusia waited patiently. It took two and a half years.

***

In 1977, Marusia received a letter with her daughter's address. The search for her daughter was a phased, multi-stage process. It started with the Red Cross, then the case moved to the Kemerovo Criminal Investigation Department. They used their channels, making inquiries to the regional police and various organizations. The person is not a needle; they found Marusia's daughter!

Marusia and her daughter started corresponding. It turned out the daughter lived in the Altai region; she was happily married and had a son. Aunt Marusia was so delighted that she had a grandson!

Then the daughter came with her little son to the asylum; you can imagine Marusia's happiness. Two years later, when the daughter gave birth to her second child, Aunt Marusia went to the Altai to help her daughter with her children. She never returned to the asylum…

Two months passed, and we were still waiting for Marusia, thinking that probably she would stay with her daughter and would never come back. Just to be sure that Marusia was all right, Olga Fedorovna sent a letter to the daughter. She replied that her mother died in a hospital during an epileptic seizure.

That is how Aunt Marusia's story ended. But at least she was able to find her daughter and had the opportunity to caress her grandchildren.

It is good that she did not die anonymously in the asylum; she was buried by her family, and her grave will be visited by people whom she loved…

In spite of so many misfortunes in the life of Aunt Marusia, I envy her. But what a destiny — she just found her family, and then she died. I also would like to die at home, and to be mourned by someone close to me. Alas…

They Try to Protect their Families from me

It had been three weeks since I was brought here from the Bachata orphanage, and I tried not to think about anything bad. We had sunny days; the summer was in full swing.

On one of those days, Aunt Marusia opened the window. I saw white clouds, floating serenely across the blue sky, reflected in the window glass and a profound sadness filled my soul. Here they are again — these calling clouds. They were calling me, making me nostalgic.

I was caught in this mood by the nurse Lubov Kuzminichna, who lived with her family in our building, behind the wall. The asylum used to be the house for disabled people of general type, who were later transferred to the village Insk, near the town Belovo. They built a new building there with an improved layout, and new people arrived from the Kirovskii psycho-neurological boarding school, not far from Kemerovo. Along with the new patients, half of the staff came to the Prokopyevsk psycho-neurological boarding school. This is why there were apartments for the staff on the territory of the asylum.

"Toma, are you sick?" Lubov Kuzminichna asked with care.

"I just feel nostalgic," I answered, on the verge of tears.

"Can I call a doctor?" the nurse suggested. "There's a city doctor here, a psychiatrist; she can prescribe something. Let me prepare your medical records for her."

I shrugged my shoulders, doubting the help of a psychiatrist. My longing could not be cured with pills. These sedatives give only a temporary relief, and when their effect was over, your longing would come back like the wave of a return tide, throwing you into the velvet night — depression.

Close to lunch time, the door to my room opened and my mother, Ekaterina Ivanovna, entered with a radiant smile. I reached out to her and suddenly started crying bitterly. My mother sat on my bed, holding me and wiping my tears.

"Mommy, take me home! Even for a week, even for three days! It's very close to Novokuznetsk from here!"

I used all my arsenals, trying to convince her how desperately I needed this little vacation. I put together all the arguments: my ardent desire to stay at home; my urgent need of communication with her and my sister Olga; my craving to see other relatives; and the proximity of Prokopyevsk to Novokuznetsk. I swore that I would overcome the inevitability of leaving and coming back to the asylum. I tried to convince my mother that I just needed a little reward.

"How can I take you? How can I bring you to the fifth floor? And who will stay with you? I have to go to work; Olga has to go to school." My mother repeated her usual impervious excuses like a parrot. She did not mention her new husband.

"You have your sisters and brothers; they are young and strong; it won't be difficult for them to carry me! I'm light! They only have to take me to the fifth floor just once! Then when I have to leave, they could bring me down, just once! They can carry me in turns, one floor after another; it's not a lot, five floors! Take me home just once! Just for a while! On your vacation! Or on a holiday!" I was howling.

My mother was silent; tears were running down her cheeks, but her eyes remained indifferent. I knew her tears were for the public, and I knew that by refusing my passionate request, this woman protected her family, where there was no place for me. I should not be there, because for the members of her family, friends and acquaintances, I did not exist.

***

In one of my last days at the orphanage, I received a letter from my father, which was a great surprise to me. My mother had not hesitated in finding his address for me through the address bureau. I had written him a letter — I was sure he would never answer. However, contrary to my pessimistic predictions, the answer had come. I was so happy, but after they opened the envelope and gave me a lined page, taken from a school notebook, my joy faded — the letter was not from my father, but from his daughter from his second marriage.

I read: 'Dear Toma, your father has become my father. My name is Lena, I am eleven years old. Toma, send me your photograph.' The rest of the page was covered with zigzags made by a ballpoint pen; obviously these scribbles were more eloquent than words. Now I am sure that Lena wrote her simple sentences herself, but that time I was so vulnerable, I suspected they could be written at her mother's dictation. The letter rendered a message that my father belonged to them, and I tended to believe it was sent not by Lena, but by her mother. Analyzing this unpresuming sample of writing, I assumed that Lena did not know anything about me — in what kind of place I lived, and in what condition I was. Oversensitive about the lack of empathy in my family, I decided that it could be even worse — Lena's request to send her my photograph was suggested by Lena's mother with the intention to show her daughter what a wretched creature I am. And why didn't Lena send me her photograph? These were my thoughts — obviously, I crossed the line between confidence and uncertainty.

I did not answer the letter, but I said to myself: 'Please, Lenochka, take my father for yourself, I give him to you.'

I believe my father had his right not to reply to my letter. He had his new family, in which there was no place for me — I accepted this crystal-clear state of affairs.

***

And now, crying in front of this woman, who was entitled to the word 'mother', the most sacred word in any language, once again I realized that it was more convenient to her to keep me behind the asylum walls. The fact that my family had thrown me into the Home of Sorrow, and that I did not exist for them, created an effect of non-existence. So nothingness became my home; its other name is exile, as nothingness is exile. Will they ever know the truth about my exile?

Doctor Olga Fedorovna came when she heard me begging my mother to have mercy on me. She said, "Toma, why are you upsetting your mother? Look at her, she is crying!"

"Toma will calm down." My mother cheered up as soon as she received support. And her tears disappeared at once. Then she skillfully shifted to another subject, and all my attempts to convince her to take me home were ineffectual.

Then my mother gave me a clever explanation, that her present home is not the home from which I was taken. It is her home, where she lives with her family. This home has different walls and inhabitants. She let me know that I should not think that I belong to this home. She was direct, gently explaining that my home is the asylum, aka the psycho-neurological boarding school, and I have to understand I will have this home for the rest of my life. I could summarize her discourse: I am regarded as a disgrace and an embarrassment to the family; in other words, the black sheep does not belong to the family.

On the Social Security Mercy

Isn't it wonderful that we have nights? Night is the time when people are asleep, and you are left alone with yourself, fearless of all. You can open your tearful soul and tempt the pillow without hiding your weakness. There are so many things hidden in the depth of your heart and mind which can be revealed at night! The night is your only luxury, as during the day there is no secret chamber or private corner where you can cry out your bitterness.

It had been a week since my mother's last visit. I was quite turbulent at that time. In the morning, everything seemed normal; I appeared to be a quiet, humble girl, submissive to reality, demanding nothing and insisting on nothing. And at night, where did it come from? Wild dreams were mixed with reality! Please believe me, my beautiful reader — I have never had an intention to act out. I did not have either mood or interest in creating a pretentious performance.

Aunt Marusia had been taking care of me. My mother was informed about her volunteer help; the staff gave her a hint that it would be a good idea to pay this invalid woman Marusia ten rubles a month as gratitude. But this made my mother even more elusive than she normally was — she was a master of elusive art! She did not want to understand such hints; she was sure that her miserable daughter should completely rely on the state, and her life support was entirely the responsibility of the government, as well as all her other problems that should be solely solved by the boarding school and not be passed on to the parents.

One day, in order to repay Aunt Marusia for her kindness, I asked my mother to bring me a stick of salami as if it was just for me. My request outraged my mother. "Am I a millionaire? Do you know how much this stick costs? Seven rubles!"

Then she gave a pompous speech about her abject poverty; her family lived on the verge of starvation. I even feel embarrassed to recall this monologue. After all, Ekaterina Ivanovna worked at the factory canteen; she was not poor, not to mention that her complaints about hunger were slightly exaggerated. But it would not hurt if occasionally she brought a little piece of salami to her disabled daughter.

It was later when she would put sometimes three rubles in an envelope, which I immediately gave to Aunt Marusia. It made me so happy that I could do something nice for this kind woman.

Aunt Marusia... I don't know why this woman, so seriously ill, never abandoned me, and offered her care until her last day in Prokopyevsk. But it was so hard for her to take care of me! At first, the nanny on duty helped to bathe me, but later Aunt Marusia alone took care of me. She had debilitating seizures of epilepsy, which led to total exhaustion. The morning toileting was impossible, as I could not bring myself to disturb her. I lay in bed, suffering tremendously because of this very natural physical need. Then I cursed myself for being alive, for being a burden to people and for being a burden to myself.

Sometimes Aunt Marusia had an epileptic attack during lunch. She would feed me and suddenly a seizure attack started. I would look at her cramped hand, in which she was holding a spoon of food, but because of the seizure she was not able to move it further, and I just wanted to scream, "Aunt Marusia, dear, don't care about me, just leave me!" But she cared and she never abandoned me.

Life went on... my mother would visit once in a while. She could help my volunteer caretaker to wash me, but she never offered her help. One day I could not stand it any more, and I said, "Please, help Marusia!"

In return, I heard "You have nannies; it's their sacred duty to look after you!"

When I tried to explain to her that taking care of her child was in principle the sacred duty of a *mother*, she rolled her eyes upwards, sending me a message through her shameless facial expression. 'Yes, yes, yes, you saw a horse with five legs, but I don't believe you.'

One day I needed to be washed. Aunt Marusia cleaned the bathtub and put me in. Apparently, the bathtub was still cold; I felt an unusual stiffness of my muscles, and my body made a violent twist. The symptoms of spasticity and hyperkinesia escalated because of constant stress while in the Prokopyevsk asylum. Aunt Marusia chastised me. "If you do it again, I will use the mop; it will straighten you up immediately!"

This sudden reaction made me cry, but I found within myself the strength to smile through tears and forgive her impertinence. I saw Aunt Marusia was embarrassed by her breakdown; I knew she did not feel well.

When I saw she was not in a good mood, I limited my requests. But in my plight, how could I not address my savior when I was completely dependent on her? When I was so upset, I would refuse food or grow silent, and I was surprised to see the misunderstanding of my actions. They would say, "Today you are a good girl."
But lying in the ward, contemplating the walls and ceiling, or sitting outside, where one of the staff would take me, was unbearable. It was always the same vicious circle of procedures and the same limited space, which I tried to overcome, but in vain. Thank God, a year after I joined the asylum, they finally gave me a stroller, and I could at least be in the hallway.

An Attempt to Escape from the PNBS

It was one of the most difficult periods in my life, which is still so intolerable in my memories that I want to forget it. I heard from the medical staff that the conditions at the Insk home for invalids without mental disorder were much better than at the Prokopyevsk PNBS. Should I ask if I could be transferred there? At first, I hesitated, then I decided to fight for my future. I needed a doctor's report to be transferred. I started preparing myself for the meeting with the doctor.

The doctor whom I met was an old woman wearing glasses, with dyed red hair and an impenetrable face which looked like a wax mask. Her name was Tamara Fedorovna. The name Tamara is not rare, but I found some symbolism in the fact that we had the same name. However, sitting in front of my namesake, whose face was unreadable like a blank page, I started feeling an unpleasant chill, and my prepared thoughts fled away.

"What is your name?" she asked, with a slight movement of her thin lips.

"Tamara Cheremnova," I answered. I wanted to add, 'your namesake', to create a warm contact between us, but the expression of her face was so stern that I did not dare to express friendliness. I continued. "I wanted to ask you for a medical evaluation. I need it to move to the Insk home. I heard there are many young people there; I want to continue my studies. I am only twenty years old!"

"Did you study?" she asked indifferently.

"Unfortunately, we didn't have regular classes at the orphanage. But I completed many classes... You can find my grades and teachers' evaluations in my medical history."

Tamara Fedorovna looked in my medical history and shrugged her shoulders. "There're no records. How many classes have you finished?"

I could not give her the answer, but I exclaimed I was among the best pupils, and I mastered the curriculum on my own. I repeated we did not have regular classes, but I learned physics on my own, using textbooks for the sixth-grade students. I was about to demonstrate to her the laws of physics, but then I realized that because she was too old, she would not remember them. Then I decided to show her my notebook with poems. I took it with me, presuming that it could be a useful piece of evidence proving that I am not retarded, but creative.

"I even write poetry. Here!" And I handed her my notebook.

Tamara Fedorovna turned a few pages, then gave me my treasure back. But I could not take it from her hand as stress brought on a prominent hyperkinesia; I just could not move my hand.

"I can't give you an evaluation based on your poems. Your seizures exhibit signs of mental illness." This is how my namesake stamped me with her resolution.

I believe any doctor should act ethically. The categorical medical judgment which I had just received was pronounced in such a harsh tone! And she pronounced me mentally ill only because of my erratic physical movements!

That night was sleepless again. With my imagination I could see myself clearly from the side — a deformed creature, bound to a wheelchair. This imaginative viewing filled my heart with sorrow and pain; my soul grew devoid of hope. There is always a sorrow inside the sorrow. Being inside the House of Sorrow, I entered my personal chamber of sorrow; I wanted to hide myself from people, so no one could see me. But where could I hide?

There was a thought in my head that seemed to me worthwhile. If I were no longer alive, then no one would see my monstrosity. Thoughts of death had visited me quite often in the orphanage. I longed to die, seeing in death the end of my suffering, but I did not attempt to act; I just waited. My recent encounter with the doctor was so humiliating and made me more conscious about my decision to leave this world.

So why should I long to die and wait, when I can speed things up, when I can do it myself? Especially since I had the reliable lethal drug in my hands — a bottle of Parkopan-5 pills; a large dose of them is fatal — they would certainly affect my impoverished body. I was glad I saved them. Suicide came to me as a comfort. Soon I will not exist, I thought.

At the time when the pale morning arrived, I made my decision to commit suicide. Then I fell asleep, calm and confident.

The day started as usual. The nannies brought breakfast. Aunt Marusia asked me if I would like to eat. I asked for tea and tried not to arouse suspicion. Lying in bed, all I could think about was the bottle with pills inside my nightstand. It was simple: all I had to do was to swallow these offensive pills without water and not choke; otherwise, my plan would fail. Was it true that in a few hours I would not feel anything? I would not see those walls, I would not receive those offensive gazes, I would not hear those murderous words. I would not have pain in my soul; I would not have myself as I am right now.

And finally, people around me, to whom I brought so much trouble, would be free of my presence. Aunt Marusia would not have to strain any more because of me; my mother would be free, my father would be notified, and he would sigh with relief, and probably would not even wonder where I was buried… And my parents would no longer have to protect their families from my encroachments.

After lunch and a little rest, my neighbors went outside; I pretended I was sleeping. Finally, I was alone. I sat in my bed and bent to take the pills from the nightstand. I got them and put them under my pillow. For dinner we had milk soup; they knew I never liked it.

"Would you like some milk soup?" Aunt Marusia asked me.

"No." I made a sour face. "Just a cup of tea."

After dinner, they all left again, and I was alone in the room. I took out the bottle with Parkopan-5 pills; I examined it, trying to remember the regular prescription in order to calculate the lethal dose.

Parkopan treats the stiffness, tremors, spasms and poor muscle control of Parkinson's disease. When they prescribed it to me, I hoped it would stop these jerky movements, and it would be easier for Aunt Marusia to feed me. But it didn't work so well with me — the pills made me so lethargic that I decided to stop taking them. As for a cure, they had no effect on my hyperkinesia. After a few days of taking Parkopan-5, I had asked the doctor Olga Fedorovna to replace it with a different medication. But she said that it was the best treatment for hyperkinesia. She advised me not to argue with the professional medical specialist, especially when I had no idea about the science of medicine. I assume that Parkopan-5 did not affect me because I had constant depression, and on its background no pharmacopoeia drugs work. In addition, hyperkinesia needs to be treated individually with physiotherapy and continuous adjustments of medication; it is a complex process. However, they had just one method in PNBS — take pills and do not reason.

Of course, I did not speculate on methods of medical treatment at the time of suicide, I was too far from any reasoning of that kind. I brought the bottle to my mouth, pulled the cork out with my teeth, and put as many pills as I could into my mouth. As my hand was shaking, half of the pills fell on my bed. With some effort I swallowed the pills, but after that I already felt exhausted. I did not have strength to pick up pills which scattered all over my bed.

The dose of Parkopan-5 was enough to put me in a half-sleep and to induce a week-long hallucination. It seemed to me I could see everything; I could hear and understand, but it was the world of fantasy which I experienced. I had the impression I could see through the wall, that I could see our little girls from the orphanage playing ball in the hallway, and I begged them to come and console me...

When I came to my senses, I saw the nurse, Lubov Kuzminichna, sitting next to me. She said with a reproach, "Tomochka! Why did you do that? You might not have come back!"

"And it would be better," I whispered and returned to reality.

***

Six months later, when I managed to obtain more pills, I tried to commit suicide again. But the staff were alert. As soon as they saw me unconscious, they opened my blue lips and poured inside me two cans of water with potassium permanganate to clear my stomach.

***

So I was not able to get out of the PNBS at that time —either to the Insk home or to the Other World...

From Atheism to God

I grew up in the era of militant atheism. In the orphanage, we were instructed that there was no God. Religion was an invention of ignorant people, and man was not God's creation, but a product of evolution. I posed an innocent question that embarrassed my teacher. "Why isn't evolution happening now? The circus bears have been trained and trained to behave like humans; they are even dressed in men's clothes; why don't they become humans? And they do so many experiments with monkeys, trying to develop them, but they are still monkeys."

"Don't make fools of us!" The teachers denounced me and changed the subject.

I acknowledged the absence of God, but sometimes I wondered: What is it? Something luminous and gentle that has been saving me all these years. When I examine my life, I find a few episodes when I was so close to death. This is your end, Tomka! I would say to myself. Take the accident in the river when I fell face down in the water. A sick, paralyzed child would not be able to get up on their own. I was so scared, my hands cramped, I felt a lump in my throat and I could not scream. But I distinctly felt that some power, unknown to me, lifted me out of the water and placed me straight. If I had tried to make any movement by myself, I would have been drowned in the river. Who helped me? What was it?

And wasn't it the same power that saved me after my suicide attempt? Gradually, I realized that life was given to me by God, and I should not interfere with His plans.

Back in the seventies, I did not dare to pronounce the word 'God'. Later, when religious toleration became acceptable, I was not afraid to say, yes, it was God who made me. He has given me life and entrusted me with a certain mission. I am loved by God and I intend to do my duty-bound mission during my lifetime. God determined the beginning of my life, and God will determine its end without my help.

It is not just me; every human being has a mission. And the only way to do it is to be with God. And no human being has the right to kill another human being, morally or physically. They do not have the right to kill themselves.

When I wanted to end my life at twenty, I did not think about God or the sin of suicide. After I had received the cruel verdict of this medical doctor, I started thinking about whether I was allowed to commit suicide. Taking my notebook of poetry to the meeting with the doctor was probably more significant than just my intention to win my case. I was very influenced by poetry, and then I started thinking about my suicide. I was also thinking about the suicides of the great poets who took their lives voluntarily: Sergei Yesenin, Vladimir Mayakovsky and Marina Tsvetaeva. I was thinking that Joseph Utkin, a prominent Soviet Jewish poet, also justified suicide. In 1920, when he was seventeen, he joined the Red Army and participated in many battles during the period of the intervention. When the Germans invaded the Soviet Union in 1941. He was praised for gallantry in action. He lost his right hand in one of the battles. He was killed in an airplane crash in December 1944.

> There is the horror of the impassable road,
> Which is the end of the horse!
> And for what you did, Serezha
> I don't blame you at all.
>
> Rebellious and wild,
> You boiled to the bottom.
> Who needs empty glasses?
> Glasses without wine?
>
> The homeland is blooming,
> But you cannot sing!
> And besides the right to live,
> There is the right to die.

I thought that the horror of the impassable road gave me the right to die… If such an exit from the void was chosen by the great poets, who were valuable to the world, then it would be even more natural for me, useless and miserable, to take this exit…

How fortunate I was that my attempts to take my own life failed!

I also realized that society should not isolate me, lock me up, and hide me behind the asylum walls. There should not be a gulf between me and other people: I am not a criminal, I am not dangerous, I am quite harmless. And I have the right to appear in society, and not just to be locked down in an asylum. And those who cannot look without shuddering at a crippled being in a wheelchair — let them not look! But if God created people like me, then we must be *accepted*, and let others who are not outcasts get used to us, and to our presence in common living space.

The Relocation to the 'Weak Quarter'

My best young years had passed as a dark succession of suffering; divided by four seasons, as in Siberia we have them all. I am returning to the most difficult period of my life, when I did not want to live, but I had not succeeded in leaving this world.

I wanted to meet the doctor again, but she refused to see me, saying: I know this patient, it's useless to prescribe to her any treatment. Nothing can help her!

The nurse told me about this — her eyes were wide open; I saw she was shocked. My brain refused to understand these horrible words…

***

Aunt Marusia went to visit her daughter, whom she found through the Red Cross, and never came back. I lived in the same room with Aunt Marusia between 1974 and 1979; she constantly took care of me. And now whoever was available among the residents took care of me. One day, the manager from the 'weak quarter' approached me. "Toma, would you like to move to us?" she asked. "I set up a separate room for young girls like you; you'll be able to read in peace."

I read a lot. Newspapers and magazines were subscribed to by the administration and brought from home by employees. There was a library left by previous residents. Books were brought by employees and relatives of residents as gifts from outside the asylum walls.

Like in the Bachata orphanage, books were mostly fiction. I needed books not only for reading, but also for my studies, because my goal was to complete the school program by myself.

I started thinking about the manager's proposal. I remembered my first dreadful day in the 'weak quarter'… I doubted that it would be possible to read and study without intrusions — how could one reason with wild patients and screamers?

But there was no way to stay in my current building without Marusia. All the people around me were in poor condition and not able to physically care for me. The staff were inconsistent in my care; one day I was fed, the next I was left to go hungry from lack of help. I thanked the manager for her offer, but did not immediately accept it — I needed time to decide what to do. In the evening the nurse Galina Nikolaevna came to our room. I told her about the conversation with the manager.

"Tamara, you have to go there, because here no one can take care of you. Sveta, who feeds you, isn't suitable for this; she works in the pig sty. It's dirty; she may give you some infection. So take the offer!" advised Galina Nikolaevna.

I weighed up pros and cons, and in the morning, I reported my decision to go to the 'weak quarter'. My friend Tatiana, who sometimes assisted me with my strolled promenades, helped me to pack my things and took me to the well-known odious building. I sensed cold in my chest, assuming another great twist in my life, but my eyes were dry.

***

At the entrance, we were met by a nanny who accompanied us to the room. I passed the hallway, sitting in my stroller with my head down, without looking at anything. Usually, I was very observant and examined carefully every detail, trying to plan ahead where I could do my activities.

I was taken to a room furnished with four beds, nightstands and a table.

"Here is Luska. You wanted to have a younger roommate. Welcome your new girlfriend," said the nanny to the black-haired girl sitting on her bed.

I greeted the nodding Luska and looked around.

"All right, girls, I have to go," said Tatiana, who obviously was not enjoying the 'weak quarter', my new roommates and my indifferent mood.

Then I saw an old friend of mine, Luba; she was sitting on the floor. A memorable day immediately appeared before my eyes — how we were together in the truck on our way from the orphanage to this asylum, how we spent a terrible night being locked up in the infirmary, how Luba was fed with chlorpromazine. Then I saw an old woman standing by the window. I noticed she could hardly walk. So, I am in the company of 'girls'!

"What's your name?" I could hardly hear Luska's voice.

"Tamara. You can call me Toma. They said they would put me in the room with girls. This grandma is a girl too?" I just could not resist the joke.

"She will be moved to another room when the next group of young people arrives. Only the young will live in this room," Luska said.

Then a nanny came to the room. "Oh, the new girl arrived," she said.

"I'm not new. I came from the women's building. My friend who took care of me died. I asked them to transfer me here. I'm not able to feed myself, but I can climb into bed and dress," I reported bravely, though not telling them that my performance without assistance would usually take a lot of time.

"All right, let me bring food for you." The nanny was not very enthusiastic about my report; she left the room.

Did Luba recognize me? There were zero emotions on Lubaher face. Probably she forgot me during these five years in the asylum, and we never met outside; each building had its own courtyard.

Luska's physical condition was much better than mine, with functioning hands and normal speech, but because of problems with her knees and lower legs, her mobility was limited to a wheelchair. With such a condition she could still study. But when Luska lived at home, she finished only one grade — her legs became worse, and she stopped going to school. Why didn't she study at home? And why was she assigned to the PNBS? I was embarrassed to ask her these questions. Luska had a disabled brother, Lesha, he was in a much worse condition. Lesha had lived in another PNBS, and then he was transferred to this one.

***

They brought lunch. I was waiting for the nanny. No one came and I started thinking that it would be the same bedlam with feeding as I had before. Finally, the nanny came, and she would leave immediately if

Luska did not ask her to feed me. Then the nanny started feeding me. I could see she was not very enthusiastic about this job.

In the evening, I sensed something new in me — it was a mixture of bleak calm and dull indifference. I did not like my mood and I decided to resist it. I said to myself I should never give up activity; otherwise, I will become like those chronic patients whose paralyzing immobility was caused by this unchangeable pattern — always remaining in the same position, lying in bed… And I should never be bound to bed!

However, despite my internal resistance, my life in the 'weak quarter' started declining. I became more indifferent to myself, the nannies had less and less interest in feeding me, people around exhibited the minimum of attention, and I did not ask them for anything. I realized with my sober mind that if I did not find the way out of this situation, I would end up in Ward No. 25, where I would join clinically insane patients, who also needed to be fed by spoon. The idiots had their own nanny. There was a special feeding method when they put all the food in a big bowl that looked like a trough. So, they mixed all food together: they crumbled a loaf of bread, poured soup, added other materials, and so on. They fed the concoction to the unfortunate idiots. They fed them like pigs! But the idiots ate this awful pigswill with pleasure, without gastronomic claims. I was physically inferior to Luska and even to Luba. I assumed I would not be different from the idiots if I were attached to their shared feeder…

***

One day, the nanny Ninka, a foolish lass, came to the room. All her talk was always about sex — even if she started with something different, she would inevitably end with sex. She used to come to talk to Luska, who was considered the most normal compared with the others: she did not have strabismus, spasticity or hyperkinesia, and her speech was clear.

Ninka was telling Luska about her adventures in a park, where there were men, with whom she had great success. When Ninka was leaving, she turned to me and made a grimace: such a cross-eyed creature!

Yes, cross-eyed, it was I. Now I would find what to say to this Ninka, but then I just put my head down. Yes, my strabismus worsened, and it was not possible to improve it — it was very painful to realize. Strabismus is the misfortune of people who suffer with cerebral palsy. My strabismus was not congenital; my eyes look directly in photographs taken in my early childhood. It developed in adolescence. At the initial stage, it could have been corrected by constantly wearing the custom-made special glasses. They were not expensive — one and a half or two rubles, or at most three.

The orphanage workers showed some concern — from time to time, they asked me not to read so much, even frightening me that my love for reading could make me more cross-eyed or completely blind. Reading all day long, without special glasses, certainly affected my eyes, but I could not live without books. At the Prokopyevsk PNBS, I never had an eye exam, and I did not have any glasses. I would have bought them myself, but I could not do it without a prescription and help. The women with whom I shared the asylum space were so generous in giving me their awful predictions:

These books won't do you any good, Tomka… You will become blind!

By this age, I already knew that people who insulted me had a lot of anger, as they failed as individuals. During their lives these poor souls had been constantly abused and flogged and came to the point that they did not like themselves. They would spit out their anger at someone who seemed to them even more miserable than they were only because they did not have self-value.

The American psychologist Dale Carnegie speculates that no one ever hits a dead dog. What is the use of kicking a dead dog? There is nothing to be jealous of about him. But if you attack someone, you find something to envy in this person. This is what it was: they were envious of me…

The Knitting Shop

I became friends with my roommate Luska. Sometimes she fed me but I did not feel comfortable asking without offering something in return. And I offered her an exchange service. One afternoon, she was sitting on her bunk, kneeling down — it was her usual position in bed after she woke up. I said, "You have healthy hands. Why don't you knit items for children? You can earn money!"

This was 1979 when stores lacked an assortment of merchandise, and knitted things were in short supply. Children's sweaters, hats and scarves most often were created by grandmothers.

"I know some patterns, but when I knit, I get confused. I just can't do it!" Luska said.

"Let me work with you. My hands are bad, but I know the art of knitting. I helped the girls at the orphanage. In the beginning they couldn't knit at all, but under my guidance, their skill grew. I will teach you and I ask for your help in feeding me."

"But we don't have materials for knitting! We don't have money to buy the yarn!"

"Yes, we don't have money; we can use my sweater."

"Won't they scold you because of your sweater?" Luska said, doubtful.

"It's my personal sweater! I can do whatever I want with it." I was proud of my resourcefulness.

The sweater was still good, but we started transforming it into the yarn. I was very anxious to start the production. Luska started disconnecting threads, making knots when the threads broke and rolling them into a ball.

First, I taught her the English style of knitting, because it was the easiest. I tried not to be too instructional; I did not want to offend Luska, and here my bitter experience in the orphanage helped me. I was taught to behave modestly. They would always put me down when I expressed my pride, though it was more the kind of pride of Lermontov's Demon, who was alone in the universe, abandoned, and without love or hope. The irritating shrieks of Anna Stepanovna Levshina are still ringing in my ears, so I had my lessons. When Luska had mastered the English style, we proceeded to the Western knitting techniques. This is an ancient style of knitting, which spread from Arabic culture to the Iberian Peninsula. With our joint efforts, we were able to create a baby bonnet, which was immediately bought by a young nanny.

Then Luska and I created more knitted things for babies — they immediately found their customers. Our earnings were intermittent and small: two or three rubles, but the attitude of others towards us had changed. Everyone complimented my organizational skills and Luska's knitting skills. We were often praised together: "Well done girls! What a great thing you started together!" I was proud of our little knitting workshop.

Now the nannies would bring us old things to transform them into new ones using the art of knitting. Luska would unpick the old knitted thing, and I would also participate, holding it to help Luska in her work of transformation. In the process of knitting, I tried not to emphasize that I was leading Luska, because people do not feel comfortable when they are instructed all the time. I did not have a problem any more with feeding, as Luska fed me properly, and I was no longer dependent on nannies.

Our success was not an achievement of great grandeur, but I was glad that I took an initiative to teach Luska and solved my problem, at least temporarily, with feeding. When Luska learned the knitting art, she did not need my help any more, and she stopped feeding me. In life we never lose friends, we only learn who true friends are — I was not disappointed when our exchange service came to end. At least Luska learned how to knit!

Oh, how complicated it was with feeding! Sometimes I would ask Taska to feed me; sometimes I would ask other girls; so feeding required a lot of management from my side.

My dear people, please appreciate that you are able to hold a spoon and bring it to your mouth! Value your capacity that enables you to take a glass of water or a cup of tea independently! And if your hands can work with such instruments as a fork, a knife and other cutlery, you are a very lucky person!

Fears in the "Weak Quarter"

At night, I would dream that sooner or later I would meet a doctor who would eliminate this horrible verdict of 'oligophrenia at the stage of debility', which some ignorant doctors attached to me like a stigma of disapproval, a discrimination distinguishing me from other members of society.

Living in the 'weak quarter' was scary. One day Luska was sitting on my bed, and we were just talking about this and that. Suddenly, a mad man barged into the room and grabbed Luska, trying to kiss her. She maneuvered her head, resisting this strange suitor. But he was a big man, much stronger than Luska, and I was close to nausea, seeing that he almost reached her lips with his stinking mouth. And without thinking about the consequences, I used all my strength to strike this beast, kicking him with my paralyzed legs.

The beast flew over Luska's wheelchair and banged on the floor. I did not think he would attempt to repeat his action; actually, he could hardly walk. After this strenuous physical exercise, my legs were tangled up in pain, so I could not kick him again. I saw this beast convulsing on the floor, but still trying to reach Luska. Then I screamed, "Luska, crawl into the corridor; call the orderly or nanny!"

While Luska was making her way to the doorstep, this imbecile punched me in the face. After that, he left the room. I saw he could hardly walk, but his face expressed some satisfaction — he was able to balance his failure in kissing Luska by his silly action of hitting me. I was so glad that I did not become the object of his insane desire. The nannies came when it was over. After a heated debate about how to prevent such intrusions, they expressed solidarity, advising us to block for the night our door with some heavy object like the bunk. But who would move the bunk? I did not have the strength to relocate the bunk; neither did Luska. Then we learned they had moved the intruder to the second floor, where the surveillance of such patients was stricter than in other facilities, and where they provided them with heavy tranquilizers as an everyday treatment.

But the worst was that the whole shift on duty got drunk as a lord every night. At times like that, I would lie in my bed thinking: what would happen to me if I didn't have my roommates who helped me? If I needed to go to the bathroom, I could scream and no one would come. What would happen if I had heart attack? They would certainly find me dead in the morning. These were my fears in the 'weak quarter'.

The nurse on duty had to make daily medical rounds, but she ignored her duties — she never visited our ward. She wrote her morning report on how her shift went — so her so-called care was just described on paper. And the shift went so well because the entire staff enjoyed drinking so much. By morning, the staff sobered up and started working, if I am allowed to call their performances under the influence of alcohol 'work'.

The qualifications of the junior staff left a lot to be desired. Not all nannies knew how to serve the patient bound to bed with a pan to urinate. They preferred a simpler solution — they covered the mattress with a piece of plastic and over it they placed a sheet, which they changed twice in twenty-four hours. They did not care if a patient urinated three or four times and lay wet to the ears in their bed. They would replace the wet sheet only at a certain time, according to their schedule.

They would roll over the same urine-soaked sheet, using it to wipe the plastic, then they would place a dry sheet over the plastic which would immediately become wet from its contact with the plastic, and the job was done — only the edges of the sheet were clean and nice when the patient's body was still wet. This method was the easiest for the nannies and fatal to the skin of the patients, which was constantly irritated with uric acid. Diapers started their existence in the nineteenth century in many parts of the world; in the United States the first mass-produced ones arrived in 1887. They entered the Soviet Union in 1979, but were used only by some elite individual families and hospitals; they were still unavailable for common citizens, especially for those who lived in the provincial land.

Most of all I was afraid of becoming weaker and having the treatment similar to that I just described. I was afraid that my body would be constantly wet and the mattress beneath me would start to rot, then live worms, bacteria, and fungus could be developed in this favorable environment — such things happened in the PNBS! So every day, no matter how weak I felt, no matter how dizzy I was, no matter how painful my spine was, I forced myself to stand up on my feet by my bed, holding it to keep my balance, and trying to be in this position between ten and twenty minutes. I stood as long as I could.

Thanks to my tenacity I have learned how to stand on my feet, strengthening my leg muscles to climb into the wheelchair without help. I experienced 'animal angst', the condition of an animal who is locked inside a small cage, when I imagined I could become completely motionless, bound forever to bed, miserable and unkempt — this encouraged me to do these physical exercises. I tried to do my best with my resistance to difficult circumstances in my life.

Important People

There were people whom I met at Prokopyevsk PNBS and who became important to me for various reasons. At least, I will never forget them.

Our volunteer assistant Tasia — what a wonderful person she was! Tasia was born as the eleventh child in her family, and she was the only one who survived. But, alas, her mental condition was so defective, that according to the hierarchical order of mental maladies, it was the most severe case of debility that defied any kind of correction. At least, her mental condition was considered incurable at PNBS. Up to ten years old, Tasia's parents kept her at home until they were unable to take care of her, then they sent her to the orphanage of the city of Berezovsk, where she lived until the age of eighteen, and after that she was transferred to our Prokopyevsk PNBS.

When I was transferred to the 'weak quarter', Tasia began her acquaintance with me by poking a glass in my face, which resulted in a black eye.

She knocked me with the glass without bad intention; it was her way to mark a new person. I was not ready for such action — I had not known yet how I might be treated by patients like Tasia. In our orphanage, children with severe mental problems were kept in a separate building, and we had no contact with them. And here Tasia communicated with everyone without restrictions; she was not considered as a problematic person — on the contrary, she was so humble, doing almost all the work the lazy nannies were supposed to do.

She visited our ward willingly; she did all kinds of physical things we were not capable of doing — she carried, moved and lifted things, and the nannies used her at their pleasure, giving her all kinds of assignments. Tasia's physical development was excellent. Her arms and legs were strong, though her slurred speech showed she had mental problems, and her disoriented head betrayed her as well. Sometimes Tasia would help with housekeeping, then she would approach Luba and say something that I could not understand. It sounded to me as if she asked for lemonade. It was strange. One day, I asked Luska. "Luska, why does Tasia always ask Luba for lemonade?"

"Oh no, she does not ask for lemonade, she always says 'mine'." Luska laughed. "Listen to her attentively; she says 'Luba is mine'; the way she pronounces this, missing some syllables, sounds a little bit like 'lemonade'."

Tasia turned to Luska and repeated her favorite phrase in another version. "Luska is mine."

"No, not yours!" Luska teased her.

But she should not have refused Tasia's whimsy, as Tasia grabbed poor Luska and started shaking her, repeating loudly, "Luska mine! Luska mine!"

She almost pushed Luska from her bunk, repeating, "Mine, mine, mine," until Luska gave up and pacified her with the words 'yours, yours, yours'. Tasia's whimsical behavior can be interpreted in this way: she needed the confirmation that Luska and Luba completely belonged to her, then she would believe she was loved by these girls. Only after this confirmation would Tasia calm down.

***

The twenty-year-old Tasia resembled a thirteen-year-old teenager: she had no breasts, no thighs, no other feminine features; her face looked like a teenager's face. And intellectually she was just a real baby.

One day, a hot-water heater leaked in the toilet, and the nannies, as usual, sent Tasia, whom they used as an obedient maid, to wipe the water. The nannies always extensively used all the walking invalids who could even slightly work with their hands. Since morning Tasia had worked in the toilet, diligently cleaning the water, which continued arriving. And apparently, she became tired of her monotonous activity, which did not bring any result. She was obviously annoyed with the hot-water heater — she snapped it off the hook on which it was attached, she disconnected it from the pipes and dragged this horribly heavy metal object to the hallway.

Luska and I were sitting in the ward when we heard metallic clangs coming from the corridor. I drove my wheelchair to the hallway. I saw Sasha, the plumber, a man of enormous proportions, and his two colleagues, also of monstrous proportions, dragging with great difficulty a huge object, which happened to be the hot-water heater, to the toilet. The three men were using bad language, cursing the nannies. The nannies were also at the spot; they denied their participation in disconnecting the hot-water heater and taking it to the hallway. The nannies were using bad language too, cursing Tasia. Sasha was sure that the nannies used their collective efforts to relocate the hot-water heater just to irritate him. The nannies tried to prove that the hot-water heater was removed by Taska, which Sasha just could not believe.

I read psychology books quite regularly, trying to understand my own diagnoses, and I knew from these books that patients like Tasia were easily excitable and in moments of extreme excitement, they were able to lift heavy things, four times heavier than their own weight. This was what Tasia did. As they say, one does not need a lot of intelligence to carry heavy things. After the hot-water heater story, the nannies used Tasia's working potential cautiously and with an eye on her mood.

***

I got acquainted with another person whom I consider significant in my life in my understanding of human nature and of altruistic support. There might have been other reasons than just friendship or love, but we always consider friendship and love as the most important motivations. I believe this woman was my guardian angel, which is equal to friend. On the second day of my stay in the 'weak quarter', in the afternoon, someone knocked on the door and a young woman entered our ward. She said to Luska, "Would you please give me your wheelchair for a while? I want to bring my Vitka to the park, but we didn't bring our vehicle."

"Of course, take it," Luska responded.

The woman, passing by, politely greeted me; she took the wheelchair and rolled it outside.

"Who is she?" I asked Luska when the woman had left.

"That is Katia Luzianina. She assists in room twenty-five, where idiots live. She is my friend; she always visits me," Luska explained. "Katia's husband has no legs; she needed my wheelchair for him."

I survived the horrors of my life in the asylum largely thanks to Katia. She never refused to help, although I was not part of her official duties. Katia always agreed to wash me when I asked. She always visited me during her shift. When I caught another cold or did not feel well, she begged the medical staff to give her pills for me.

***

Once Luska and I had an intimate conversation, as it could happen between two Russian girls — we Russians like confessions. She asked me, "Toma, have you ever tasted vodka?"

"No, not once," I confessed.

"Would you like to taste it?" Luska asked me, and I did not know what to say.

I hesitated. "I can taste just to find out what it is. But we may be punished if they find out we drank vodka."

"Who is going to find out? Look — everybody drinks here." Luska frowned. "Vodka helps you to live happily. It's the best thing to relax and forget!"

I tried vodka... It did not give me anything good! And it is not the best thing to solve problems! I drank a whole little cup, making small gulps. In Slavic languages the word 'vodka' is the diminutive for 'water'. It suggests the meaning of 'water of life' and 'spirit'. Anna Akhmatova called it 'fire water'. Indeed, at first this fire water released my body; it seemed my problems and resentments retreated to the background. I sensed the lightness of being, and even my incurable hyperkinesia disappeared. Then I fell asleep blissfully. But the next morning, everything came back in multiple dimensions, with all problems and indignations, along with the depression mixed with fear... and not to mention the headache and pain. This stopped forever any desire for vodka, which I actually never had again. It seems that God guided me in the right direction, keeping me away from wrong things.

I did not know my future at all, and I certainly did not think that one day I would be successful as a writer; nevertheless, I see my life as a preparation for my literary vocation. When I look at my life, I see a distinctive path that goes heroically in its own direction, in spite of all obstacles, and no matter how much I would resist taking this path — it seems the path goes on its own — and now I can see it is the path of my destiny.

***

Six months later, the new girl Svetlana moved to our room. She was a girl who was raised inside the family; she was opposite to the street girl. She belonged to the minority population of Shors or Shorians — the Turkic ethnic group, inhabitants of Mountain Shoria, in the southern part of the Kemerovo region. They were also called Kuznetsk Tatars in some of the documents of the seventeenth and eighteenth centuries. Sveta's mother died, and her aunt submitted her to the PNBS. Sveta had cerebral palsy, but she was able to walk, supporting herself by holding the wall. She was able to eat; she did her laundry. But she did not speak well. She could not write or read, she could not even sign, and she suffered from epilepsy. Sveta's mental condition was not hopeless, and I think she could have studied, but apparently, she did not. Sveta replaced our roommate, the old lady, who was moved to another room on Sveta's arrival. This rearrangement followed the plan — to create a ward for young girls.

It was difficult for Svetlana to get used to PNBS. It was disappointing that on the first day, she had a serious argument with Luska. On the day of Svetlana's arrival, Luska was taken by her friend to a birthday party, from where she came back tipsy. When she saw the new girl, she attacked her for no reason. "Why didn't they ask my permission before they moved this strange girl to my room?" Luska attacked me. "Why did you let her move in? She could steal my things while I was not here!"

"Luska, calm down; Sveta didn't touch your things. I was here all the time." I tried to stop the conflict which I already sensed in the air.

But she would not listen, and she kept yelling at me and Svetlana. "Why are you defending her? So she's good for you? Let her feed you!" Luska was so angry. But what do you expect from a drunken woman?

"I don't think she took anything from you, but you can check it out tomorrow. Just calm down and go to bed!" I continued, calming her down.

I perfectly understood Sveta, who had just left home and had appeared in this public setting, which was not particularly friendly. She had just buried her mother; after that she was moved to a strange place to be cursed on the very first day... I heard Sveta crying at night. This situation was painfully familiar to me.

Three days later, Luska and Sveta had a fight. Sveta could not forgive Luska for accusing her for nothing, and she aggressively reminded Luska of her insult. Although I explained to Svetlana that Luska did not have bad intentions, but she was just intoxicated with alcohol, it did not help. Then the action started — it had its logistics, strategies and goals: Luska crawled to Svetlana's bunk, which was by the window, next to my bunk, and Sveta slid to the floor, and placed herself by the hot-water heater. I was lying in my bunk, and I had no desire to be involved. However, when I saw that they were camped by the hot-water heater, I was terrified because they were about to start banging each other's heads against it and they would kill each other or make themselves even more advanced invalids than they were before the fight!

"Girls, at least step away from the hot-water heater!" I commanded.

But they did not pay attention to my mandate. So I slid down to the floor too with my mission to separate the girls before the trouble happened. Svetlana was closer to me; I was facing her back, and I grabbed her dress and pulled it in my direction, so she fell on the floor. I screamed to Luska, "Run and call the nannies!"

While Luska was crawling to the hallway, I tried to reason with the wild Svetlana. "Svetlana, sweet girl, just calm down. I won't hurt you! I'll let you go if you promise you will not hurt anyone."

This was how I tried to bring her to her senses; at the same time, I thought with fear: God forbid, she will not release herself from my hands! If she does, she might scratch my eyes out. I was safe as long as

I was holding her, but if she liberated herself from my custody, I would be in trouble.

"Let me go! I will not do anything bad to you!" Svetlana begged. I trusted Svetlana, and I let her go.

But when I got up and climbed to my bed, I had a sharp twitch (Oh! This horrible hyperkinesia!) and I snapped my left arm. My arm immediately became swollen, largely increased in its size. Later the nurse came and applied bandages to my hand, but it hurt for a long time.

Luska and Svetka never reconciled; they became the worst enemies until Svetka's death in 1985. Before Svetlana's death they had been fighting all the time. I was very upset about this; our fourth roommate, the feeble-minded Luba, did not care. She was very quiet and did not interfere in anything. We had never had problems with Luba; she had been always fine. Sometimes I wondered about Luba's state — a blissful condition where she did not want anything, did not strive for anything — it was similar to the state of a domestic animal, which can be satisfied when warm and fed.

The death of Sveta was a blow to me. According to the official version, she died of epilepsy. In reality, Svetlana poisoned herself with Lysol, a floor-cleaner, which was kept in the toilet. She killed herself intentionally. She was brought to our ward from the bathroom at eleven p.m. She could not get accustomed to the PSBS conditions…

The 'Weak Quarter': The New Place

The winter of 1979 in Kuzbass turned out to be fierce; it was minus forty degrees Celsius, and our 'weak quarter', which was already in decay, did not withstand the pressure of winter — all heating pipes were frozen. They had to remove wooden planks from the floor in order to reach the pipes, which they heated with a blowtorch. We were in bed with all our clothes on, even wearing coats and jackets. It was ice cold in the room; if we touched the walls, the frozen lime immediately fell off. The 'weak quarter' turned out to be weak in all respects. It would be cruel to keep even cattle in such a room! Our shameless director had already been fined several times, but he did not pay the fines out of his pocket, and he did not care deeply about us or our ward.

Somehow, we survived the winter of 1979. In September of 1980, the authorities decided we should not wait for the cold winter, so we were transferred to another building — it was considered to be the strongest one in the PNBS. We were moved to one of the two large wings, where we were placed in rooms. The second wing was occupied by the administration with their accounting office, personnel department, director's office and medical facility. The wings were separated by a small hall, and we had the common exit to the street.

The empty 'weak quarter' was put on the costly capital repair to correct previous defects and degradations with all necessary replacements and rebuilding. After the restoration of the ex-'weak quarter' was completed and approved as a qualitative work, all administrative services were transferred there.

Even though a lot of bad things happened to us after the relocation, I was happy about moving.

***

One day, all nannies were drunk as skunks. In those years, they had salaries which were considered decent —a hundred and twenty to a hundred and forty rubles a month — they had just got paid. Usually, the wages were paid in two steps: as advance and salary. So the joyous event of receiving money happened twice a month — a good reason for every employee to celebrate it and get drunk. There was a woman, more or less young, Alka Gavrina; she was one of the nannies on that unforgettable shift. She ran to our room. "I'm dying to go to the toilet! I'll leave my bag here!" She threw her bag on the floor, not far from Luska's bed and ran away.

She was gone for quite a while — later we learned that after she had used the toilet, she ran directly to receive her advance. Then she came back to take her bag. Analyzing this pitiful story with a detective mind, I can conclude that she came back with the money in her pocket. She did not open her bag — she rushed off, as she was impatient to take part in the cocktail party.

Three days later, Alka started her shift with drinking, bringing herself to the condition that she completely lost her mind, then felt like she had to deal with a challenging situation. This was how a storm in a teacup started, though this storm was quite brutal. She came to our room and started speaking scornfully to Luska. "Where is my money? What did you do with my money?"

Luska had not touched Alka's bag, and it was clear to us that Luska was innocent. As a matter of fact, using deductive logic, the fact that the bag in question was left with us before Alka received her advance, but not after, also supported our conclusion that the event of theft did not happen in our room. I did not believe that Alka would leave her bag so carelessly if she had money in it. And if there was some money in the bag, she would check it — though this is more related to logical reasoning than to reality — in reality the employees usually did not have money before they received their next payment. Another thing was Alka's longing for alcohol; sometimes a person with such longing for a drink can even forget about her mother in a sick bed, not to mention a bag which obviously did not contain any money.

Luska calmly replied that she did not touch the bag. "Why didn't you come to me when you discovered your money was missing?" Luska said.

Then Alka became mad, and as an answer to Luska's meek but reasonable question, she started hitting her in the face, doing it as a meticulous succession of hard blows at high speed, saying. "That's why I didn't come here!"

Luska's head was shaking from the blows in all directions — mostly back and to both sides, touching her shoulders, as if she was performing some flowing Zen exercises for her neck. She would be more than willing to stop this painful routine, but she was completely defenseless against Alka's attack. If she could walk, she would have been capable of some strategic manipulations: to stand up or to take a step back, or even to fight back. But how could the feeble, handicapped Luska compete with the strong and not-handicapped Alka?

At the screams, Alka's colleague Lisa entered the room. She had poor vision, the reason she had the status of a handicap of second degree; in addition, she was retarded. She was not a bad woman; she began to reproach her colleague. "Alka, stop beating the girl! Do you hear me? Stop!"

But this docile intervention made Alka even more infuriated. I screamed, "Lisa, call the nurse on duty! Alka could kill Luska!"

Lisa finally left the room in a slow fashion. About ten minutes later the nurse showed up.

"What's going on here?" the nurse asked in a strict tone, as if she did not see the drunken nanny Alka was beating the handicapped Luska non-stop.

The nurse sat in the chair and began giving commands, shouting, "Gavrina, stop beating the sick woman!" Then the nurse decided to take action. "So, where's the orderly on duty?"

Alka did not pay any attention to the nurse; in her rage, she continued hitting Luska. Someone knocked on the door; the nurse left her chair and proceeded to the door. There was an orderly standing in the hallway by the door. His appearance was not promising for saving the poor Luska; it was not a hero who came to rescue us from this Alka, but a monster. Saliva was flowing from the mouth of this antihero; he was snorting and making growling and barking sounds. The body of this lowlife sample was swinging from side to side — he was trying to keep his balance but in vain.

"Oh, my God, the whole shift is drunk, and you are drunk too! You! Miserable drunkard!" the nurse screamed intensely.

Then she sat in the chair again and began to lecture Alka, who continued beating Luska. I could not take it any more, and I yelled at the nurse without thinking about the consequences. "Zinaida Ilinichna, what's the point of talking? Gavrina doesn't understand! Why don't you call the police?"

The nurse pretended she did not hear me. But Gavrina heard me; she turned to me. She looked at me as if I were not worth considering seriously; she just imitated me, making a monkey face, frowning at me. "And you're a wreck, galactic bulge!"

"So what?" I threw at her. "But I don't drink like a pig!"

"Don't talk to Gavrina! No one!" ordered the nurse, apparently fearing that Alka would attack me as well. But I wanted Alka to give me her attention, so Luska would have a chance to crawl away. Finally, Gavrina stopped, because she became tired of beating Luska; I am sure she spent all her physical resources, probably sadistic too — everything has its limits.

We hoped that Gavrina would be brought to justice for her violence; we hoped she would be fired. However, we were wrong — Alka escaped any punishment, except a slight fright; she was affected by the case just a little bit. Following the complaint of Luska's mother, a certain grande dame came from the Regional Social Security Department. In her presence, the director acted like a good judge, shaking some legal papers in front of the subdued Alka, reading from the sets of laws for her and the grande dame who witnessed this theater of the absurd. The director did his best, threatening Alka with initiating a criminal case for assault and harm to the patient's health. But he only announced a reprimand for her being drunk at work and non-performance of official duties. That was the end of it. There was no question of dismissal. Well, the director can be understood — nannies were in short supply; even for a decent salary, only a few people wanted to clean up after the sick. Only those who were rejected for 'clean work' were taken into the system of hospitals for the disabled.

Later Lisa told us in secret that after Alka had received that ill-fated advance, she attended a great party, which probably lasted all night. In the morning, Alka discovered that her money was missing. But she was too clever to start a fight with her friends who supposedly had stolen her money; they were not invalids and even stronger than Alka. So she decided to play out her misfortune on Luska, who unfortunately became a scapegoat. I also have to admit that it was a little tragedy for Alka to lose forty rubles; she had four children. But anyway, this ugly drama can expose so many weaknesses of human beings; sadism is one of them.

***

It was no secret that non-invalid men from the nearby village, after they got drunk, visited young disabled women who lived on the second floor. Or these disabled women would run to their village, and in the morning, they would come back to their rooms as if nothing happened.

Once, on a beautiful summer night, one of those waggish suitors started hanging around our building. But his circulation started even earlier; it started in the afternoon. We were in our room; some of us were asleep, and some were just lying in bed. We lived on the first floor; our window was open. Suddenly, we saw a big monster jump through our window; he crossed our room, opened the door and hid in the hallway. At first, we thought it was one of the workers rushing to the scene of an accident in our building. But why did he enter through our window? Ten minutes later, this giant flitted again through our window, crossed our room and disappeared in the hallway. We called the nurse to find out what was going on.

"So he climbed through your window! We kicked him out the door, and he jumped through the window! What a villain!" the nurse exclaimed with rightful indignation. "Girls, close the window, so he can no longer get through."

"And who is he?" Luska asked curiously. "We thought it was a plumber or an electrician."

"A plumber! Oh no! He is the 'beau of the girl from the second floor; we pushed him out, but he came back again. Don't let him use your window any more!" The nurse rebuked us in a bizarre way, as if we invited this character. Then she left.

We were excited because of this peculiar intrusion; we closed the window and calmed down. However, closer to the night this circus began again. The night nannies always blocked the door of their room with a wardrobe, so they could sleep until morning peacefully and without interruptions. The nurse locked herself in her office with a key; she did not have to barricade her door. So until six o'clock in the morning, the staff were not visible, not heard, and they could not hear a sound from us. We had already started to doze when the annoying 'beau' scratched like a mouse on the closed window. We got alarmed and sent Taska to wake up the nannies. Taska pounded on their door, but no one answered; she could injure her hand with no response from the other side. Then she knocked on the door behind which the nurse rested like Sleeping Beauty; it was dead silence behind her door.

We survived that night. In the morning, we complained to the head nurse. So the nurse who was on duty on that unfortunate night came to our ward with the orderly, and they both threatened us — it was like a singing duet in which each was singing: we should stop complaining, otherwise, we would regret it.

"You all! Get up! Your happy life is finished! Now you will get up very early!" the orderly yelled, turning on the light in our room. "If you don't get up now, I'll throw you off your beds to the floor!"

But none of us moved. I covered my face with my dress which I pulled from the back of my bed — I did not want them to see that I was laughing. I imagined how the orderly would start throwing the girls, who were not capable of walking, off their beds to the floor. And then what? He would be forced to put the handicapped girls back in their beds.

Winds of Change

In the autumn of 1982, Leonid Ilyich Brezhnev, who seemed to be eternal and irreplaceable, died. Soon after his death, the 'iron curtain' slightly opened. Just a crack, but it was enough to leak dangerous information — many foreign countries were doing a lot better. And especially the life of the disabled was much better abroad.

One afternoon, in 1984, I went to the hallway just to get some air. I drove up to the window in the lobby, and I saw a ragged newspaper on the windowsill. I took the paper in my hands; my gaze caught an unusual headline: Is this true? I thought.

I put the paper on my knee and started reading; it took my breath away. The article stated that special auxiliary schools had begun to accommodate children with intellectual disabilities, as well as children with preserved intellect. If the child failed the school curriculum, he or she was immediately sent to the school for the mentally retarded. The article said they placed children in the asylum unreasonably fast, without any attempts to help them. The term 'mentally retarded' was abbreviated in this article to MR. I lifted my head and looked around. And, like a professional thief, I put the precious paper under my shirt and rushed into my room. I climbed to my bed and started rereading the article — I reread it five times! Where did it come from? Who brought this seditious material? The article gave me the courage and desire to fight for myself as I belonged to the category of unjustly classified MR.

That night, I could not sleep. I kept thinking that I should act, but how and where to start? There were plans in my head, one bigger than the other. I fell asleep in the morning; in my dream I saw myself in a classroom.

I would go back to this ragged, wrinkled piece of newspaper too often. Each reading was like a breath of fresh air. It came to be my last hope, a gateway to the future.

That newspaper was not the only thing that awakened me.

It is true that fate squeezes man mercilessly and then it gives a reward for all his torments.

In those years, we had a visiting psychiatrist, Ludmila Alekseevna Yenina, at the Prokopyevsk PNBS. She attended advanced training courses and would bring medical journals to work. In 1985 one of the journals came to me.

Nadia, the girl who was able to walk, liked to visit our room, helping with one thing or another. She was a good girl, but she had a bad habit — everything that she liked would be innocently stuck to her hands, even things which she did not actually need. Then she would give the stolen thing back, but before she did it, her victims would look for the missing thing everywhere and become upset. To give her credit, she did not take anything from us, knowing that we were deprived of the freedom of movement, with our deficiencies it would be difficult for us to look for a missing thing, and we would be certainly more affected by her games than the people who could walk.

One day Nadia came to our ward, holding the 'S. S. Korsakov Journal of Neuropathology and Psychiatry'. Sergey Sergeevich Korsakov was the first professor of psychiatry in Russia and founder of the Moscow school of psychiatry. Although he was head of the psychiatric clinic of Moscow University for only twelve years, his clinical approach and organizing skills influenced the direction in which Russian psychiatry developed and put it on the international map. The major topic of the journal was: All about the children with 'backward intellect'.

"Nadia, give me this journal! I'll give you all the candies I am going to get for lunch!" I said.

"Take it!" Nadka gave me the journal.

It was clear to me that the journal belonged to Ludmila Alekseevna, and apparently it was her own — there was no library stamp on it. So I decided that if she found out her journal was missing, and tried to look for it, I would say, "I have it," and I would ask her if I could keep it for a while. I was sure I would solve the problem with the journal. What was wrong with wanting to learn about my diagnosis? Luckily, she did not look for the journal, and I read it cover to cover. It was a gift of fate. And was it just a coincidence that I came across this journal?

Who would conduct these causes and effects so meticulously? And how can powerless human beings control the future? There is only One who set things the way they are supposed to be; there is only One who controls our destinies and our lives, and it was One who always led me by the hand. God showed me how I would solve the problem, but it had to be me who did all the work.

In the evening, when the bosses left the asylum and the girls went to watch TV, I was alone, reading scientific texts in the journal. First, I feared that I would not understand anything — the journal was for professional psychiatrists. But all the articles were written in a simple and fascinating way. I was able to understand the Wechsler Adult Intelligence Scale (WAIS), an IQ test designed to measure intelligence and cognitive ability in adults and older adolescents. Reading the journal, I smiled: how simple, I thought. Of course, some formulas were too complicated for me, but I understood the rest. And I stopped torturing myself with my thoughts of how I could prove that I was not an idiot. It was written that the oligophrenic does not perceive subtext, that is, between the lines or the double meaning of the written. This was my thinking: should I write poetry? I could not write novels because I had not seen much during my years in prison. I just thought: I have to do something! I have to write something that could prove to these heartless doctors that I was capable of thinking and reading subtext; I was able to read between the lines.

At that time, I was impressed by Eduard Uspensky. I considered the children's writer the highest vocation in the world. So I decided to try to write for children. However, there were no children around me in my imprisoned environment. And how could I be a writer if I had never tried to write even a short essay? I never went to school, and I have no idea how one should write even an elementary composition. But I put all my doubts aside; I made the first move.

I could not write on my own — my paralyzed hands were incapable of such delicate movements as one would need to do handwriting. If someone was holding my hand, I could write a few lines. I asked Luska to write down under my dictation the plots I had invented. I promised her I would pay for her job of a scribe. Luska agreed and wrote down three of my fairy tales. But after that she did not want to write any more. I did not criticize her for her refusal; she just did not like to write under my dictation. I thanked her for doing me a favor and paid her the money I had promised before. Where did I get the money? I would beg my mother to give me some money, and she would nag and reproach me, but in the end, she would give me five or even ten rubles.

Thus, my first fairy tales were written by Luska's hand: 'Vovka's Snowman', "'From the Life of the Wizard Mishuta' and 'The Blue Centipede'. Later, 'Vovka's Snowman' and 'From the Life of the Wizard Mishuta' were published, but the manuscript 'The Blue Centipede' was irrevocably lost, and I cannot even remember the story, only the name.

The Writer from a Madhouse

With the process underway, I started writing! And, it seems, I managed to write not primitively, not superficially, but with subtext, so that it was possible to read between the lines, which, in fact, was my task — to convince the doctors to withdraw the degrading diagnosis.

And what should I do with my texts? How would I know if my fairy tales proved not only my ability to write with subtext, but were also worthy of publication? How could I send my opuses to the publisher? Should I send them by mail? I was overwhelmed with emotions that now I could write fairy tales, and I already anticipated bright prospects.

And again, I was helped by mysterious angels.

In 1986, Lena Medvedeva arrived at our asylum from the city boarding school, where she finished the eighth grade of high school. She would continue her studies, but at twelve, after a fight in a pioneer camp, where older girls beat her head against the wall, she developed epilepsy. With such a disease, she could not be accepted to any school or get a job. So Lena was sent to the PNBS. She suffered from severe epileptic seizures, but otherwise she was a completely normal girl. As soon as she arrived, Lena immediately began visiting us. This was understandable; she had lived with normal people, but here she could not find any kindred spirit, with whom she could talk and open her heart. Every weekend she went to visit her teacher of Russian language and literature, who always welcomed her.

I asked Lena to show my writing to her teacher. Lena took my fairy tales, written by Luska on separate sheets. She said that next weekend she would go to the teacher again and bring them back along with her opinion about my work.

All week I was on tenterhooks. When you are waiting for something, time passes slowly; it crawls like a tortoise, and the week seemed to be like eternity. The long-awaited Sunday came, and in my anticipation of an answer, I huddled into a ball in uncertainty. Then suddenly I felt that soon I would be a recognizable writer and I felt like I had wings behind my back and I could fly, at least in my imagination. I had been restless in my expectation of precarious news until five o'clock when Lena finally came back. She told me that her teacher was very impressed with my opuses; she was very surprised. She had said, "Did Tamara come up with all this herself?" And she advised me to show my fairy tales to the local newspaper, 'Shakhterskaia Pravda' (Miners' Truth). There was a literary section, as well as a local literary circle, whom I should contact.

I begged Lena to go to the editorial office of this newspaper. The next week of waiting proceeded in a slow motion, but I no longer cringed into a ball, but impatiently flapped my grown wings. However, Lena still could not accomplish the task — the working hours of the editorial office coincided with those of her job. As soon as she arrived at the asylum, she was immediately forced to work with the coypus, which belonged to the director, who tried to make a profit with anything. I impatiently waited until Saturday, when Lena was released early from the director's animal farm.

But it turned out that Saturday was a short day at the editorial office. What a disappointment! I begged Lena to take a day off during the week to visit the editorial office, and she was permitted to take a day off. Her teacher gave her the address; Lena knew the city very well.

The editor of 'Miners' Truth' turned out to be my namesake — Sergey Ivanovich Cheremnov. I found this a strange coincidence. He took the sheets from Lena, reviewed them, and promised to deliver them to the local communication center where the literary circle meetings were held. There was a woman named Rahil.

A week later, on a Saturday, Lena went there and brought such news that not only did my wings spread, but my roof was blown to pieces — Rahil was going to come and visit me, and Sergei Ivanovich read all my stories and praised me!

He said that I had a 'very warm literary language' and advised me to read some books, probably manuals on how to write. Unfortunately, Lena did not remember and did not write down the titles of these books.

We had the girl Marina, who liked to spread gossip. And she told all the staff that I was writing fairy tales, and these fairy tales were going to be read on the radio. This Marina was a real fake news person! One afternoon, I took a nap and I heard a loud conversation behind the wall in the manager's office; I heard my last name pronounced.

"Can you believe we have a writer in the madhouse? Cheremnova is a writer!" The manager was sniggering. "Such things don't happen very often in madhouses!" And such a cackle rose that it made me blue. But I tried to cheer myself up — that is true — a writer from a madhouse is rare.

Three days after my public mockery, an old woman from the nearby village of New Constructions came to us — her own daughter threw her out, and our head nurse asked her colleagues to give her shelter in our asylum. Just like that, without any official documents — they were going to provide these papers later. You cannot leave a human being outside in the cold autumn! But the roommates of the old lady resented the bringing of a normal person into the asylum. They believed that she belonged in a nursing home, and they sent a complaining letter to the 'Miners' Truth'. If before, our asylum was considered officially as a boarding school, as part of our full name was missing — in other words, 'psycho-neurological' was absent in our address, after the letter of the good roommates, the secret about our full status was disclosed.

And after this 'declassification', Rahil from the literary circle did not come. Many times, Katia Luzianina called this particular Rahil, but she only fed promises. And then she hung up on me as soon as she found out who was calling.

It had been three bitter months. Lena Medvedeva was taken home by her uncle, and I was left without help and support…

But I am a stubborn donkey by nature — if I grab onto something, I won't give up for a long time. I dictated my fairy tales to other girls who had good writing hands. And they did not charge me, and they said they were interested in my stories. And I worked so hard to make my stories interesting to my scribers and to children, my future readers. And gradually, I learned how to work with the elements of the narrative.

I am so lucky!

I am so lucky! It would be a great title for this chapter! My fairy tale began with the television set which appeared in our room. In 1986, Irina, who was local from the city of Prokopyevsk, was admitted to our asylum and assigned to our room. She was younger than all my roommates and me. We started gently calling her Irishka. She suffered from cerebral palsy as I did, though her hands were healthy. She could crawl on the floor quite sufficiently; she did not need assistance for eating and dressing herself. Irishka's mother was the opposite of my mother: she visited her daughter all the time. She did all kinds of things for her daughter: helping her with the toilet, washing her, and even cleaning her ears. She did not express contempt, disgust, disrespect and a wide range of hostile emotions towards handicaps, which was my mother's character defect. While Ekaterina Ivanovna avoided any action to improve the conditions of her disabled daughter, Irishka's mother would communicate with the doctors and staff about the possible measures for her daughter's health, requesting special medication and various physiotherapeutic procedures. How jealous I was of Irishka! I was even ashamed of myself — how could it be? The grown-up Tamara is jealous of the young Irishka. A few months later, to make Irishka more comfortable, her mother brought her own TV to our room. And of course, it was never turned off. This was our window to the world.

In 1987, a series of landmark events happened in my life. It began with a television broadcast. One night I was sitting on my bed, thinking about another fairy tale story. The girls were watching the regional news on TV. Suddenly I heard: "Today, we have invited to our studio the Kuzbass writer Zinaida Aleksandrovna Chigareva."

When Chigareva was announced, I was all ears. I started listening intently. In the orphanage I had read her book 'Golden Hills of Childhood'. I learned that Chigareva had written a new book, titled 'Cruise'. She was invited to the television station in regard to this book.

In the middle of the night, thinking about some big plans, it dawned on me to write to Zinaida Aleksandrovna Chigareva and ask her to read my fairy tales. But then what? What would happen? Let it happen! I do not know how I got this idea, but I fell asleep with new hope.

The next day, I begged Luska to write a letter under my dictation to the address office of the city of Kemerovo — at that time it was possible to get the address of any person by mail. I had the audacity to lie that I was Chigareva's niece, that I had entered the home of the handicapped, about which my aunt did not yet know. I asked them humbly to send me her address.

Two weeks later, I received Chigareva's address. With all this luck, I was jumping on the bunk until I fell to the floor and knocked my head so strongly that multicolored sparks fell from my eyes. The girls looked at me as if I had lost my mind until they found the cause of my excitement.

With Luska's help, I wrote a letter to Zinaida Aleksandrovna, in which I thanked her for the wonderful books and for the important subjects raised in them, and at the end, modestly and unobtrusively, asked her if she could read my fairy tales. I wrote: 'It is important to me to have your opinion as a professional writer if I should write fiction at all?'

I did not dare to dream that I would receive an answer to my flamboyant letter, but three weeks later it came. Zinaida Aleksandrovna wrote that she was in the hospital, recovering from her third heart attack, and that as soon as she recovered, she would read my fairy tales. After reading the letter, I felt like I had acquired wide wings behind my back — first they rose to the ceiling and covered all the beds in our room. I was filled with joy, and at the same time, I was terrified! What if Zinaida Aleksandrovna did not read my fairy tales? What if she did not like them?

My fears were in vain — Zinaida Aleksandrovna found time to read my fairy tales and she blessed me for writing. At first, I did not want to tell Chigareva the truth — that I was handicapped with cerebral palsy and incorrectly diagnosed as mentally retarded, and living in an asylum. Then I confessed. Zinaida Aleksandrovna took it calmly, and did not fear asylums like Rahil. She even sent me an article about typical medical errors. She promised me she would help me with literary advice. I never doubted the last one, because I already felt I would not be betrayed this time. And for the rest of my life, I will remember the encouragement from Zinaida Aleksandrovna: 'From now, Tamara Aleksandrovna, we will have ongoing communication'.

I was so lucky to enter the literary stage and be led by such a guiding star! After Zinaida Aleksandrovna finally recovered, she wrote: 'Tamara Aleksandrovna! I read your fairy tales, I typed them and gave them to the book publisher with my recommendation. But I want to tell you this might not work. I have very little influence in the publishing house, where others command everything, so be prepared if they refuse.'

No matter how much I prepared for rejection, I still felt the joy. For my sorrowful life, God has given me such a reward — the ability to write fairy tales and to meet the writer Chigareva!

One night I had a dream that I was tearing my medical history into pieces. When I woke up, I thought that the dream was prophetic; it was painfully saturated with reality. I always wanted to tear apart this pile of tattered pieces of paper glued together that had been used to humiliate and destroy me for so many years.

And it was on that afternoon that an envelope with a government stamp — a letter from the book publisher — arrived. I felt like I fainted inside — was it a positive response or a polite refusal? The envelope was opened, and I looked through the lines, and I did not understand anything — typed letters were jumping in my eyes.

I asked someone to read the letter; now I do not remember who this person was. The letter said that Tamara Cheremnova's fairy tales book had been approved for publication. It was going to be published!

I took this news with such a candid avowal that I felt if I did not let my emotions come out, I would explode like a balloon. And I produced such a mighty cry which probably required not just all my emotional resources, but all my auditory capacities as well! That is probably how a wild animal howls when he reaches his prey. That was the jubilation of the winner. Then after I had expressed myself in such an uncivilized manner, I cried discreetly with tears as a cultured person. My crying was joined immediately by Luska, then by all others who happened to witness this unforgettable moment of triumph — we all cried together as a well-tuned lyrical ensemble, exhibiting euphony and joy. It was a collective victory of the spirit.

I immediately wrote to Zinaida Aleksandrovna about the letter from the publisher. And in a few days, when I was contented with joy to my heart, I decided to boast about my success to the doctor Yenina, and at the same time, I wanted to express my views on psychiatric topics. I told her that their time had come to an end, that I refused to be diagnosed with oligophrenia, because my head was fine. However, she listened to my tirade with a lean face and a glued smile, and then she just put me down. Was it so difficult to her to praise me for my success? Well, for some reason, she had to kick me. "That means nothing that your book is going to be published. Dostoevsky was sick in the head. He had epilepsy. And Gogol was mentally disturbed. He had horrible seizures! And Pushkin was so unstable and prone to psychosis. And at the Kemerovo Psychiatric Hospital we have a poet with schizophrenia who writes such fantastic poems!"

It was so strange that Yenina, the psychiatrist, responded to my request to remove the diagnosis, which she and her colleagues had attached to me, by comparing me with the Russian classics and the Kemerovo poet, who according to her, were all insane. I could have taken her response as flattering, but I felt humiliated.

"I wonder what would happen to these Russian classics if they lived in our time; would they be put in lunatic asylums?" I confronted the psychiatrist with a trembling voice.

"You haven't even attended school, which means you're mentally retarded!" Yenina tried to put me down by all means. She crucified me and ignored completely the delightful news that my manuscript had been accepted for publication.

After I had recovered after Yenina's blow, I decided to take some actions. I was an adult individual, I was thirty-two, and I could defend myself!

A Letter to the Ministry of Health

Finally, I pulled myself together and wrote a letter to the USSR Ministry of Health, addressed to Minister Yevgenii Ivanovich Chazov. I described my medical situation, which, from the point of view of common sense, was out of order. And at the same time, I expressed all the bitterness which had accumulated in me. I sent my letter through Zinaida Aleksandrovna. I asked her to help me — she added a few lines.

My daring letter to Chazov worked! Three months later, I received an answer. They wrote that the diagnosis would be reviewed, and I would be assigned a home of general type. This was what I had been dreaming all these years!

Yenina found out about Chazov's answer; she immediately ran to our ward and started screaming right from the doorway, "Cheremnova, why are you jumping over heads?"

At first, I did not understand what Yenina meant, because the last thing I could do would be jumping, especially over someone's head. But when I got into the essence of the claim, I snapped, "This is my principle to jump over heads!"

During our correspondence, Zinaida Aleksandrovna repeatedly suggested that I should start acting on my own through the asylum's doctors. But I evaluated my situation in a more sober way than my friend, knowing what kind of doctors we had in the asylum. Only Yenina's reply about me jumping over heads was worth it to understand her style of psychiatry.

"Publishers don't pay attention where these literary works come from; they don't care!"

My silent response to her abominable words was, "They don't care, of course, but I do care where I live!"

Two months later, in October 1988, following the order of Chazov's administration, Pavel Petrovich Kuzin, deputy doctor of the Prokopyevsk Psychiatric Hospital, arrived at the asylum to conduct a personal examination of my person. I do not remember what debate I presented from my side, participating in our dialogue. However, I answered his questions rationally as the results of the interview and testing not only confirmed the preservation of my intelligence and normal mental development, but also brought the decision to transfer me to the boarding school of general type.

Before Kuzin's visit, I was extremely nervous. Suddenly I realized the seriousness of my situation. I was scared: What am I doing? They will see my hyperkinesia, spasticity, twitching and other uncontrolled movements — I can't hide them! What should I do? I was so exhausted with my doubts that I begged for help. It is ironic that I turned to Yenina, asking for advice — otherwise, I would collapse. For the first time, she acted as a professional psychiatrist. "You can try hypnosis to remove this compulsive fear. You have to apply to a hospital which uses hypnotherapy. A lot of psychiatric hospitals do that. And it wouldn't hurt if you get physical therapy at some neurological hospital…"

And being encouraged by her advice, I got the courage to talk to Kuzin. "Pavel Petrovich, please take me to the hospital or send me to the neurological ward; otherwise, I'll be very sick. I've been insisting on leaving this asylum; I've already lost my faith. And then, when things started to move, suddenly, I got scarred, and fear haunts me day and night."

Kuzin looked at me attentively, smiled and said, "You just haven't had much contact with people — this is why you are in panic. You were in closed places all the time. Unfortunately, I can't send you to neurology. I can take you to my hospital. Would you like to go there?"

"I'll be so happy to go!" I said.

Three days later, for the first time in my life, I was taken to the psychiatric hospital. However, all the examinations and tests were carried out 'at home' — in the asylum. I think no one in the world would be so excited about going to a mental hospital. But if I had not asked to go to a psychiatric hospital, I would not be able to get rid of emotional stress — those who know the specifics of cerebral palsy will understand me.

In the Madhouse

I was admitted to Prokopyevsk Psychiatric Hospital in late November 1988 and spent about two months there. Upon arrival, I was first interviewed by the head of the department, Tatiana Ivanovna. I was taken to her office; she greeted me and asked my name.

"Tamara Cheremnova, I answered.

"What's your patronymic name?"

"Aleksandrovna," I squeezed out, embarrassed.

Doctors were seldom interested in my patronymic name, and in communication addressed me by surname and the informal 'you'.

"Tamara Aleksandrovna, we have an unusual psychiatric hospital. Did they warn you when they brought you to us?"

"I know. I requested that they bring me here."

"You'll stay here until we get the proper paperwork for the boarding school; we'll treat you with vitamins. Did they give you pills that reduce spasticity at the asylum?"

"I take only phenazepam; unfortunately, the other medication is not right for me," I replied.

Another doctor came to the office. Tatiana Ivanovna introduced her. "Tamara Aleksandrovna, this is Elena Vasilevna Diakonova; she will be your physician."

They decided to put me in the ward with permanent nannies' assistance, but they said they would let me have promenades in the hallway.

***

At first, I could not get used to the fact that there was no noise, so typical in my orphanage and the asylum. I felt tense, and as soon as one of the nannies approached me, I shuddered in fright.

"What are you flinching about? Who are you afraid of? Don't worry, no one will hurt you here; we won't let anyone you hurt you." The nannies calmed me down.

But the most unusual for me was that the nannies assisted me so humbly — I did not even have to beg them, and no one ever complained that it was difficult for them to take care of me. In the past I had always heard that feeding me was an enormous burden. And for the first time, I felt like not a miserable cripple, but an ordinary person.

When Elena Vasilevna went through my medical history and read the evaluation written by Pavel Petrovich Kuzin during his visit to the asylum, she was indignant. "This medical history is not written professionally; no home for the disabled will take you with such medical history! Everything must be rewritten; we have to write a new medical history. I know what to do. Let us treat you for a week or two, you will calm down a bit, then we'll do the paperwork."

And they started treating me. They did not hypnotize me, because they did not have hypnotic treatment in this hospital. But the treatment they provided was effective, and my fears went away, and the hyperkinesia significantly reduced.

***

I started looking closely at my roommates. They were brought here in poor condition, during the exacerbation of their diseases. During the attacks, they were completely dysfunctional, as if they were in another dimension. But the attack passed, and they would become ordinary people, living in the real world. All of them had families who visited them.

The first woman I got acquainted with was Tatiana. She did not have severe seizures during which one loses function, but she worried about her son and old mother whom she had left at home. Tatiana expressed her enthusiasm about our friendship and her willingness to take care of me.

Then another woman had just recovered from her seizures. Later I learned that she worked as a teacher at a vocational school. Then another poor soul regained consciousness. And they all looked at me amazed as if they had seen me for the first time, though I had been living with them for a few days. Then the bookworm was brought in — this girl studied too much; it was too strenuous for her head and as result, she was brought to this hospital. And then a very young girl came in; she was in her nineteenth year, a trainee paramedic. She started working at the hospital, and then she started having schizophrenic attacks; she even stopped recognizing her own mother. There was a woman in the ward, who had just had a baby, and she had a post-partum psychosis — she stopped talking to everyone. She would lie all day long, in silence, and if you asked her anything, she would answer the question, and then she would sink into oblivion.

After I had spent a week at the hospital, they started taking me to different clinics located in the city for further tests. It was a trial for me: I felt so humiliated to be carried in the arms of women of my age. Every time when I returned to the hospital from a clinic, I cried so hard, one could think it was me who had a stomach ache, not the poor nannies who carried me in their hands along the stairs to my room on the third floor.

Tamara, we rest afterwards and our stomachs don't hurt a bit, they would say to me.

I did not hear a single complaint from them about carrying me in their hands, and this physical activity was quite hard, especially for women.

I am so grateful to these women for their kindness and compassion!

***

Oddly enough, spending some time in this psychiatric hospital, where I did not have intensive medication treatment, either physiotherapy or hypnosis sessions, and without the participation of neurologists, my acute hyperkinesia completely disappeared. I only twitched a little bit when I started to move. From time to time, I would flinch because of angst; this almost disappeared too. I calmed down. And of whom should I be afraid? After all, I would soon have a new medical history without the diagnosis of oligophrenia and with recommendations for maintaining the improved condition.

My roommates were discharged after they recovered and went home as normal people. I did not dare to envy them, because it was not final recovery, but remission; the attack could reoccur unpredictably. But when I saw them in normal condition, I was a little bit envious because they felt better, and I was condemned with cerebral palsy forever.

In January 1989, the paperwork was complete. I was discharged and taken back to the asylum to wait for a trip to the boarding school.

***

When I tell people about how I was treated in the psychiatric hospital, I often hear the following assumptions.

They must have treated you with psychotropic drugs, but they didn't tell you!

No, I was treated only with vitamins and the prescribed phenazepam. They were taken out of the boxes right in front of me. Plus, we have to consider their kindness, tactfulness, good care and my peace of mind. And of course, we have to consider my psychological condition. I looked into my future; I was strongly promised that I would be transferred from the asylum to a different home where I would live with normal people.

What a wonderful psychiatric hospital it was in Prokopyevsk! And what qualified and sincere employees they were! The attitude towards me was not dictated by instructions from the Ministry of Health; they treated all patients in the same way. This is what a health policy should be. And this attitude towards patients also implies the Hippocratic Oath, which doctors take when they receive their medical degrees.

When I returned to the asylum to wait for my transference to the boarding school of the general type, our nurses were delighted when they saw me.

"Tomochka! How wonderful you look! And where did your hyperkinesia go? And your spasticity went away…What did they do for you?"

"Yes, it's gone," I answered proudly.

And the girls in the ward noticed that even my voice had changed; it became quieter and happier.

But as soon as one becomes nervous and bursts into screaming, the calm mood vanishes like smoke. And everything returned to that which it was before — my voice and broken speech, spasticity and hyperkinesia. As if the magic spell vanished… And I returned to the condition in which I was before. I was waiting for my transference…

The Day Came...

And then the long-awaited day finally came. I was informed that my transfer papers had arrived. It happened in early May 1989.

My joy was overshadowed by the decision of the regional council to send me to a place which was far removed from the center of civilization, so to say. The fact that I was from the asylum did not give me many choices, and I had to be thankful that they considered me to be transferred to the most inferior boarding school. Even our doctors resented the fact that I had to be transferred to the boarding school in Blagoveshchenka. Blagoveshchenka is a little-known village in the Mariinski district, which can only be found on the detailed map of the Kemerovo region, far from the city of Mariinsk, in the eerie wilderness. The boarding school was inhabited by people who were released from prison and did not have a place to live. The inhabitants without prison experience were in the minority. In the future the ex-violators of the order would be relocated to a special boarding school which was built just for them.

I was so afraid to go to Blagoveshchenka! Someone stronger should be sent there instead of me, a defenseless being with unmanageable hands and legs, bound to the wheelchair.

Andrei Petrovich, our new doctor, suggested, "Tamara, since they gave you the ticket to be transferred to the wrong place, let us wait with your transfer. Maybe there will be another ticket, more decent. I'll try to exchange the bad ticket for the good one at the city council."

But how long should I wait for another transfer ticket? What if it came in a year? Will the city council agree with the doctor that I need a better ticket? How long will it take to negotiate, correspond, and reconsider my 'case'? I rejected the offer of Andrei Petrovich. "Thank you, Andrei Petrovich, for all your concerns. But I shouldn't wait. I'll go where they send me."

And I thought to myself that in this Blagoveshchenka I could arrange a transfer to another boarding school. How could I be so sure? Probably

I followed the voice from above; it was the voice of One who had saved me before so many times and led me in my life.

"Well, then be ready at four o'clock tomorrow morning." Andrei Petrovich was relieved; he had one problem less.

The staff and my roommates were helping me collect my simple belongings, and I said goodbye to everyone. I tried to say something kind and reassuring. But to speak with hope in such a hopeless place, which I had tried to leave with all my efforts... I must have sounded hypocritical.

The night before my departure, I did not even go to bed; I knew I would not be able to sleep. I just stayed in my wheelchair.

Lie down, they said. If you cannot sleep, at least get some rest. The trip is long — four hours from Prokopyevsk to Mariinsk, and God knows how long you have to drive to this boarding school... All tried to convince me that I needed rest. But how could I rest?

My last night at the asylum... I was sitting silent in the dark. The girls were quiet; they were sleeping or silent out of decency, giving me the opportunity to be alone.

I could not believe that in three or four hours I would leave this sorrowful establishment — the moment had come for which I had been waiting all these years! And if I have the opportunity — or rather, achieved it myself, gnawed it out with my teeth — why should I agree to wait until I had a better transfer to a more dignified place? I was right to reject the kind offer of Andrei Petrovich. What if this was the only chance? And then there would be no tickets, no places; they would change laws and rules, and they would forget about me, and my case would be thrown to the dogs. Anything could happen.

This was my last night in the asylum. Sitting in the wheelchair, I was silently saying goodbye to every resident, every employee and every person I had known. And again and again, I asked forgiveness from the girls with whom I had lived such a long time; I asked them to pardon me for everything that I did wrong. I understood what they felt: I was leaving, but they were staying. If I had the opportunity, I would have taken all of them with me, away from the asylum...

Unwittingly, I compared this last night — the good night — to my first night at the asylum, which was a nightmare... how lucky I am to get out of here! I experienced a long-awaited happiness, my martyred reward.

And then a car rattled outside the window. Well, that's all, I sighed.

And I already felt myself outside the walls of the asylum.

The nanny came to the room. "So, Toma, you already woke up? Are you ready?"

"I'm wide awake! I'm ready!" I almost sang.

They pushed my wheelchair outside to the street. A minibus was parked near the porch. I was placed conveniently on the seat inside the cabin, and we moved off. We passed the gate; the minibus picked up speed and rushed toward dawn, toward my optimistic future…

Part 3
The Insk Boarding School

The Insk Boarding School

The minibus that carried me from the Prokopyevsk psycho-neurological boarding school to the Blagoveshchenka boarding school raced along the highway, faster and faster. We left the dark night and entered the break of a beautiful dawn. Through my semi-closed eyelids, I had been observing that there were more and more cars on the freeway, and in accordance with this, our speed slowed down. It was like I was watching TV footage, but then I smiled at myself: no, it was the real world behind the cockpit window, and it was me who was sitting inside the cabin! It was me who was on my way to a new life. I did not want to think either about the past or the future; I just wanted to enjoy the road. I have had little experience riding in a car: just a few times in my life.

It was a long trip. Even driving at high speed, it took four hours to reach Mariinsk, and then two and a half hours from Mariinsk to the Blagoveshchenka Boarding School. When we were passing the village Blagoveshchenka, I noticed it was clean and nice, a place of trees and flowers. After crossing back roads, we finally arrived at the boarding school. The nurse who accompanied us left the minibus and went to process the documents. I was taken to the isolation room, which differed remarkably from that of the Prokopyevsk PNBS where I was locked for the night fifteen years before.

The isolation room of the Blagoveshchenka Boarding School looked like a regular room; it was very clean. There was a babushka on duty who took her position very seriously. She was kind and friendly; she helped me undress and made me feel comfortable on the bed. Then the less gracious staff came in all at once, and they stared at me with wonder. I was examined by their gazes and was confused. I thought they were displeased with my unusual state, and I thought it was probably the first time they had seen an example of cerebral palsy. But it turned out to be something different: the Prokopyevsk nurse had told them that I had come here to write books, and I needed an assistant who would write under my dictation. She did it for a good reason, or more likely, she was just bragging about bringing a writer who writes fairy tales! And it was quite shocking to the staff — they never had such inhabitants, especially in the 'weak quarter', where I was going to be transported. Again, I was surprised with the terminology — they used the expression 'weak quarter' in the same way as it was used in my orphanage and the PNBS, but they used this expression differently in each institution. In the Blagoveshchenka boarding house the 'weak quarter' was for physically weak people, completely infirm, who could not hold a spoon. It was clear that I fitted in the 'weak quarter'.

I was brought on Wednesday, and on Friday I was moved to the 'weak quarter', to a room with two old grannies. And soon I realized that there was a whole quarter of income earners that the staff could barely keep up with. Who could help me with my writing? Thank God if they help me with feeding and bathing… If I stayed here, it would be not only the end of my starting writing career, but it will be my end.

"Tamara, don't worry! Our director will return from his vacation and he will sort everything out." The staff tried to comfort me.

The days crawled at the speed of a turtle. One day, a tall representative entered the room — it was the director. My granny roommates came to life when they saw him. He was attentive to every single granny, asking her about her health and private business. Then he approached me. "They told me you are new here."

"Yes," I gasped and shamefully burst into tears.

"Don't cry; tell me what happened. Maybe I can help."

I had a lump in my throat. I could not say a single word. I pointed with my eyes to the letter from the publisher announcing my book publication. The director read the letter and frowned. "Have they lost their mind in the Social Welfare Office? They don't know where they have to send you? Don't cry; I'll go to Kemerovo on Wednesday. I'll try to help you."

I did not have much faith that they would solve my case so easily; it would not be possible to leave this boarding house immediately. But I was mistaken!

Two days later, the director came into our room; a glint of triumph lit his gaze when he said, "There you go; I have two tickets. One is to the

Kemerovo Boarding School; the other is to the Insk Boarding School. You choose! Where do you want to go?"

I felt shy and embarrassed, but I managed to choose Insk. The director was amazed at the choice. Why not Kemerovo? He was surprised that I did not want to be closer to the regional publishing house where the book was supposed to be published. I explained that in Insk I have many acquaintances who were transferred there from the orphanage; I heard that living conditions were good there, including that the staff was sufficient and not limited, so it would be easier for me to adapt.

"Well, get ready; you will go there tomorrow. Or maybe you want to stay with us?" he said with a smile.

"I would have stayed here if I had the chance to work," I answered. "Thank you so much for everything, absolutely everything! And thank you for doing it so fast!"

In the morning, the nannies dressed me up, and here I was again on the road — now the car rushed to the Insk Boarding House. The village of Insk is in the district of Belovo. And Insk Boarding School is the place I have been striving for so passionately, starting my last year in the orphanage and during the fifteen years of my life at the Prokopyevsk PNBS. I anticipated the meeting with my childhood friends and acquaintances, who unlike me, were not aggravated by the heavy form of cerebral palsy, along with the incorrect diagnosis of oligophrenia, and were sent there directly from the orphanage.

I was in the Blagoveshchenka Boarding School for a little over a week, and I took off lightly like a butterfly. Forgive me for such comparison; I was able to get out of there too easily. I truly fluttered, was carried out, flew out.

The New Home and Old Friends

I arrived at two p.m. at the Insk Boarding School and was taken to the isolation room as scheduled. Oh, such an isolator! It was a luxurious room, with two bathrooms, two beds and a couch. They put me on the couch. I fidgeted, trying to cope with the overwhelming excitement — I wanted so much to see my orphanage girls! A woman entered the room; she was apparently a staff member. I asked her, "Would you please tell me if Natalia Volkova and Valentina Pozdniakova live here?"

"How do you know them?" The woman was surprised.

"We lived in the same orphanage," I explained.

The woman, without saying anything, left. And I sank into my childhood memories. Natalia dragged me down the stairs in the orphanage... Valiukha, the determined battle girl, taught me a good lesson — how not to behave in some situations...

And what a miracle! Natasha and Valiukha flew up to me! They stared at me for a second, and screamed with joy. "Tomochka!" And they started hugging me.

The chief sister entered the isolation room, introduced herself as Lidia Rodionovna and asked the girls, "Do you know Tamara Cheremnova?"

"She was with us at the orphanage!" my family girls screamed in one high-pitched voice.

But now they were not girls, but adult women in their thirties. We left the orphanage fifteen years ago...

"Well, then take your Tamara and take her to her room," ordered Lidia Rodionovna, hardly suppressing her laughter caused by the emotional meeting of the orphanage pupils.

At first, I was taken to the assigned room on the second floor. It was occupied by elderly women. But the excited Natasha and Valiukha dragged me to their floor where the youth lived; they found a free bed and made a quick deal with the administration. I was placed with three nice girls, who lived and worked as nannies on different floors. They had boyfriends, and after work, they would go on dates. The Insk Boarding School provided separate rooms to the established families.

In one week after my admission, I was given a wheelchair — it was old and shabby; it was used before by a handicapped man to ride to the shower. They said it was a temporary vehicle; later they would provide me with a new one. And they did, and it was an excellent comfortable wheelchair.

***

The Insk Boarding School was probably the most comfortable in the whole Kemerovo region. Every room had a sink with hot and cold water — what a comfort for a handicapped person! Nobody yelled at you, demanding that you must wash your face faster. And hygienic conditions were much better — strangers would not come to your room to wash up or to do the dishes; they had their own sinks.

The elevator in our building functioned until eleven p.m. in the summer; there were no restrictions with promenades outside. And most amazing was a great garden outside — it was a real karaagach garden! The word 'karaagach' is taken from the Turkic languages: 'kara' is black; 'agach' is tree, so 'karaagach' can be translated as 'black tree'. It is also called 'elm tree'. There were wooden benches placed beneath the trees. I could drive to the garden in a wheelchair, using my weak arms, to hide from the hot sun in the shade of lavish branches. I could feel the pulse of life, sitting inside the inner space of the spherical crown of the karaagach tree. The access to this magic karaagach garden was comfortable too.

Near the Insk Boarding School there was a water reservoir — the artificial sea by the Belovo hydroelectric power plant. And the village of Insk was green and clean. One had free access to the Insk BS and did not need a special permit as it was in the Prokopyevsk PNBS with its prison regime, where IDs and permits were required.

***

Perhaps it is necessary to mention the essential change during the dashing nineties and after the collapse of the Soviet Union and how it affected the life of the Insk Boarding School. Yeltsin's program of radical, market-oriented reform came to be known as a 'shock therapy'. The readers may think that due to our isolation, we were able to escape the shock therapy of the state. Of course, the adversity of this difficult period for the whole of Russia had been felt by us too — it was manifested in many things, including the reduced content of food and the lack of essential items for living. However, the good news was that in 1991, after the election of Yeltsin as President of the Russian Soviet Federative Socialist Republic (RSFSR), residents of psycho-neurological boarding schools and boarding schools for the disabled started receiving per month a quarter of their disability benefit. Before this, we had not had any pension, even a penny; our pensions were sent to the boarding school administration. So for the first time in my life, when I was about thirty-six years old, I had my own money. The amount was small, but I was so happy! Then inflation hit; money depreciated. Pensions were not indexed, but we could buy very little for the miserable amount of money we had in our possession; nevertheless, the thought that the state paid me something was consoling.

***

Unfortunately, in 2010, the wonderful, comfortable Insk Boarding School was disbanded, and its residents, despite the fact that many of them had lived in this house for more than twenty years, were moved against their will to various locations. And they reformed this wonderful boarding school into a psycho-neurological boarding school. Why did they do this? At those times it was very expensive to build new homes with all amenities for the mentally disabled. The cost of land, building materials and labor had increased, and the existing psycho-neurological boarding schools were overcrowded. The administration of the Kemerovo region decided to give the Insk Boarding School, equipped with all the necessary facilities, to the PNBS, and most of the former residents of the Insk Boarding School were moved to the building which was used as a holiday and vacation house, and the rest were distributed to other boarding schools with available places.

It might be a reasonable solution, but the residents were not enthusiastic about the prospect of leaving their home. They sent letters to authorities in which they expressed their unhappiness about leaving their home. But the decision was made and it was not welcomed for discussion. The residents were transferred to places assigned for them: to the Holiday House and to the boarding schools of Kemerovo and Novokuznetsk. People suffered tremendously in their new homes; they could not get accustomed to them and missed their native home, recalling happy times. As a matter of fact, I was nostalgic as well about the Insk Boarding School where I had lived between May 1989 and October 1997.

Looking for a Scribe

My days at the Insk Boarding School went smoothly. The living conditions were decent; the food was good. The only sad thing was the lack of communication. No one was interested in me; they all forgot about me. Natasha and Valiukha were busy with their private matters and work. Valiukha worked in our dining room as a cleaning woman, and Natasha worked as a plaster painter. From time to time, Valiukha would visit me and feed me; it was more complicated for Natasha to take time off. I did not make friends, and I was counting so much on communication! The most important reason I had chosen the Insk BS was communication! I was naïve thinking that someone would come to me and wonder if it was true that my book was about to be published. I dreamed people would ask me what my book was about. 'What are you writing now?' I anticipated a great interest because they had been talking about me as a writer…

But no one was interested in me or in my literary achievements. And I already regretted my choice of the Insk BS. Why did I not choose the Kemerovo BS? It was closer to the regional publishing house.

The days passed indifferently one by one, and I lived in a vacuum. There was no one to write under my dictation. Even in the Prokopyevsk PNBS I had more opportunities with the scribes. I had written so many fairy tales; they were in my head and I had no one to write them. I was so disappointed!

The first people who volunteered to help in the search for a scribe were completely illiterate: Valiukha and Mikhail, who was also diagnosed with cerebral palsy and moved on crutches. They were illiterate, but it was not their fault; no one taught them how to read, considering it redundant. Mikhail suggested that we talk to Nadezhda Vasilevna Ilkaeva, the director. Despite her strong character, Valiukha opposed this idea categorically, believing that the director would find our idea to find a scribe extravagant and she would even be scolded. In the evening, when Shura, the nanny, who agreed to take care of me, came from her main job to feed me, I asked her to sit next to me and I dictated my letter to the director. Shura kindly agreed to be my scribe, though she was not fluent in letters. We worked together on each letter to compose my petition.

A week later, the director had a tour through the administered properties, about which I learned from the noise that I heard in the hallway. The door to our room opened; a slender, attractive, middle-aged woman entered. She asked, "Who is Cheremnova Tamara?"

"I-I-I-it's m-m-m-m-ee," I stuttered.

I saw in her eyes wonder mixed with doubt. It was easy to read her thoughts: this is the writer? But why didn't anyone from the social welfare office warn me about this writer? And maybe this writer is not quite right in the head after all?

I could not restrain myself after reading her thoughts. I experienced such a tension that my body jerked in such a violent fashion that it embarrassed the director, who immediately turned away with disgust, pretending she was observing the room, seeing if it was in order.

"I will send your note to the Social and Cultural Commission; they will think of something," she said and left

The Social and Cultural Commission, abbreviated to SCC, was recruited from the residents. They dealt with violators of order, studied complaints, listened to all kinds of gossip, resolved scandals and so on. They also found solutions to situations like mine.

Three days later, a perky beauty, a representative of the Social and Cultural Commission, drove to our room in a wheelchair. She saw Maxim Gorky's book 'On Literature' on my night table and raised her brows in surprise. "And you understand what is written here?"

"If I didn't understand, I wouldn't read it," I replied.

"Tomorrow our Social and Cultural Commission has a meeting; I will try to find you an assistant," she said and drove away.

Two weeks later, I met her in the hallway. Seeing me, she approached me with a radiant smile. "Well, how are you? Getting used to our home?"

Frankly, I was embarrassed, and she apparently was embarrassed too. Meanwhile, she continued. "I raised your question in the meeting, but no one agreed to write under your dictation. You can see, everyone here lives on their own…"

***

And yet I found an assistant scribe in the person of the illiterate Shura. Then I had to find my own little corner where I could work in peace. I knew if I did not organize myself, no one would do it for me. I talked to Shura, and she agreed to live with me in the room for two, helping me in everyday needs and in writing. We wrote a memo to the director, explaining the situation, and she agreed to move Shura and me to the room for two, for which I was immensely grateful.

Shura's expertise in writing left a lot to be desired — she barely knew literacy, just very basics, and she wrote very slowly. She confused the Russian letters 'ш' (sh) and 'щ '(shch), also 'т' (t) and 'д' (d), constantly asking which letter to put, and if the letter should be with a tail or without. I tried to teach Shura how to write faster. After all, it was not easy when you dictate each word by syllables and repeat each letter several times. While I dictated the first sentence, I would completely forget the second. Physically, such a protracted dictation was hard for me. Nevertheless, my efforts were not in vain — over time, Shura acquired some skills. She began to write faster and understand me better, and she made fewer mistakes. And it was with Shura that I recorded several fairy tales, including the first versions of 'Fairy Tale for a Little Coward' and 'Where the Fairy Tale Lives', as well as sketches of the sequel about Mishuta. I subsequently modified these tales, slightly altered them, and they were published. And then I learned from letters that my young readers liked them.

The Wizard Mishuta

Finally, at the end of May 1990, my little book 'From the Life of the Wizard Mishuta' was published by the Kemerovo regional publishing house: eighty thousand printed copies, priced ten kopecks apiece. It was available to any family, even with a small income. I was highly surprised with this huge circulation. Later I was told that all book shops of the village of Insk and the city of Belovo sold out my books with lightning speed. I was happy to hear it!

As expected, they sent me ten copyright copies. Shura helped unpack the parcel and pulled out colored books with merry covers. What a wonderful design! The postman who brought the parcel did not leave immediately — he was extremely curious about the interesting parcel he brought. When he saw ten similar copies and read aloud the title, 'From the Life of the Wizard Mishuta', he said in disappointment, "Why did they send so many identical books? All ten about the Wizard Mishuta?"

"This is my book! I wrote this book!" I announced, trembling with excitement, but the postman did not understand it; he shrugged his shoulders and left.

And I, left alone in the room, was staring at these colored books and expressing all my emotions at once: I was crying, howling and laughing. This was my first book! And the Wizard Mishuta was a real magician, because the release of my book was his magic! And over time, the second book, and then the third one, and then others would come out... They would definitely come out — I had already composed so many fairy tales and stories for children.

I gave the first two copies of the book to the director and the deputy director and waited for congratulations and praise. Maybe the boarding school would somehow celebrate this event? No, I waited for the celebration in vain. The director did not visit me; she only conveyed congratulations through a third party. The deputy director did not express a word. Today I understand better why the administration of the Insk

Boarding School was not enthusiastic — at that time everything had to be coordinated with the Social Welfare Office (SWO), even public events such as celebrations of publications. And the SWO could hardly consider the publication of a book written by a disabled person living in a boarding school as a significant event, although logically I could not understand why my accomplishment was not significant...

Soon my joy faded away; my euphoria ended. And again, I faced the problem — how could I continue my literary work? Shura was overjoyed at the release of my book, but her writing speed and literacy were stuck at a very low level, and such scenes of writing under dictation exhausted us both. It was clear that sooner or later Shura would get tired of her work as a scribe, and I would fizzle out.

Deer Fear

Suddenly, I found myself very unhappy in the Insk Boarding School, the place where I had been striving for so many years. It was not just my disappointment that that there was no one who would be willing to write under my dictation and that my hands were not capable of writing, it was something else. A new perception of myself and people around me entered my psyche. I started believing that all disabled people from my environment were better than I, physically and mentally.

The words of the Prokopyevsk psychiatrist Tamara Fedorovna were stamped in my memory; I just could not forget them. She said that my hyperkinesia, which is manifested in uncontrolled movements, twitched so sharply and chaotically that sometimes it frightened people around me, and was a sign of my mental illness. When I went outside, I was afraid to move, for fear of attracting attention by involuntary twitching. The psychiatrist's words that my hyperkinesia was the sign of my mental illness had been engraved in my memory.

And what was strange was that people who had acquired hyperkinesia after being traumatized physically in an accident or another unfortunate episode were not considered to be mentally sick. They would just receive the first diagnosis of physical disability without indication of mental disability. And we, people with cerebral palsy, are assigned to oligophrenia, or congenital dementia. Our status of mental pathology is based on hyperkinesia. And this had been practiced to this day. I would like to hear the answers of experts to this question. However, there is no answer to this day.

The diagnosis of oligophrenia is still molded to the majority of patients suffering with cerebral palsy, although most of them, three quarters according to medical statistics, have intact intelligence. And it is uncertain if there is a difference between Cheremnova, who bowed under the weight of the world above her laptop, writing fairy tales for children and journalism for adults, who despite all the intrigues, almost independently mastered the laptop, and those who are really mentally retarded and uneducable. With this inferiority complex, I drove myself into a corner. Moreover, sometimes I would be scared to wake up — it seemed to me that if I woke up, I would again find myself *there*, in a madhouse, and they would send me back, punishing me for my disqualification. I was the most miserable in the world! It could not be worse!

Absurd fears and constant tightness wore me down and I was very tired of my condition. It seemed I had accepted this home and got accustomed to it. I had decent living conditions, and no one harassed me, but if anyone looked at me askance, I would become scared and want to hide. I would immediately become paralyzed if someone just cast a long look, which was not necessarily unkind or malicious. The science of fear calls this state 'deer fear' and explains why we find ourselves paralyzed like a deer in headlights during threatening situations.

Rummaging through my medical papers, I found a notice from the Kemerovo Regional Clinical Psychiatric Hospital (KRCPH), which informed me about an appointment of recommission. I received this little piece of paper when I still lived in the Prokopyevsk PNBS. I took the risk of writing a letter to the deputy chief physician of the KRCPH — his name was Georgii Leonidovich Ustiantsev — requesting to receive me and to help me to remove this overwhelming feeling of constriction and irrational angst. At that time we did not have our own psychologists at boarding schools. This was already the year 1992.

"What a character!" one of the psychologists of this psychiatric hospital exclaimed — later his words were conveyed to me. "It is not enough for her to experience the Prokopyevsk PNBS and the madhouse; she demands to be treated in our hospital. She decided to try all psychiatrists in the world!"

But I needed a cure and my greatest desire was to remove the diagnosis 'oligophrenia in the state of debility', which still loomed on the first page of my medical history, although the results of the examination refuted this diagnosis and demonstrated my mental health.

The answer came very soon. Ustiantsev gave orders, and I was admitted to the open border department of the KRCPH. They found out what exactly worried me, and prescribed vitamin injections as well as elenium and relanium, which are used as sedatives, reduce stress and anxiety, relax skeletal muscles of the spine and relieve spasticity for a long time. At this point the treatment ended, but the feeling of tightness and anxiety did not disappear. I wanted to remove these problems with the help of hypnosis, as the psychiatrist of the Prokopyevsk PNBS, Ludmila Alekseeva Yenina had recommended in the past. But the psychotherapist of the KRCPH, Leonid Stanislavovich Koshkin stated that I did not need hypnosis; I had enough of my own willpower. They gave me a leaflet with the descriptions of the auto-training based on the methods of the psychotherapist Vladimir Levy, and that was it.

I would like to tell you in a separate line about the neuropathologist, but I will not release her name. When she saw me in the hospital, she cast at me a puzzled look and then she made a face which was supposed to represent horror. One day she came to my room and started showering me with questions without waiting for my answers. "Why did you come here? Have you been married? So, you've never been married! Why did you come here? There are only psychos and wimps here!"

I tried to answer something to such a strange set of questions, but she did not let me say a word, going on about psychos and wimps. If all patients for her were psychos and wimps, to which category she would assign me? I became so upset and reacted naturally for my illness — I jerked so violently that I almost fell from my bed. What should the doctor do in this situation? I believe, first of all, they have to comfort their patient. However, the neuropathologist jumped away from me; she made the nauseated face and left the room still wearing her extraordinary facial expression.

Of course, I burst into tears, and just like that, all in tears, I had another visitor, this time the leading doctor, Lidiia Yakovlevna Nokhrina. She asked me about the reason for my tears; I told her about the visit of neuropathologist, discreetly skipping the offensive words 'psychos' and 'wimps'.

"She treated you in such a harsh way because she wanted you to get rid of your tightness," Lidiia Yakovlevna reassured me, believing I could not distinguish cruelty from a shock therapy.

***

Thank God, the next episode lifted my depressed mood. The daughter of one of the hospital nurses, a schoolgirl, came to the hospital with my little book 'From the Life of the Wizard Mishuta'. She showed it to her mother. "Look what an unusual children's book I just bought from the bookstore. It costs only ten kopecks! What a great gift for my friend!"

Her mother replied, "The writer of this book is in our hospital. We cure her nerves. She is so sensitive and easily excited. All writers are like that."

This story was told by my nurse with great admiration.

***

Before I was discharged, Lidiia Yakovlevna showed me my medical history. There was no mentioning of the ominous diagnosis 'oligophrenia at the stage of debility' in the recent records — they described sufficient intelligence and adequate behavior, but the stigma was still present — it remained on the first page and was not removed. But people always see the first page! And after they have read the diagnosis, they do not want to proceed further!

"Why is the old diagnosis of oligophrenia not eliminated?" I asked with disappointment.

"We do not remove old diagnoses, we write current diagnoses. As you see, we didn't mention oligophrenia. What are your complaints?"

"I will do all possible to refute this wrong diagnosis," I promised.

"It's your own business," the doctor said; she did not like my resolute mood. She pressed her lips and left.

***

I left the hospital feeling upset and defeated. Probably my condition would be more typical for patients arriving at the hospital than for those departing. I regretted that I asked to be admitted to this hospital. The Kemerovo regional psychiatric hospital differed significantly from the Prokopyevsk psychiatric city hospital where I was cured in 1988.

However, I had an extraordinary record in my medical history, which always confused my doctors: 'T.A. Cheremnova was hospitalized at the Kemerovo Regional Clinical Psychiatric Hospital (KRCPH) at her own request.' How could it be? She wanted to go to *the madhouse*? She wanted to be with 'psychos'? Yes, indeed, it was her request, but she needed the doctors in order to get rid of 'deer fear', which made her life unbearable. She also had another goal: to get rid of the stigma — this diagnosis of oligophrenia in the state of debility. I also hoped — of course naïvely — that in the regional center of Kemerovo I would find support and I would meet intelligent people with whom I would share my ideas. But alas and ah!

I invited people to visit me in the psychiatric hospital, but no one came. I can understand; just the word 'psychiatric' can frighten anyone. But I do not regret that it turned out that way. But what result had I achieved in this Kemerovo psychiatric hospital? I had the opportunity to be examined by the doctors. And Lidiia Yakovlevna's words which she said to me before my departure sank into my soul: "You yourself must find the way out of this situation. What you have to do is write, write, write. Write at least with someone's help under your dictation, even with the help of the illiterate person. But do not overdo it, otherwise you may lose your interest not just in dictation, but in writing too."

Oh yes, dear Lidiia Yakovlevna, if you knew how much I struggled to receive the right to write. And I found this right living inside the society which is completely deaf to the requests of disabled people! I found this right to write having in my possession paralyzed hands which cannot hold a pen!

***

I received the official refutation of the wrong diagnosis 'oligophrenia at the state of debility' only after many years; at that time, I lived in Novokuznetsk.

Olga Racheva

Exhausted after many defeats, I was quite shaken. And Shura was already frankly bored to write under my dictation and began to run away in the evenings. She was more interested in being with others, and especially with the deputy director Nina Grigorevna, who favored her. Sometimes Shura would go to the object of her adoration without even acknowledging me or turning on the light in the room. And I would lie in bed, waiting for her in the dark. One day she showed up at twelve o'clock midnight. I asked her, "Shura, where have you been?"

"At Nina Grigorevna's. I helped her to pickle cucumbers."

"Shura, why didn't you come home and turn the light on before you went to Nina Grigorevna's?"

"Nina Grigorevna said that in the evening, the girls on duty should take care of you," Shura answered carelessly.

"You should have asked the nanny to come to me before you left. You left, and I lay in the dark until midnight, and I didn't watch TV, and I wanted to go to the toilet; I was not very happy."

But for Shura, these conversations were just empty. I, trying not to offend her, delicately asked, "Shura, would it be fine with you if I ask another girl to assist me? You are young; you are really bored with me; you always run away from me."

"I only go to Nina Grigorevna's," Shura said. "And I am not bored with you at all and I like to write under your dictation."

But I could not bear Shura's unpredictable absences; it was a shame to waste time lying alone in a dark room. On the one hand, I did not want to offend Shura with my decision, but on the other hand, if I was determined to do something, I would do it anyway. Lying awake at night, I analyzed the situation and looked for a way out. How could I arrange my unsettled life? And on one such bitter night, I recalled my secret dream.

Living in Prokopyevsk PNBS, I, against all odds, imagined that I lived in a separate room with one of the girls from our Bachata orphanage. And most often I imagined Olga Racheva near me. Olga was a deaf-mute girl who was brought to the orphanage by her neighbor-babushka. She was my age; we even had our birthdays in the same month. I have my birthday on the sixth, and she has hers on the fifth. For a while Olga took care of me. She was not very agreeable — if she did not want to come to me, even being forced, she would never come. However, in my dreams, most often I saw Olga as my assistant and not other girls, who treated me better and resignedly helped in everyday affairs. I communicated with Olga in the orphanage infrequently, although I learned sign language. So why Olga? I could not find an explanation for that.

***

In 1992, my relationship with Shura became worse. I saw that she was already weighed down by me. She was right: well, what joy for a young girl to spend hours sitting near an older associate? One day I asked the deputy director Nina Grigorevna to call Nadezhda Konstantinovna Trushina.

Trushina worked in the regional social security administration; she checked the boarding schools' living conditions. I was introduced to her by our director and eventually Trushina and I became friends. Every time she came to the Insk Boarding School, she visited me, and we talked about everything. And I decided to ask her to be my mediator.

"Tamara, what happened to you?" the deputy director asked me anxiously.

"Nina Grigorevna, nothing special — my usual problems, how to live this life." I led our conversation in a joking manner. "I need to consult Trushina. Please ask her to visit me as soon as she has the opportunity."

Two weeks later Trushina arrived and immediately came to me. I explained to her in general terms my intractable problem. Nadezhda Konstantinovna immediately understood everything, without requiring details and clarifications. I asked her to find Olga Racheva in the village of Bachata and invite her to live in the same room with me.

It was easy to find Olga; I knew that our specialized orphanage was transformed into PNBS, and Olga had stayed there. And it was easy to transfer from PNBS to the boarding school of the general type — Olga was physically healthy, except she was deaf and mute. She had the diagnosis of 'oligophrenia in the stage of imbecility', but such a diagnosis when it is embraced with a good physical condition was not an obstacle to transfer. All the nurses who worked in the Insk Boarding School had similar diagnoses — these girls, more or less healthy physically, were brought from orphanages with the purpose of taking care of the physically weak. Other homes for disabled people had many nannies in similar condition, and everyone was satisfied with their work. And I already described how generously they gave the diagnosis of oligophrenia, without speculating too much about real intellectual capacities of persons, giving them easy diagnostic awards.

The paradox was that the diagnosis of 'oligophrenia' was not an obstacle for the nannies to work at boarding schools of the general type. And for me, diagnosed with cerebral palsy, the boarding school of the general type had been like a forbidden fruit for a long time. I was repeatedly refused transfer there only because I was diagnosed with oligophrenia. That is, diagnoses were assigned and distributed only for the convenience of the staff, and they had nothing to do with the cure and treatment!

Nadezhda Konstantinovna spoke with our director, who was pleased with the state of affairs — finally they found the solution of constant care for Cheremnova! So she agreed with the proposal to transfer Olga from her place to the Insk Boarding School with the assigned duty of my caretaker. A week later, the director drove to the Bachata PNBS in her car; she talked with the administration and she talked with Olga as well. She led a conversation with the deaf and mute Olga through translators — Olga's roommates, who knew sign language. When Olga understood the situation, she danced with joy. She was not very happy living in the Bachata PNBS.

My 'project' received collective approval. Olga quickly packed her things, the legal papers for her transfer took just few minutes, and Nina

Grigorevna brought her to the Insk Boarding School in her car. Olga was immediately brought to my room. And whom did I see in front of me? A 'scared bunny'!

That was in August 1992.

Help from the All-Russian Society of the Disabled

I received solid royalties for my book, 'The Wizard Mishuta', and I immediately purchased a mechanical typewriter. For two years I could not adapt to it, only look at it sadly, scolding myself for the senseless purchase. Sometimes I even wanted to throw it off the nightstand! How could I master the typewriter, if my hands twitched and my fingers refused to press the keys? And I had no one to dictate my texts to — Olga could not record; she was deaf. She had little literacy; she knew all the letters, but she could not write anything. I had a literary pause or intermission because of the absence of a scribe — I had nothing on paper, but my head was full of stories.

At that time, in 1993, Valentina Ivanovna Shakhova, the chairman of the Belovo City Society of the Disabled, visited me. Then, in the 1990s, city and village societies of the disabled were created; they were all related to the All-Russian Society of the Disabled, abbreviated as ARSD. In one of her visits, Valentina Ivanovna brought me the news that made me very happy. They had ordered an electric typewriter for me ! It was much better than the mechanical one! I understood that as soon as the machine arrived, they would give it to me. I was full of hope, and in my anticipation of the machine, I started regarding every visit of Valentina Ivanovna as a special day.

This was my mood... Well! They promised me an electric typewriter! I am sure I am going to get it right! And 1993 will be the happiest year of my life — I will start writing on my own, without help!

One day Shakhova came to visit me and said, "We got an electric typewriter. But before we give it to you, we want to be sure you will be able to use it correctly.

She handed me a postcard and commanded, "Try to hit with your finger the spot with the area code."

I poked my finger, but it hit inaccurately — the joy that stirred me from head to toe intensified my hyperkinesia.

"You see, you can't do it!" Shakhova delivered a verdict and majestically left the ward, leaving me aghast.

Oh, the society! How could you do this to me? First you raised me to heaven, then you threw me into the abyss. Well, they promised me an electric typewriter! I'm sure I'm going to get it right! And 1993 will be the happiest year of my life — I will start writing myself, without help!

However, this is not the only bitter memory associated with the assistance of the All-Russian Society of the Disabled. In 1990, when my first book came out, the workers of the bookstore learned that the author of the children's book lived in their village in the house of the disabled. They wrote an appeal to the residents of the village of Insk that I needed help. The appeal was displayed in the bookstore, but the village remained deaf to this request. Then the chairman of the Insk All-Russian Society of the Disabled (I do not remember her name) promised to help me. I had been waiting for her more than six months. From time to time, she would call the Insk Boarding School, apologizing and invariably referring to her dacha and garden. Each time when the village chairman made her telephone calls, she reported that she worked so hard at her dacha, and each time she swore, "After I harvest my garden, I will visit Tamara. My word upon it!"

The staff told me about her calls and promises; I kept waiting. By the new year, I had asked the staff to call her to remind her that she promised to visit me. They called her, but she said she did not have time. I never asked her again about anything.

Mastering the Typewriter

Despite all this, I have mastered the mechanical typewriter — I invented a way to print even when my hand was twitching. In order to reach the keys with exactness, I invented a device resembling a mushroom. It was a stick, to the upper end of which was attached a flat circle with the diameter of the palm, wrapped in tape, and on the lower end there was a stretched plastic cork which was nailed to it. Creating the 'mushroom' was fun.

When Olga was transferred to me, she began to collect all sorts of corks from bottles, scraps of wrapping paper and foam, and all these materials she used for making toys. Her toys were so amazing that they immediately took first place in a competition of the applied arts. What a talented girl! And then one day, in 1993, coming from the street, Olga showed me a whole handful of colorful plastic corks. I angrily turned down her find. Olga had a bad habit — whatever she found, she would put it in my face. When she bought anything new, she would put it in my face. It was not very nice. I even yelled at her a few times, asking her to get the show object out of my face. And when she dropped this on the keys of my typewriter — the cork sat securely on the key — it was a little larger than the key. I had already opened my mouth to comment: well, are we going to store corks on the keyboard, but the comment froze in my throat. At that very moment I had a mental picture of my device — it looked like a mushroom — I saw its design with my inner eyes.

Then everything went smoothly — I asked Olga to cut out from the thick cardboard a circle the size of a palm. We gave this circle to the carpenters to cut the same design out of plywood. And under my guidance, Olga and our neighbor Masha attached the cork to the wooden stick and the plywood circle. The construction looked like a mushroom.

I started typing, putting the 'mushroom' on the right key and hitting the circle with my palm. The cork pressed the key, and no matter how severely the hyperkinesia affected my hand, the letter was printed right.

So pressing the 'mushroom' over the keys, I managed to type quite long texts.

The typing process was slow; it was very tense and physically exhausting, but I was no longer dependent on assistants. Now all I had to do was to sit down in front of the typewriter, stick paper in it and then type.

***

I received the electric typewriter, which I was promised by the All-Russian Society of the Disabled, but much later. I was already in Novokuznetsk; it was in 2000. It was personally brought to me by Zinaida Gavrilovna Chernovol, the editor of the newspaper 'Invalid' and a member of the Russian Union of Journalists (RUJ). The typewriter belonged to the 'Kuznetsk Worker Newspaper'. When it was discarded, Chernovol took it for me. The machine stalled, it tore the paper, but it was much easier for me to type on than the mechanical one. Using the electric typewriter, I pressed the keys with my fingers, not with the 'mushroom'.

Lena Medvedeva

Moving to the Insk Boarding School in 1989, I immediately recalled Lena Medvedeva, who was so helpful during the first stage of my writing at the Prokopyevsk PNBS. This was the girl who showed my work — my first 'pen test' — to her teacher of Russian language and literature. I knew Lena lived near Insk. I wrote her a letter and invited her to visit me. After receiving the letter, she came. Now she was a married woman, the mother of two sons. She worked in the dining room at the coal mine. Her epilepsy had gone away — I was so happy for her — she had recovered after she gave birth to her first child. They were afraid that the second birth would cause a relapse, but fortunately, everything had gone well.

Lena Medvedeva eventually became my friend. Surprisingly, we were not close when we lived in Prokopyevsk in 1986. Lena had not stayed there long, only a few months, and in such a time a strong friendship cannot develop, especially when she spent all day at work — at the animal farm of our director. And the ten-year age difference has also to be considered — at the time of our acquaintance, I was thirty-one years old, and Lena was twenty-one. But over time, the gap in our age was not noticeable.

We corresponded; Lena visited me. We could not call each other — Lena did not have a home phone, and I could only call from the medical post, which was not very convenient. After all, there were no automatic phones around. Those who needed to call went to the nearest post office; the transport to our boarding school was free. It was not far, but for me to go there was problematic — I could not use steps. At that time, personal mobile phones were owned mainly by businessmen. So the main way of communication for me and Lena remained the old-fashioned correspondence by regular mail.

How happy Lena was when my book about the Wizard Mishuta came out! I gave her a copy and signed it. I was helped during the process of signing — they were holding my right hand. Lena's two sons read my book — it suited their age.

Lena kindly agreed to help me in my literary affairs. After I had adjusted to the typewriter, I again relied on Lena, as once it was in 1986. Lena distributed my typed works outside the boarding school. After all, it was very important for me to gather as many opinions, impressions, reviews, and responses as possible to my works. It is important to know about the reception of your works: reading is a fusion of text and reader. I was interested in whether the plot of my fairy tales captured children and what questions children would ask adults after reading them. It was especially important to me since I wrote not so much for adults but for children. There were no children in the boarding schools where I lived, except a few children of the employees.

***

Everyone in the boarding school already knew that I was writing, and quite successfully. And those people, to whom I gave my book about the Wizard Mishuta, passed it to others. The book went from hand to hand; people approached me, praised me and expressed admiration. And gradually, people started treating me with courtesy and warmth.

Searching without success for a personal scribe, I had invented my 'mushroom' device and tamed the recalcitrant typewriter; after that I was not so dependent on other people. My independence freed me from unnecessary agitation and calmed me down.

I did not think I was the worst person in the world any more. Moreover, it turned out that no one considered me so. These were my personal fears and prejudices. It came to be that our locals always treated me with respect. And when you feel love, admiration and respect, you love yourself and you love the world, instead of despising both.

***

Once in 1994 I read the regional newspaper Kuzbass and I came across the column 'Your Own Voice', with publications of young local writers. I decided to show them my works, and I sent my fairy tale 'The Spring

Girl' to the address I found in the newspaper. Then I waited for an answer.

It had been a month and a half of silence. One day when Lena came to visit, I persuaded her to go to Kemerovo to the editorial office of this newspaper. Kemerovo is not far from Belovo. Lena left her children with her aunt and went to Kemerovo. Luckily, they liked my fairy tale, but they closed the column 'Your Own Voice'. In those troubled 1990s, many industries were closed and eliminated, including the business of books, magazines, and newspapers.

The Kemerovo Regional Professional Book Publishing House and many periodicals were closed, and those that remained decreased in volume. My hopes for publication were dashed…

My literary path was so thorny! I would solve one problem, and my fate would immediately bring new ones. As in the story of the Lernean Hydra from the Greek legend, a gigantic snake with nine heads, one of which was immortal, anyone who attempted to behead the Hydra, found that as soon as one head was cut off, two more heads would immediately emerge. But I reassured myself that I still achieved the main thing — my independence!

The Belovo Herald

The director of our boarding school also played some role in my fate. Life has shown me that when you do something on your own, people do not remain indifferent to you; they offer help. On this basis, I dare to give you advice — do not let your life flow on its own; be active. When the director saw the results of my literary activity and how I mastered the typewriter, she invited the correspondents of the local newspaper, the 'Belovo Herald' to take an interview with me.

The visit of the journalists astounded me — I did not expect anything like that. Imagine a cloudy day; I am sitting in my room, pondering another story. Suddenly two strangers come, both young, a man and a woman. They introduced themselves as correspondents of the newspaper the 'Belovo Herald'.

The woman's name was Larisa Viktorovna Lezina. I missed the patronymic name of Aleksei Ovsianikov — I was too excited — I just could not believe that they came from the newspaper to see me. I was thinking: are they going to write about me in the newspaper? I saw a frank bewilderment in the eyes of the journalists — they were astonished too when they saw me in my deplorable physical condition. They were probably thinking: how could she manage the typewriter? For the first few minutes, they were just silent. When the pause became quite awkward, Larisa asked the first question.

"Tamara, tell me please, how do you find plots for your stories? Are there any prototypes among real people?"

I understood that this was an on-call question, a formal one, but I had to answer it somehow. I said, "The characters of my fairy tales and stories reflect my own personality. My characters express my Weltanschauung, in other words, my world view. I can even admit that there is my dream hidden between the lines of my fairy tales."

"What are you working on now?" Aleksei asked shyly. Before that, he was looking at me silently in amazement — I understood why and forgave him for his revelation — my appearance was out of the ordinary.

"Now I am writing a story about a disabled girl who does not require validation from anyone, who didn't find love, but love found her." I blurted out my words in one breath. I was afraid that if I hesitated, I would not be able to put my point across, because of my timidity, or because of my excitement that could cause spastic movement and affect my speech.

"Could you show us your story?" Aleksei asked with more enthusiasm.

"But I have not finished it," I said.

"But would you please show us what you have?" Aleksei insisted.

I hesitated — after all, this was a draft version, and I, like anyone who does not have absolute perfection in the language, did not want to show my spelling mistakes and typos. But looking at Aleksei's face, which showed his sincere interest, I gave up. I asked Olga to submit the two sheets I already typed on the typewriter. Olga gave them to the journalists, and they started reading.

"Look here." Larissa Viktorovna pointed out some lines to Aleksei.

I was trying to remember what I wrote — so remarkable that it attracted her attention. Did I write something that shocked her? Noticing my uneasiness, Larissa Viktorovna explained, "Tamara, I am fascinated by these lines." Then she read, "Why should I be offended? If I look like a blade of grass, it is not that bad. The blade of grass possesses its own distinct beauty; it is a thin flexible leaf that grows in a magic clear field. They say that during a powerful storm the wind rips out the mighty oaks, but the thin and flexible blade of grass bows to every wind. It will stand any tempest, and then it will rejoice again in the blue sky and golden sun."

Oh, I felt relieved… They did not resent my writing, but admired it.

They asked a few more questions and then left, saying goodbye and wishing me creative success. Later I learned that Larisa Viktorovna Lezina was an experienced, talented journalist. She had a nickname, the 'Golden Pen' and directed a workshop for young journalists.

Aleksei Ovsianikov was at that time the beginner. Larissa Viktorovna was his advisor and supervisor; this is why they came together. And it is good that she entrusted writing an article about me to him — sometimes a young, inexperienced pen is more sincere than the golden one…

***

A few days after the visit of the journalists, the newspaper the 'Belovo Herald' published Aleksei's enthusiastic article. Here are lines I quote from memory: 'Looking at Tamara Cheremnova, it is difficult to imagine how she manages to work when she cannot eat and drink without assistance, and she needs a lot of effort to speak. We admire this woman for her courage!' And so on — they praised me for my resilience. The article offended me a little bit — there were too many compliments and mentions about my plight and physical difficulties, which I overcome. After all, by that time I had more or less gotten rid of my fears, inferiority complex, and thoughts that I was the worst person in the world. In addition, I saw disabled people in a much worse condition, and I believed their life was even more difficult than mine. But in general, the article was touching, sincere and written from the heart. And the author was very right in one respect — the work exhausted me completely, and it was quite disappointing.

Sitting all day long by the typewriter in an extremely uncomfortable position and constantly pressing my hand with the 'mushroom' clamped in my fingers, over the keys, I would fall dead after my work — I had an incredible pain in my muscles, head, and eyes. But my arm muscles were only half the trouble. The muscles of my entire body were strained during my work — all the muscles, the skeletal and smooth muscles. And these tense muscles clamped blood and lymph vessels, bronchi, and so on. And such a tense state does not lead to anything good, especially if it is constant. And with my body affected by cerebral palsy, I went too far. So when they took me to have the annual fluorography, it was found that the overall condition of my chest had deteriorated significantly. My muscles avenged me for my constant working sit-down sessions — I got acquired cervical chondrosis in the thoracic section and permanent cramps, both in front and back.

You may ask me: who was chasing me? Why did I work in a hurry? My answer is no one. Just that when a story was born in my head, I wanted to splash it out at once, otherwise it would not be possible for me either to eat or sleep. And I wanted to see as soon as possible how it would look on paper. Writing is like the birth process that cannot be stopped. It is not accidental that they say: the birth of a story, the birth of a novel, the birth of a painting.

***

In the mid-90s, my fairy tales were printed one after another: 'The Crystal Cocktail', 'The Girl Spring' and 'The Saga of the First Love'. After Aleksei Ovsianikov's article, published in the 'Belovo Herald', I became known to the city of Belovo as a writer…

'Hope'

In 1996, the city department of social protection gave me a ticket to the Recreation Resort. It was the first ticket in my life to such a place. There was a beautiful vacation area called Targay located in the suburban area of Novokuznetsk. They decided to open a medical wellness complex for the disabled, and the first candidates who were chosen to enjoy health benefits were the so-called gifted disabled people — this is how flatteringly they christened us. And there came gifted disabled people from all over the Kemerovo region. However, the MWC for the disabled did not last very long. Targay was given to children with disabilities, also under the same cause of the MWC, and a new health complex for adults with disabilities was never built.

It was in Targay I met Zinaida Gavrilovna Chernovol, editor of the Novokuznetsk newspaper 'Invalid'. Zinaida Gavrilovna is a journalist; thank God she is a healthy person, but she deals with the problems of the disabled.

I took with me to 'Targay' the manuscript of the story 'Milasha's Holiday' in a draft version to finish it and polish. I showed it to a nurse, to someone from the staff, and new acquaintance, Tatiana — the poet. Tatiana was also disabled; it was she who introduced me to Chernovol, whom I asked to read my story. Zinaida Gavrilovna read it and approved, then she sent it to the newspaper of the All-Russian Society of Disabled People (ARSDP) — the name of this newspaper was 'Hope'.

In February 1997, the newspaper 'Hope' published my story 'Milasha's Holiday'. It was a great success, because this newspaper was spreading all over Russia. The newspaper 'Hope' gave me hope for everything — for my health improvement, for fruitful work and wide fame.

Once again, the newspaper 'Hope' justified its name many years later, in 2008. I fly sometimes in the sky, so I lost the newspaper copy with my story 'Milasha's Holiday', and I needed it to include in the list of my publications in order to join the Writers' Union of Russia. What could I do? I asked my friend, who lived in Moscow, to call the editors of 'Hope' to request the information about my story, not really expecting that they would search in their archives for the old publication of Tamara Cheremnova. So I turned to 'Hope' with hope. And my hope was justified! The editorial office not only found in the archive the number and page of my publication, but also sent me the newspaper, removing it from the archive.

The Transfer to Novokuznetsk

In the late nineties, life in the Insk Boarding School was not bad. The assistance care had been more or less adjusted, my work went well, my friend Lena Medvedeva was on my side, but... In the evenings I suffered with the spiritual emotion which is known to most people in the world, but the word which defines this emotion exactly can only be found in Russian language. In Russian we call it 'тоска'. The word 'тоска' can be translated to English as 'longing', 'emotional pain' or 'melancholy', but these English words do not transmit all of the depth of this very elevated suffering. Actually, many Russian folk songs have this element — 'toska' (you stress the last syllable). Vladimir Nabokov wrote: 'Not one word in English can transmit all the nuances of toska (тоска). This is a feeling of spiritual suffering without any particular reason. On a less dolorous level, it's the indistinct pain of the soul... vague anxiety, nostalgia, amorous longing.'

It was a nebulous thought that tortured my soul, a vague idea that my future was not here... Not in the Insk house, not in Belovo. A poignant feeling that I was not in the right place had been tormenting my heart... My toska was a sum of longing for a magic place and probably for loving people, mixed with my obscure interpretations of my condition, because as an analytical person, I always tried to understand the psychological content of my experiences. I also have to say that this toska affected my health, which was already compromised.

And then there were problems with Olga. She suffered with hypertension; often she had high blood pressure. She had been suffering with this medical condition for a long time, but the administration kept it silent when they transferred her from the Bachata PNBS to our place. It did not take a long time for her hypertension to manifest itself. Taking care of me, who was aggravated with many health problems and bound to a wheelchair, was not the best job for the hypertensive Olga. Frequent increases in blood pressure led her to a micro stroke; thank God, she recovered. I worried about Olga, when I realized that sooner or later, they would send her back to the Bachata PNBS. After all, the Insk Boarding School recruited physically healthy people, who would be able to do difficult work. Olga with her health problem should not have been getting up at six in the morning and going to wash the stairs, and then also taking care of me. I looked at her, asking myself if I would let it happen if they decided to take her back to the place where she was so unhappy. Olga was full of joy when she received the news she would be moved here; she liked to be here, and it would be a nightmare to her to return to the place where she was before.

And I made my choice — I helped Olga to stay in Insk. And I do not regret it, despite the frequent problems I had with her care. If I had agreed to send her back, against her will and based on the motivation of her poor physical condition, it would have been a betrayal for which I would never forgive myself. I already knew what it was like to experience the betrayal of a loved one, and for Olga I was the closest person. Olga's mother died when she was two years old, and her father, coming out of prison somewhere in the seventies, periodically took his daughter to visit home, but in the early eighties he died. I never asked Olga for which crime he was convicted; if she wanted to tell me, she would tell me without asking. She had two cousins: one in Magadan, the other in Kemerovo. But they never visited Olga, only sent her postcards and sometimes money for holidays.

***

And in general, how one can throw a living creature to a place where they will be notoriously cold and hungry… I could not put outside Olga's cats, with whom she was obsessed and who made our life a little bit chaotic. As a passionate cat person, Olga would feed any cat she met on the street. All the walls of our room, including the wardrobe, were covered with pictures and images of cats.

When Olga was brought to Insk, she noticed immediately that some rooms were inhabited by cats, and she also wanted to get a furry friend. Valiukha gave us a kitten that promised to grow into a lush smoky-colored Siberian cat. We named him Mishka after my literary character from 'The Wizard Mishuta'. Mishka is a nickname for the bear in Russian. Mishka had something of a bear in his appearance — he had a robust physique and looked clumsy.

Once I was sitting in front of the typewriter, writing another story, and suddenly I heard Mishka crying wildly as if his life was in danger. I raised my head and saw Olga, holding Mishka under her arm above the sink and washing Mishka's derriere with soap. I started to communicate with the deaf and mute Olga in sign language, sending her my visual-gestural signals: what are you doing? Cats should not be washed! They clean themselves, licking their coats with their tongues! And Olga answered me in sign language that Mishka licked his behind, and this was not good, because it was not proper; he could get an infection and get sick. With great difficulty I managed to convince Olga that cats have their own feline hygiene politics. It turned out that Olga did not know that cats are famous for their general cleanliness and can take care of their coats even better than some people do. Mishka grew up to be a hefty cat. As a cat with a character, he was not satisfied spending his life inside the room. It became too troublesome to keep Mishka. He liked to go to the basement; from there he would come home with fleas and sores after his fraternity battles with other cats. We loved Mishka, but we agreed that his life was in danger. Living with a good family would be much better for him, so we gave Mishka away, to good hands.

Then, longing for a kindred feline spirit, Olga begged Valiukha to give her another kitten — this time it was the black and white Vaska. Vaska became our companion. One day Olga went to work and she forgot to feed him. There were two portions of fish soup on the table; they were leftovers from lunch. The two bowls of soup were covered by two other bowls. Few felines could resist this temptation. Vaska yelled for about five minutes, and when he realized I would not feed him, he decided to take his own action. He jumped on Olga's bed; from the bed he jumped to the table. He came to the bowls, gently moved the top cover with his nose, and the soup was exposed to this little gourmet. He began eating the soup, purring with pleasure. I would have dragged Vaska by the nape of his neck with my hand, if I could move and perform this action. And of course, I would have fed him but in a proper way; he had his own little bowl. I tried to negotiate with Vaska, appealing to his conscience. Like a good rhetorician, I tried to denounce him, moralizing and preaching about manners and friendship, but Vaska continued eating the soup.

The scene was exactly like that in Krylov's fable 'The Cat and the Cook'. Leaving the tavern, the cook left the kitchen in the care of Vaska the cat, so that he would guard food supplies from the mice. But, returning home, the cook discovers that the cat is working on the chicken. The cook, seeing this, started appealing to the cat's conscience: "Now all the neighbors will say that Cat Vaska is a rogue! Cat Vaska is a thief! Cat Vaska is corrupt!" and so on. 'But Vaska listens and eats' — this is the famous line from Krylov's fable.

I moved from my moral discourse to threats. "Look, Vaska, you are eating Olga's soup; here she comes, and she will beat you with her slipper!"

Of course, I did not allow Olga to beat Vaska. I gave her my bowl of soup which Vaska did not touch, realizing it would be indecent to eat my soup in my presence. Also, one bowl of soup was enough for him; he was still a little kitten. I appreciated Vaska's delicacy and perpetuated Vaska in one of my fairy tales.

***

My trip to Targay in 1996 helped me to make a lot of friends from different parts of the Kemerovo region. I actively corresponded with them, and information reached me that a new boarding house for the elderly and disabled — spacious and equipped with the latest technology — had opened in Novokuznetsk.

Oh, I wanted so much to go there... I was attracted to the house with comforts and amenities, and this was my home city Novokuznetsk, where I was born and lived during the first six years of my life — my happiest and cloudless years. Nadezhda Konstantinovna Trushina, who always supported me, no longer worked at the Regional Department of Social Security (RDSS); she had been transferred to another organization. So I ventured into writing to the RDSS myself. I wrote a detailed letter-request, objectively describing my life at the Insk Boarding School — I am treated very well, but there are some technical difficulties and so on. I presented my arguments: originally, I am from Novokuznetsk, and I ask for two tickets to the Novokuznetsk Home for the Elderly and Disabled for Olga and myself. I always thought about the two of us. If I left Olga, they would transfer her back to the Bachata PNBS, as unqualified for professional fitness. As a nanny, she was not able to do her job because of health reasons, and she was kept solely as my personal assistant.

How much I wanted to return to the city of my childhood! Just on pronouncing the word 'Novokuznetsk', sweet memories started flooding — our house, my grandparents, my loving father and mother... I was loved at that time...

I also had an ignoble desire for revenge on my relatives for stopping loving me. I wanted to remind them just with my presence in Novokuznetsk about being sent by them to the orphanage. For being forced to leave Novokuznetsk. For rare visits. For not being invited to visit them. Such a childish desire for revenge — oh, you did not invite me to come to Novokuznetsk? Here I am, I came here without your help!

The answer from the RDSS did not come, but I stubbornly repeated to myself that I would go to Novokuznetsk. And in 1997, my wish to go to Novokuznetsk was fulfilled. One day, when I went down to the accounting department on the first floor, suddenly I heard, "Tickets to Novokuznetsk arrived for Cheremnova and Racheva."

I was very surprised; I had been about to give up and stop waiting. The next day I went to see the director — to get details on the move. Waiting in line to go to her office, I saw the doctor Sergei Aleksandrovich Chervov. He had just started working at the boarding school, but we quickly established a good relationship.

"Tamara, why are you here?" he asked.

"I came to discuss my transfer," I said.

"Where are you going?" he asked.

"I am moving to the Novokuznetsk house."

"Tamara, why do you want to go there? Here you have your peers, and in the Novokuznetsk house, there are mostly elderly people."

"Sergei Aleksandrovich, I am not so young too; I am in my forties."

"There will be people in the nursing home twice your age."

"Well, I had some experience with older people in Prokopyevsk PNBS; I got along with them very well." I smiled, thinking of my wonderful three Mashas.

"Tamara! Here you are known; you are respected here. The whole town of Belovo reads you; you are published in newspapers. What kind of life you will have in Novokuznetsk? Think of it! Why should you leave?" Sergei Aleksandrovich could not stop warning me.

I just shook my head. Sergei Aleksandrovich's arguments were reasonable, but if I have rushed forward in my thoughts and convinced myself of the extreme necessity of something — it is already irrevocable... All that I had to do was agree with Olga and pack things.

***

And now the car rushed along the road, like it was eight years ago, but this time it would bring me to my home town, the city of my childhood, from where I was taken away at the age of less than seven years old... And now I was back, but I was six times older; I was almost forty-two!

Seven multiplied by six equals forty-two... I lived one time period in Novokuznetsk and five subsequent similar segments outside it, and had never been there during these five segments...

***

During the eight years of my life in the Insk Boarding School, I experienced all sorts of things. They were good and joyful and bad and sorrowful. But they treated me there with respect, they listened to my opinion and they tried to help me. And most importantly, I continued my literary path — I created my works and typed them on my typewriter. My tales and stories were published, and I was called a writer without sarcasm.

Part 4
The Novokuznetsk Boarding School

Arrival and Acclimatization

In October 1997, Olga and I were taken to the Novokuznetsk Boarding School No. 2 for the elderly and disabled. Belovo and Novokuznetsk are fairly close together — a hundred-plus kilometers. We arrived in no time, but we were lost in Novokuznetsk, as the driver was not familiar with the area.

I looked out the car window, hoping to find something familiar. I was so naïve — much had changed in thirty-five years! After all, I was taken away from Novokuznetsk in 1962, and now it was 1997.

At four o'clock in the afternoon we arrived at the boarding house. The nurse who accompanied Olga and me went to fill out documents. The director of the boarding school looked inside the car. She did not introduce herself, but one of the people nearby whispered, 'She is the director'.

"Who came here?" She asked dryly and sounding unfriendly. Her greeting should have been friendlier. From this harsh treatment I cringed, and was gripped by the same coldness I experienced in days gone by. The director gazed at me indifferently, then she turned away and left.

After a while, Elvira Alekseevna, the chief nurse, came to us. She cheerfully greeted us with a smile and asked our names. I introduced the mute and deaf Olga and myself and briefly told her about us. After reviewing the transfer papers, our belongings were unloaded from the car. The nurse and the driver who brought us here from Insk said goodbye and left.

So now Olga and I were sitting in the lobby with our belongings. It was unusual and embarrassing to sit like that in public when everyone looked at us with a strange curiosity. I could do nothing about it, and I started looking around — the hall was large and light, it had a marble floor and looked like the lobby of a hotel, which I had seen in films. Then the friendly nurse came and asked us to follow her. "Come with me; I will show you your room."

Olga and I in my wheelchair hurried after her. I was glad that I had my wheelchair — the Insk director Nadezhda Vasilevna was very kind letting me take it with me. I decided to transform my first emotions of coldness which I perceived from the Novokuznetsk house into a little triumph, proudly riding along the corridor on my personal transport.

The nurse opened the room which was prepared for us; there were two beds with fresh sheets; everything was proper and clean. The interior of this room was exactly like a hotel! And the feeling of being in a sterile hotel did not leave me that first evening.

***

After a week, I felt a great discomfort. At first, I did not understand why I was so uncomfortable. Then, being on the street, I understood why I felt like I had been put inside a box. There was a lot of space in the Insk Boarding School — nothing blocked the perspective and distance. The Novokuznetsk house was surrounded by many multi-storied residential buildings, and only in one place could one see a distant forest. Accustomed to living on the land of massive expanse, covered with green forests, I involuntarily yearned for the city of my childhood. But the city of Novokuznetsk was now inhabited by people completely unfamiliar to me, and that spot, where the house of my childhood stood, had become densely covered with ugly constructions.

I sank into depression; I did not want to read or write. I felt like running back to Insk to hide under the branches in the karagaach garden! But my common sense whispered to me that this was a temporary nostalgia; I would get adapted and my melancholy would go away. My leading idea was: I have achieved what I have always wanted — I returned to my city, Novokuznetsk.

And I began pushing this longing to the bottom of my soul, trying to suppress it with positive and constructive thoughts. Long live my stubbornness! I had not immediately succeeded in coping with my adaptation, but finally I overcame my depression. And gradually the inhospitable city changed its nature; I began to love it and my working mood returned.

The Journalist Tamara Bokhan

Three weeks after my arrival at Novokuznetsk, a nice-looking woman, accompanied by the chief nurse Elvira Alekseevna, entered my room.

"Tamara, here is the journalist from the newspaper 'Metallurgist of Westsib' our director sent to you," said Elvira Alekseevna and left.

I offered the journalist a chair; she sat and introduced herself. "My name is Tamara Petrovna Bokhan. I am a journalist. Tamara Cheremnova, may I ask you some questions? Your director intrigued me — she said you are a very interesting person."

"Of course," I said.

I was a little bit agitated — I was not visited too often by journalists, and here this journalist came; we even had the same name. I was surprised that the director recommended to her to see me and even said good things about me. She must be kinder than I thought if she recommended interviewing me to 'Metallurgist of Westsib'. I will explain to the reader that the Russian name of this newspaper is 'Металлург Запсиба'. The first word can be translated as 'metallurgist'. 'Запсиб' is the abbreviation of 'Западная Сибирь' — Western Siberia in English. So 'Запсиб' is actually 'Westsib'.

I overcame my excitement, and Tamara Bokhan and I had a warm conversation. In the future we became good friends. She is a little older than I, and she is such a wonderful person — goodhearted, kind and open — what a beautiful soul. My fate sent this namesake to me in contrast to the other namesake, Tamara Fedorovna of the Prokopyevsk PNBS, whose ruthless medical report pushed me to suicide. That Tamara almost killed me, and this Tamara gave me new vital elements.

Tamara Bokhan visited me often, and we talked about everything. When she had problems in her life, she shared them with me as an equal, and I tried to support her with advice or just listening to her and encouraging. I reached an important conclusion through my communication with Tamara: any person, be he or she successful and fortunate or not, can experience difficulties, and all people, absolutely all, even the most intelligent, wealthy, and independent, need understanding and empathy.

***

After the interview, I realized that my parents, aunts, and cousins from Novokuznetsk might read Tamara Bokhan's essay in the newspaper and find out that I was in Novokuznetsk. At that moment, none of them knew that I had moved. I really wanted them to read this essay, but probably it did not catch my relatives' eye, or maybe they did not read newspapers.

My mother found out that I was in Novokuznetsk from the director of the Insk house. In December 1997, my mother sent me a birthday card to my Insk address. The director was surprised that my mother did not know my new address and sent her card back along with an official letter about my transfer to Novokuznetsk. Later I found out that the director had marveled at my conspiracy and felt it was necessary to reveal it. But there was no conspiracy. My mother was not interested in me, so why should I notify her about my move?

You Will be Able to Walk!

I have to pay tribute to the Novokuznetsk house — as soon as I arrived here, I immediately began to be taken to neurologists — in the same year, 1997, in late November and December. They did it out of the best intentions — to heal me and cure!

But now, more than ten years later, I can say with confidence that it would have been better not to do it. I went through a succession of various stages — first I was encouraged, then offended, then humiliated, and finally exhausted — nothing in this cure could help me. My fate seemed to laugh at me; it mercilessly tried my most vulnerable places. It hissed at me with a gleeful grin: 'Now you can see! No one and nothing can help you! Did you see how people looked at you? Did you understand who you are to them?'

My fate hurt me and along the way showed me human vices — as if it decided to introduce negative characters to the novice writer for her writing.

Tamara Bokhan had a friend, who worked at the Novokuznetsk Traumatology and Orthopedics Institute, and she arranged for me an examination by the specialists. It was in December 1997. I was taken to this solid institute in a car. I was accompanied by the nurse Elvira Alekseevna and my assistant Olga. Then I was transported to the orthopedics office and put on a couch.

A young woman entered the room; she was a doctor. I was presented to her, and then she took my medical documents. She looked briefly in my medical history and began to examine me, not even offering to undress me, as it should be, according to the rules of medical examination. She asked me to straighten my back. I complied with her request. And then our subsequent conversation went astray; it seemed to me I was talking not to a doctor but to some entity whose demeaning voice I would recognize even after my death in the Other World. I do not want to give the name of this so-called doctor, as I do not want to embarrass her for being such a heartless person. But I hope she will read this book, and then she might reconsider her attitude towards patients and reduce her arrogance and carelessness. It might also prevent her giving her patients empty promises.

"Why don't you walk?" She asked this stunning question in such a tone, as if I deliberately did not walk, as if it was my cunning agenda to be bound to the wheelchair for so many years. "Look how good your back is!" she said.

"No one took my condition seriously," I said meekly. "I was pretty much avoided... Most of my life I have lived in strange places..."

The so-called doctor looked at me with perplexity. I started telling her about the psycho-neurological boarding school and how I escaped from it, but she interrupted me rudely. "As a specialist, I see you have oligophrenia!"

I showed her my little book 'From the Life of the Wizard Mishuta', which I had taken with me for some purpose. She examined it with an amazement similar to how a cow would look at a new gate, then she made an astounding conclusion. "You see, you were able to write a book, so you can walk!"

"Then take me to your hospital," I said quite magnanimously, as if giving her a chance to display some dignity.

"I can't do that! Our orthopedics department is focused on the treatment of muscle contractions and undeveloped joints. But you have spastic and hyperkinetic disorders — to remove them you should be sent to the neurology department, and then we'll see."

After my meeting with this orthopedist, I was in some confusion for a long time. On the one hand, I was affected by an unpleasant examination and the conversation in which the ominous diagnosis of 'oligophrenia', which had already been removed, stabbed me right in the back; on the other hand, this doctor appeared like an angel bringing me a holy message: you will be able to walk! How could I not believe this angel? It was a doctor after all. And if the doctor believed I could walk, then that was the way it was. The doctor would not give false promises. So I saw this orthopedist doctor as a sorceress — not like the Wizard Mishuta, but still a sorceress with the ability to attain objectives, using not supernatural means and magic, but her doctoral qualifications and medical knowledge, who could use them sufficiently and transform me into a person who could walk.

I was also encouraged by a story I had learned when I lived in the Prokopyevsk PNBS. The new girl Galina came to us. Galina had the same form of cerebral palsy as I have, with spasticity and hyperkinesia, but she was able to walk and eat without assistance. I asked her how she was treated. She told me about the psycho-neurological center for children in Novokuznetsk; among them there were also children with cerebral palsy. They were engaged in various physical and intellectual activities — those who could and wanted to learn, were taught. Until the age of six, Galina could only crawl; she was not able to walk. At the center, they gave her proper medication. Also, she went through healing fitness training and physical therapy, and after that she was able to walk!

This is why I so naïvely believed this doctor and insisted on being hospitalized to the neurology department of the Novokuznetsk City Hospital No. 29.

The Neurology and Soullessness

I arrived at the neurology department not in the best time for the Russian state — this was February-March 1998. Pharmaceutical drugs were no longer free; they had to be bought with your own money. This post-Soviet innovation is still in effect — in December 2009 I was again in this neurology department — it was the same scheme of medical care with medications at the expense of the patient.

I did not argue and I bought piracetam. They say this drug influences neuronal, vascular, and cognitive functions. Then the doctor prescribed for me pills with the unusual name 'nakom'. As I read, it is indicated for the treatment of motor fluctuations in patients with advanced Parkinson's disease. Nakom is also used after brain surgery to avoid seizures. They say that in combination with other drugs and vitamins, it gives good results. And I was optimistic. I was lucky to buy this nakom directly from the wholesale facility for four hundred rubles; at the pharmacy it cost six hundred. But nakom turned out to be 'not my drug'. In combination with B vitamins, it removed my spasticity, but nothing more. Hyperkinesia did not want to leave my body. The word hyperkinesis comes from the Greek *hyper*, meaning 'increased', and *kinein*, meaning 'to move'. Basic hyperkinetic movements can be defined as any unwanted, excess movements. Such abnormal movements can be distinguished from each other on the basis of their degree. In general, they were not removed completely by the treatment and were in accordance with my emotional state: sometimes they could disappear for several hours, and then they could suddenly come back and manifest themselves for a long time. In severe cases I took relanium.

The doctor agreed that nakom did not help me, and I needed another medication. But she could not do anything, because finding a proper remedy was problematic; they did not have a wide selection of drugs and did not use the individual approach when prescribing drugs. As a matter of fact, they used the same drugs for each patient. And I dutifully took nakom and waited patiently for the time when my body would acquire balance. I dreamed that I would be able to walk...

From time to time, the physical education instructor would come to the ward to do exercises with us. I tried to do my best, but I had a problem with my hand. Sometimes my reluctant left hand did not want to bend, so I would hide it behind my back. Then the instructor barked, "Well, you hide your left hand behind your back again! Bring your hand in front! Let it be free!"

I understood her righteous indignation, and I would pull out my left hand, letting it be in 'free flight', but this maneuver affected my exercises not in an advantageous way. And the instructor could not do anything to correct and direct my movements. And she did not understand that she should not offend her students, even if they were clumsy and did not have grace and flexibility.

***

I want to tell you another story about my experience in the neurology department. It happened during the first week of my hospitalization. As Olga assisted me on an everyday basis, she accompanied me; however, they did not provide her with a bed.

Being without her personal bed, Olga could only use a bed which was available at night, as the patient to whom this bed was assigned was absent during the night and came only for morning procedures. During the day Olga could only use a chair. Naturally, she began to get tired, her headaches increased, and often she had high blood pressure. This aggravated my doctor — instead of helping to find a bed for Olga, she demanded that Olga should be sent back to the boarding school. But then who would assist me? Alas, without assistance I would be in a difficult situation.

And then I asked the doctor to call my mother and ask her to help me with my everyday needs. I addressed my mother only as a last resort, but this was the case. Moreover, other patients were visited by their relatives, who usually came directly after work, and in spite of tiredness, took care of them.

My mother responded to the doctor's call — two days later she came with her sister Maria. My mother has four sisters and one brother; they all lived in Novokuznetsk. After learning about my affairs, she turned her eyes upward, which was her typical expression of annoyance. "I can't quit my job! Even though I'm officially retired, I still work part-time. I need to earn money for my old age, otherwise I am going to starve!"

Her sister Maria immediately put in her two cents: "Tomka, why do you go through this treatment? You're incurable anyway. You are just wasting your time and money. If you were curable, you'd have been cured as a child."

"Can you look after me at least once in your life?" I exploded.

"How dare you to demand anything from us? We are old!" my aunt said.

I wanted to tell them that she never helped me when they were young. But my roommates were ahead of me. "Shame on you! Why do you take her last hopes away from her? No one has the right to do that, not even her mother!"

But it was not easy to deal with my heartless family. After my roommates' reproach, my mother and Aunt Maria began to discuss if it would be a good idea to pay the nanny for taking care of me. But after reflecting upon this idea, they decided that it would be unnecessary. Then my mother went to the hospital kiosk to buy some pills for Olga who had headaches and high blood pressure.

Very soon the sisters left, believing that their mission had been accomplished. After their refusal to take care of me, the hospital administration took some measures — they provided Olga with a vacant bed.

***

My treatment was coming to an end in March 1998, and there were no bodily improvements. My expectations of getting up and walking disappeared. I realized that the prediction that I would transform, from a person bound to a wheelchair to one who would be able to walk, was just another fairy tale. I accepted the bitter truth: no treatment would help me, and all kinds of medication and procedures were powerless in my case.

Of course, I had no desire to see this magician-orthopedic, who had promised I would be able to walk if they removed the spasticity and hyperkinesia. Spasticity and hyperkinesia remained with me, and this was just my reality beyond any magic.

And then another wave of depression took hold of me; a melancholy had taken on my being... All day long I cried as if my eyes became fountains of tears — I wanted to stop this source of water, but my body knew better than I. Contrary to my will, it threw sobs from its depths, and I felt like I witnessed an eruption of my personal volcano.

I wished the doctors would attend to me, but it did not happen. Attention is vitality, but I was unworthy of it as the status of an invalid is lower than that of her healers. I certainly disappointed them because I did not live up to their lofty expectations and did not satisfy their professional ambitions.

***

After returning from the hospital to the boarding school, I periodically fell into an insensitive stupor; this continued for three weeks. I would sit looking at the wall, immersed in nothingness, and then I would come back to my senses to find out that my face was all covered with tears. I did not even notice that I was crying, and I was surprised; why was my face wet — was I exposed to the rain, or did I take a shower and did not notice it? One day I was caught in this condition by the nurse Larisa. She asked, "Why are you crying?"

I opened my mouth to answer, but instead of words, the sobbing started all over again. Larisa reached a paradoxical conclusion. "I see you fell in love!"

At that moment, I just wanted to kill her, and I tried to find some ironic expression to pay her back, but instead, I burst into laughter. Larisa shrugged her shoulders and left. And I was immediately healed from my depression and got back on track. Thereafter Larisa continued making fun of me: "Well, when will you fall in love again and cry because you are in love?"

The Orthopedics and Craftsmanship

The next time I was taken to the orthopedist at the Institute of Orthopedics, I was accompanied by our boarding school doctor. The orthopedist looked at my medical history, and then she examined me, this time undressed. During the examination, I was sitting in the wheelchair; she did not ask me to move to the couch. I noticed our boarding school doctor was astounded when the other doctor said, "I see you have been treated very well in the neurology department!"

There were no significant changes in my condition. Maybe the orthopedist could see the future success in my treatment through her clairvoyance? She started flipping through my medical history and asking questions. "What pills were you prescribed?"

"Nakom, the complex of vitamins B1, B6, B12 and niacin."

"What pills? I didn't understand," she said.

I spelled out 'nakom'. She raised her brows, trying to recall the drug, but probably she had not come across it in her medical practice.

"And now will you take me to your department?" I asked with hope, though I knew that the previous obstacles — spasticity and hyperkinesia — still remained in my body.

"I will not. It is impossible to heal someone with such bad hands. If you had muscle contractions, they would be treated by us. But you have spasticity and hyperkinesia; you also have reduced joint mobility." This was how she justified her rejection.

It was obvious that being so confident, she would never apologize for her irresponsible promise to heal my legs. She was not aware of her own professional unfitness, though like a juggler from the circus, she showered me with many incomprehensible medical terms, which she probably believed would put me in awe. She launched into a strange diatribe speaking about effective treatments and the inability to apply them to me. Why should I listen to her? Did she want to show off her expertise to the doctor who accompanied me? Or was this medical song from other spheres where angels and demons reside? She was still a sorceress, though the one who was not able to accomplish her magic — was she mocking me in revenge? After she had thrown on us a basket of unnecessary information, she descended from heaven to earth. "Now ask your boarding school to order for you special walkers."

"Where can they be ordered?" the doctor who accompanied me asked.

"We have our own manufacturer, but he makes them for our invalids. But now he does not take orders; we order walkers at the factory. But now the factory refuses to make them for us."

So we left the sorceress with empty pockets. And she did not help us with the walkers. Actually, I have been thinking about the walkers for some time, and I even designed them in my mind. I have been thinking about the walkers from my childhood and how sufficient they were for my trips around the house. During my term in the neurology department, in my anticipation of the upcoming training of walking, I made a drawing of the walkers.

At the boarding house, I showed my drawing to Elvira Alekseevna and the director — they both praised me. Without school education, I had to become Ivan Kulibin, the eighteenth century Russian mechanic and inventor. I already designed the 'mushroom' device for typing, and now I attempted to design the walkers. I made my drawing, according to engineering rules, but where and how to implement them? Walkers and other rehabilitation equipment of custom design were made exclusively in the department of orthopedics.

I expected to arrange my walker production in the orthopedics department. I thought about the payment for manufacturing my work, and I knew where to get money. But they refused to hospitalize me in the orthopedics department! The sorceress-orthopedist gave her recommendation to master the walkers — about which I had been thinking for a long time without her involvement — however, she did not give any clue where I could get or order these walkers…

***

After my visit to the orthopedist, I still could not forget certain improper phrases she had pronounced like a confident trickster. It made my blood boil — I had to liberate myself from this bad influence, otherwise my depression would resume. I returned to my typewriter, wrote an article about my recent experience with the orthopedist, and sent it to the newspaper called 'Invalid'. I titled the article 'Poison in the crystal cocktail'.

After the publication of my article, the editor-in-chief of this newspaper, Zinaida Chernovol, visited the Institute of Orthopedics, where she was immediately attacked by the sorceress. "Do you have any idea whom you criticized? I have a special degree in orthopedics! I am highly qualified! I am a very experienced specialist!"

I was lucky — Chernovol knew the manufacturer who made custom walkers. At the moment he did not have the necessary materials, but he picked up useful pieces of iron at the dumpster and made the walkers out of them. I gave the master my drawing, and he made the elegant walkers from thin nickel tubes which were curtain eaves in their previous incarnation. At first, I did not use them, because the wheels were very fragile. Then Olga and I picked up two discarded decent wheels on the street, and the locksmiths from our boarding school attached them to the walkers. In addition to this construction, I installed the rubber, which I detached from some crutches.

So, using such a fantastic construction, I moved around the room, making steps and jumps, until I broke it. But I was lucky again: a woman from the local church came to visit us. Her husband had found two iron parts at the garbage place, which belonged before to a bed, and made for me some very strong walkers, and he did not charge me!

***

I met good doctors too — they were professional, intelligent and kind. Tatiana Balanova was one of them; she was our district therapist, and she supervised our boarding school. Then I should mention Margarita Aleksandrovna, a neurologist, who worked in our clinic. Now we were supervised by the neurologist Olga Aleksandrovna — when she came to me, I felt like I was covered with a warm cloak of care and protection.

Such doctors will never stab a knife into your back; they will never hurt you, never offend you and never humiliate you. But most importantly, they will never give you false promises. God might or might not forgive those doctors who are so incompetent and soulless.

But, anyway, all these sorrows were ground and thrown to the wind when I decided to do my work — to write my stories and fairy tales. In whatever condition I am — able to walk or not — my texts are in demand, children enjoy them, and they are important for adults too, and only for the sake of this is it worth living.

Some people sincerely believe that the home for the disabled is a quiet pier. Alas and ah! I wish that were the case. But it is tolerable here only for those who are able to walk and have healthy hands, for those who do not need assistance to bring a spoon to their mouths, and do not need service with the toilet.

The system of social protection was governed by barbaric laws, especially in hospitals, in psycho-neurological boarding schools and in homes of the general type for the elderly and disabled people. If you complained, they could provoke zealous workers to do whatever they wanted to please their big bosses.

In the Novokuznetsk Boarding School, I saw the barbaric side of some individuals in all its glory. I saw what they were capable of doing in order not to lose their jobs, and how they tried to please the director. The type of organization should always be taken into consideration, as the law enforcement agencies were not willing to look into such institutions, and if they attempted to look, it was not always possible to prove that an old person or a disabled person was mentally capable and could be trusted. It was not possible for an invalid to hire a lawyer and carry out an objective examination, which, as a matter of fact, they were not able to afford. They say there are some human rights activists, but I have never seen them in my disabled life. And these officials, who work in the city, are always connected by a network and will never do anything against each other for the sake of some helpless disabled person. I have learned this from my bitter experience — these officials always stand together like a solid block, and they support each other in anything ambiguous and equivocal.

In 1999, without knowing what consequences it would bring, I got involved with a very unpleasant business. May God forgive me both alive and dead, but if I have to write, I will tell everything, and I will describe in detail and go to the end, so that there are no dark holes in my autobiography. After all, the state and society simply do not know and do not want to know about the Russian boarding schools for old and disabled people.

I thought, in order to survive, you had to be strong and active every second only at the Prokopyevsk psycho-neurological boarding school. I thought it would be different at the Novokuznetsk Boarding School, because its residents were former workers — no comparison with us, disabled since childhood.

One day Varvara, a news presenter, who had always been the first to bring me the news, reported that a new order had come from the director or even from the higher level of the administration in Kemerovo, saying that the residents had to change the status of their personal belongings —
from now all their private things must belong to the state. Those who did not want to transfer their things to the state could sell their possessions or give them to their relatives. According to this regulation, personal belongings should not be kept in the state institution. The transition of the personal to the public had to be accomplished during ten days. So personal things were not allowed; all things should be public — these were like regulations in prison!

The residents were in panic — they began selling their possessions — TV sets, refrigerators, and all kinds of other things. And because they had a very limited time, only ten days, they sold their possessions at very low prices, although their electronics and other things were new and had cost them three times more than their current selling prices. Apparently, the alarm was created on purpose to give a chance to some dishonest people from the administration to buy valuables from the residents for reduced prices.

The order arrived, but it had a contrary meaning — all personal belongings of the residents had to be listed in a special file. But someone in the administration had wanted to make some profit, robbing the disabled and elderly blind, so they had distorted the order.

Such happenings are typical for boarding schools — their residents are vulnerable and helpless and dependent on the administration.

And what machinations they do with the apartments of the elderly and disabled! What horrible things people do sometimes! There was an official provision that an elderly person, who has difficulties living alone, has the right to stay in a boarding school for three months and then decide which place would be better for him or her — his or her home or the boarding school. But as soon as this person comes here, he or she is forced to give his apartment as a gift either to the boarding school, or to a certain person closely associated with the boarding school. And that was exactly the case of one man, who was forced to give his apartment as a gift to a person who was a complete stranger to him, but who was very interested in accepting this gift. This shady business brought the man to suicide. Today I do not have sufficient evidence and living witnesses — most of them died. And the administration chose to forget the precedent with the man who hanged himself precisely because of their cabal. But we did experience this tragedy — it put us in shock, pain, and sadness…

Many of us perfectly remember the story about the obligatory transfer of personal belongings to state possessions — it was a mini-version of ten days that shook the world, a storm in a teacup — nevertheless, filled with senseless panic and cruel hassle. And none of the staff, who were informed about the nature of the new order, during these stormy ten days had ever explained to us that the order was actually not against the residents, it was just an inventory of people's possessions, which by the way, I also found peculiar.

After having been acquainted in full measure with the discreet charm of the administration, I decided to share my experience with the governor of the region, Aman Gumirovich Tuleev. I wrote a letter in which I described the outrageous facts in the boarding school, but I decided to send it first to my acquaintance — he lived in Kemerovo.

This letter was signed by the news presenter Varvara and by the local old lady whom Varvara brought to me. This old lady was an honored teacher; she had experienced the horrors of Stalin's repression and the heroic endurance during the Siege of Leningrad, which lasted nearly nine hundred days. How could one not believe such a respected person? I should have been more careful, as the teacher was very old and not very adequate. Later I bitterly repented that I allowed these two residents to put their signatures on my appeal to Tuleev.

And here is what happened. When my acquaintance from Kemerovo received my letter, he made a copy of it. He sent the original to Tuleev and the copy to the newspaper 'The Working Novokuznetsk'. This newspaper functioned in the late 1990s; later it was closed. And in the morning, when everyone was still asleep, the chairman of the Cultural and Household Commission (CHC) came to my room and quietly woke me up. "Tamara, your letter was published in the newspaper," he said. "The director came to work furious. You did the right thing!"

First, I did not understand. What letter, what newspaper? Then I realized they had published my letter to Tuleev in the newspaper without my permission.

It was my own fault that people were punished because of this letter. When Varvara told me about the inquisition she went through when she was interrogated by the director and the members of the Cultural and Household Commission, I sensed the icy cold inside me, and I felt like I had been stabbed in the chest. I imagined this eighty-two-year-old woman standing humbly in front of these members of the CHC, screaming at her. But I did not force Varvara and the old lady to sign that letter! It was their idea to put their signatures, though I warned them that they would be responsible for their signatures. I was not afraid of my own responsibility.

Soon it was my turn to go for the execution to the director in her suite, the CHC. They sent three old men to carry me along the stairs to the second floor where the meeting took place. I looked at these elderly slaves and I realized that they would not be able to deliver me like an Egyptian queen to the place of execution; most likely, they would drop me on the stairs. And if they let me fall on the floor, they would say this happened because of my hyperkinesia, that I jerked violently and it was difficult for them to hold me. At that time, there were few people who lived on the ground floor, so the director did not allow using the elevator.

"Let's go. The director is calling you to a meeting," one of the old men said to me.

"I am not going anywhere," I replied. "If they need me, let them come here."

The three old men left. Soon the members of the Cultural and Household Commission appeared. "Tamara, the director sent us to you to investigate the complaint," the chairman said.

"Why didn't she come with you?" I asked him. "The complaint concerns her personally. I'd like her to be present. And I am going to ask her, why and who provoked the sale of things? And why did that ugliness last for ten days? Why did people panic and sell their last belongings for nothing? During these ten days it was possible to explain to the residents about the order."

The chairman gave up on any possibility of negotiating with me. "Oh, why should I be involved in this!"

Then the Cultural and Household Commission members left.

I thought it was perfectly logical and proper to bring the director to explain that situation. But apparently, she had nothing to say in her defense. The next day, she sent the chief nurse and the head doctor to me. The chief nurse sat on a stool, while the head doctor remained standing.

"Toma, what complaint did you write about the director? the head doctor began.

"This complaint wouldn't have happened if we were explained to about the new resolution regarding personal things," I answered.

But their plans, apparently, did not include listening to me. The chief nurse, with her eyes focused on my complaint, moved her finger over its lines, trying to find a mistake in the text. "And here, why is it written like that? … Why did you use this word? … Just look at this sentence."

It was strange that she tried to find grammatical faults in my writing; my letter was edited and corrected. The head doctor chose a different approach for criticizing me; she just raised her voice and gradually proceeded to screaming. Then they started yelling at me together in one high-pitched almost operatic voice. I understood that both the visitors were doing this on purpose to intimidate me. Then I decided to yell at them too. All my life I have been oppressed by these bossy screamers, and now the time came, when I could show them I have the right to answer them in the same manner. In fact, I could have said a lot to enlighten them, but the damned hyperkinesia did not allow me to do this — I fell down from my wheelchair to the floor.

For a minute, the head doctor and chief nurse stopped yelling. The chief nurse even turned to me with caring attention. And I asked her from the floor, "Please show me what mistakes you found in my letter."

"Can I help you to get up?" she said. She was calm, as if nothing had happened.

"I can get up myself." I refused her help, and after making a few maneuvers, I was able to sit down on my butt on the floor.

"Toma, write a retraction to your letter," the head doctor begged me.

I laughed and shook my head negatively. "I will not write a retraction. Why should I deny the truth?"

"So you will not write the retraction?"

"I will not!" I said firmly.

The head doctor and the chief nurse left. About three weeks later, the director fired the head doctor — she usually fired all those who refused or failed to comply with her orders. And then one evening I was sitting outside, and I saw this head doctor approaching me. She sat next to me on the bench and began complaining tearfully that the director had kicked her out.

I asked her an unpleasant question. "Do you remember how you demanded the retraction and how you shouted at me?"

"Me? When? Oh, I was so ashamed that I don't remember anything," she said sheepishly, bringing her eyes down. I saw she felt guilty.

Major and Minor Troubles

Troubles are part of our life; no one can escape them, even those who have the most prosperous life. But apparently, I am a person who attracts troubles like a magnet.

New troubles arrived in the new millennium — in 2001-2002. At this point I had been tormented by our doctors and had the opportunity to observe their specific attitude towards me and people like me. I had been through various treatments, and at the end I was empty handed. I decided to get examination and treatment in other cities. I wondered how they would deal with such patients as me, and how other clinics than those I had experienced in my Kemerovo region would compare. Of all the choices, mine was Moscow.

At that time there was a medical agency that provided paid services, including help in admission for treatment in Moscow hospitals. So I made my choice to go to Moscow, and I wrote a letter indicating my diagnosis of cerebral palsy. They answered in detail, explaining that they would make a request to a Moscow clinic which was specialized in cerebral palsy; then I had to wait for an invitation. The agency also indicated how much the examination and treatment in the Moscow clinic would cost. It was possible to receive money for the medical treatment from the regional budget administration — they provided special financial resources for patients and persons who accompanied them. I received an invitation to the Moscow clinic. The next step was to prepare a dossier in order to apply to the regional administration for money.

It was not difficult to order a special medical document in our district clinic — Tatiana Vasilevna Balanova, the therapist, who supervised our boarding school, quickly issued it. However, it required the signature of the Novokuznetsk chief neurologist. His name was Vladimir Vladimirovich Malevik, and his office was in one of the city clinics.

Our director approached me. "Tamara, your medical history should be signed by the chief neurologist. Our senior nurse cannot help you —

she is too busy. You have your friend Shishkina. As the chairman of the Society for the Disabled People she can help you. Ask her to go with your medical history to the chief neurologist."

"All right, I will ask her when she comes to me." I nodded.

Shishkina, the chairman of the local All-Russian Society of Invalids, visited us regularly — she organized events and festive receptions and helped with other affairs. I conveyed to her the director's request. She agreed; it was not difficult for her to visit the chief neurologist since she often went to that clinic because of her health reasons. Before she went to the clinic, I had told her my bitter story about my life at the psycho-neurological boarding school. She listened to me silently, with her eyes wide open, and then she said, "You deserve a golden monument! In your lifetime!"

"I didn't tell you my story to be admired, but only to avoid misunderstandings." I made it clear.

Shishkina took my medical history and went to the chief neurologist. A week later she came to the boarding school. With some sadness she delivered her report. "I gave your medical history to the chief neurologist. He looked at it, but he refused to sign anything. The diagnosis of oligophrenia is still in your medical history, and almost every page states it. You said the last records should have a good report about your mental condition, but we didn't find it. The chief neurologist asked me 'Does she draw out words when she speaks'? I said, she draws out a little, so what does it mean? And he said that this is the sign of oligophrenia; therefore, he cannot give you permission to go to the Moscow institute of neurology."

I was sitting like I was struck by lightning — her words flew into me like cosmic meteorites. I was not offended by Shishkina — she was only the bearer of bad news; you don't shoot the messenger. After this fiasco, she never visited me again; and I understood why. I also understood the bureaucrat Malevik — probably, he was given the order to put down the cases with ordinary patients, who requested money from the regional budget in order to pay for their examination and treatment. This money was supposed to be given to privileged individuals, who were not necessarily in bad health, but who had the so-called elite connections. That is, it seemed that it would be possible for an ordinary patient to ask for money to pay to the Moscow neurologists, but he or she would never receive it under any pretext. In my case, the pretext was the diagnosis 'oligophrenia' which was glued to my medical history.

But the Moscow neurologists who work with cerebral palsy have to deal with various cases — with patients with preserved intelligence and with those who are mentally retarded — in other words, they deal with oligophrenia as well. I analyzed the situation and tried not to worry. Well, they refused me permission to go to the Moscow neurologists; so what? Well, they didn't want to eliminate the diagnosis of oligophrenia from my medical history; it seems it was carved in stone. All this is not a tragedy; it is just a trouble.

There was a chain of troubles, large and small, and I said to myself: do not dwell on them, especially since you have to do your literary work, and you have so many ideas! However, I still remembered the promise I made to the doctor Lidiia Yakovlevna Nokhrina, ten years before at the Kemerovo hospital, that I would do all possible to remove the diagnosis of oligophrenia from my medical history. And now I realized that the time had come, and I had to fulfill my promise at all costs — this damn oligophrenia again stood like a rock on my path of life. But how could I accomplish my task? How could I get rid of this diagnosis of oligophrenia stated in my medical records? This misdiagnosis had been following me for so many years!

I swore that if I had even the slightest chance, even a tiny hole in the rock and a tiny loophole in the bureaucratic barbed fence, I would try to remove this sturdy label of 'oligophrenia'. I would certainly put all of them on edge to do their moral duty. But in the meantime, I just had to work: to compose and record new fairy tales and stories.

The Fresh Wind and Inspiration

In the early years of the third millennium, I was more and more concerned about my literary future, and I already firmly believed in it. And I dreamed that my fairy tales would get into some children's periodical. And I was lucky.

Once, from the 'chatter' (this was what we called the radio-speaker on the wall, which was continuous news), I heard the regional radio speaker speaking about a children's newspaper, published in Kemerovo. It published works of children and adult authors, and books for and about children. The newspaper was called 'The Fresh Wind'. It was a wonderful name, as well as being wonderful that the newspaper was focused on children. I felt like a fresh wind blew into my life. I easily memorized the address of the editorial office; it was near the regional TV center. I wrote them a letter. I received a warm answer — they promised to publish my story 'The Rainbow Drop'. 'The Fresh Wind' lifted me to seventh heaven! I also thought, if my work was be published in the regional publication, I would be noticed, and it would help me to find a permanent job.

But the fresh wind did not blow too long; I managed to publish in this newspaper, only my two fairy tales — 'The Rainbow Drop' and 'The Extraordinary Gift'. After that, the management of the newspaper changed, and I was politely refused. Of course, I was upset. But I hoped there would be more gusts of fresh wind in my life. And I was not wrong. 'The Fresh Wind' turned out to be a springboard to success.

***

At first, nothing seemed to predict that I would soon enter a new happy phase of my life. No one wanted to publish my new works, but from time to time, they wrote about me and published my old works.

One day a journalist was sent to interview me for a local newspaper. Apparently, another sensational article like 'How a completely paralyzed woman became a writer' was planned. The journalist, seeing me, was confused and frightened — either she was shocked by my appearance with twitching hands, or by my diagnosis, about which she had been notified. She looked at me with bewilderment, bordering on disgust; she mumbled her questions with difficulties. I was not mad at her. How could I be angry with a non-professional journalist? I could only sympathize with this novice. And I did not need articles about me; I wanted to publish *my own works*.

I felt that my depression was about to come, and it would cover me like water over a drowning person. And then I decided to keep my spirits high and resist all afflictions — it was my revenge to all misfortunes I had experienced — I decided to work every day.

This time I wanted to write not a fairy tale, but a novel! This desire had been maturing in me for a long time — to write my first novel. Once my neighbor Tatiana Valitova, who lived on the same floor with me, told me a story from her childhood. She was four years old when she saved a stray dog from a group of hooligans, who tied the poor animal to a fence and amused themselves, throwing stones at the dog. I started writing a novel based on the case of the victimized dog, the children's behavior and their relationship with their parents. And as the main character, I created a red-haired girl, who stubbornly sticks to the truth and wants to restore justice. I named the little girl Taiushka.

I worked so hard — in the morning I would drink tea and work until lunch. In the afternoon again, I would sit working on my typewriter. And in three months it turned out to be a good novel. It was finished, but I collapsed after sitting in an unnatural pose, typing on my machine. I developed a constant tension in my back; I was climbing the walls — the pain I experienced was excruciating. It seemed like every single muscle of my body was crying and moaning, but my soul was filled with joy from the work I had done. I felt especially satisfied when I was reading my draft.

At that time, the psychologist Olga Vladimirovna worked at our boarding school — she was such a great person. I took a risk showing her my novel, but I warned that it was just the first sketch, with spelling and punctuation errors. She took my draft home to read. At night I dreamed that soon I would get a little bit better and start correcting mistakes without anyone's help. It could take some time, but I had the spelling dictionary and the Russian grammar book, and using these books, I would edit my novel step by step.

In the morning Olga Vladimirovna opened the door to my room, holding in her hand my draft, and right from the doorway she exclaimed with great excitement, "Tamara, I read your novel last night! I couldn't separate myself from it until I finished reading it! I even cried! Reading your novel, I recalled my student years. When I reached the place where Svetlana, Taiushka's mother, tells about her life — she studied at the university, then she moved to the city, where her missing husband had lived, I burst into tears. She was so young! She moved to a city unfamiliar to her! With a little daughter in her arms! And hoping secretly she would find traces of her husband, who had disappeared in the war! What a courageous woman!"

Olga became silent and sat down in a chair. I did not find words to respond. This was how we were sitting, both silent. Olga was the first who broke our silence. "Tamara, we just have to edit the manuscript; we just have to make some corrections. But it's really great! What a great novel!"

Such sincere praise from my first reader of my first novel about the red-haired Taiushka was the best compensation for all my muscle pain.

Miracles Happen!

I did not really believe in miracles because my childhood, a time when you believe in them, was already over. And what are miracles? They are usually presented as something unexpected, accompanied by the words 'suddenly', 'out of the blue', 'serendipitously', and so on. The word miracle is often used to characterize beneficial events, wonderful occurrences and happy coincidences. And they seem to be non-natural phenomena, often dismissed as physically impossible, and far from life realities. It is not likely that circumstances arise by themselves or by some unknown laws, which one can circumvent, or on the contrary, can attract at the right moment.

But some time ago I started believing that my path was inscribed by God. Not that He decides everything for me, but He draws my life path with indistinct dots, which I recognize intuitively and follow. He carefully takes me away from the bad and ugly, pushes me to the good and necessary and offers opportunities along my path of life. But this is my own work to use these opportunities as God helps those who help themselves. You rely on God, but you have to have self-initiative. I came to believe that God helps those who dare. During the period between 2003 and 2004, I understood better the purpose of my life, and I came to believe in miracles also...

In mid-November 2003, I received a letter from Moscow, which surprised me very much. Who sent me this letter? The envelope looked quite ordinary; it was a private letter, and I was used to receiving official letters. I asked Olga to open the envelope — I could not do it myself — I was too elevated. I had a strange prophetic feeling that I had received something extraordinary. The address of the sender was not familiar to me; the name of the addressee was O.E. Zaikina. I tried to recall all my acquaintances, but I did not have anyone with such a name. The sweet last name 'Zaikina' did not bring me anything specific. The name Zaikina can be translated to English as 'little bunny' — quite a charming last name! Olga pulled out a page from the envelope. I examined the page on both sides.

On one side there was a print of my fairy-tale 'The Belated Waltz of Autumn', and on the other side there was a letter.

'Dear T.A.! Please pardon me, I don't know your full name, I only know your last name and initials. I found your story 'The Late Waltz of Autumn' on the internet, on the website for the disabled, 'disability.ru.' What an amazing story! I put the link to your story on my internet literary forum — all my subscribers read your story with delight. Where can I read your other works? What is your name? With respect and best wishes in your creative work. Please write! Olga Eduardovna Zaikina'.

When I read this, I was so surprised. Was I on the internet? How did I get there? Neither I, nor my friends had the internet; we did not even have a computer. And what is the 'link to my story'? I was familiar with the computer — I saw it in the director's office, but the rest was incomprehensible to me; it was too complicated and tricky.

I was sitting like a statue, not knowing whether to rejoice or wonder. Was it an extravagant gift of Santa Claus or just confusion? It was too early for Santa Claus; we were in November, but confusions in my life have been circulating all year round…

The next morning, I took the letter again, looking at it and not understanding anything. At times, I would close my eyes, thinking: I will open my eyes, and this letter will disappear like an illusion! But the wonderful letter did not disappear.

Then I remembered myself in the autumn, feeling so hopeless about my situation, when they stopped publishing my literary works, and praying: "Dear God! Help me publish! I have written so much! People like my fairy tales and stories. I have accumulated so much, and I have published so little. Dear God, help me just a little, just push me, and I will do the rest myself. I swear to you!" I whispered my words, looking at the autumn sky filled with clouds — these clouds which were calling me to follow them far away… But now they were no longer calling me; instead, the world of books and magazines was calling me. The letter of the Moscow stranger seemed to me to be the path leading to that world.

***

I answered Olga Zaikina only on the third day after I had received her letter. I had to come to my senses from my surprise and to thank God for the new opportunities that He sent to me. I dictated my letter to Marishka, whose hands were healthy. I could not even look at the typewriter — this was how this machine exasperated me! Using Marishka's hands, I wrote to Zaika (this was how I called Zaikina) about myself, without hiding anything. I wrote that I had a severe form of cerebral palsy. I wrote that I could not write with my hands; I could only write my signature and a few lines, if my right hand was held by someone, and my left hand is tied behind my back. I wrote that I have an old electric typewriter that rips the sheets whenever it pleases. That I don't have the internet, and I don't have a computer either. I boasted about my recent publication of 'Where the Tale Lives' in the Moscow regional magazine 'White Bullfinches', whose editorial house was located in the village Verbilki. And I timidly reported that I had written my first novel; it was still in a draft form, but it had already been approved for the publication.

Zaika did not hesitate to answer and asked me to send her all my works, including my novel. I collected all my writings, and after some hesitation, I added to my oeuvre the draft of my novel 'Taiushka'. I sent all these texts to Zaika.

A few weeks later I received an answer. Zaika admired my fairy tales. As concerning my novel, she wrote it was great in content, but I had spelling and punctuation errors, and the style should be polished as well.

I promised that I would try to write more attentively, and as soon as the pain in my back stopped, I would polish my story. But Zaika preferred a different solution: she scanned my draft, and made corrections and other necessary improvements. Then after my approval, she sent the text to a literary contest, announced by Aleksander Gezalov, a writer and a public figure from Karelia, the land which is currently divided among the northwestern Russian Federation (the federal subjects of the Republic of Karelia and Leningrad Oblast) and Finland. I was familiar with this author through his book 'The Salty Childhood'.

Zaika published my tales and stories on the internet sites of her friends. Vladimir Solomonov, a disabled activist from Samara, published them on a website for the disabled called 'The Equal'. Then Ivan Kokotkin, a Moscow doctor, created the page 'Tamara Cheremnova', which was part of his website called 'The World of Health', where he published my old fairy tales and stories, and also the new ones, as soon as I created them.

Soon Zaika told me that my works had been replicating on the internet; they were actively dragged to different sites. And they even appeared in paper publications — the St. Petersburg newspaper 'We Are Part of the Society' published two of my fairy tales. Zaika wrote: "When I use the name 'Tamara Cheremnova' in my internet search, it brings immediately numerous sources with your fairy tales and stories." I learned from Zaika some new terminology: 'virtual reality', 'homepage', 'browser', 'link', etcetera. I was happy about my virtual travels. But the language of the computer and the internet was still enigmatic to me.

My correspondence with Zaika was pleasant, beneficial and informative. She typed her letters on her computer and printed on her printer, and I typed my letters on my typewriter. I was a little bit relieved from the pain in my back — I might be rested from the everyday labor of hitting the typewriter's keys, or maybe it was God who helped me. Our tumultuous correspondence had been continuing already more for than a year. Letters had been flying from Moscow to Novokuznetsk and back without pauses — I received letters from Zaika every week, or even more often. And each of us had accumulated quite a significant archive of letters — without mutual agreement, we kept all our correspondence which we had written between 2003 and 2005. Then we switched to electronic letters.

Editing and promoting my writing was a serious labor, and I did not feel very comfortable that Zaika did so much for me. Why would a person who lives in the great city of Moscow get involved with a disabled woman from the provincial Kuzbass? Would it be possible that Zaika was also not completely normal? Was she, so to speak, my comrade in misfortune? Or did she have some problems in her life? Was she lonely, unhappy, and perhaps not satisfied with her life? I had courage to ask Zaika to tell me about herself. She wrote about her life in detail and sent me a photograph, which depicted a beautiful, slender woman with luxurious hair. And of course, she was not alone or unhappy. Zaika had a family — a loving husband and a beautiful adult daughter. Zaika had accomplished a lot in her life — she had a Ph.D. in biological sciences and worked at the Institute of Immunology. She had been writing for women's newspapers and journals; she was the author of the six-volume collection called 'The Living Lace'; she was also the author of a collection of humorous stories 'The Fat and The Skinny'. In general, everything was in order in her life and there was no flaw, which I had suspected because of my own misfortunes and with my belief that every human being has their secret sorrows.

The feeling of my unhappy childhood surrounded by the cold world was still inside me. I am very open and trustful, and the coldness which I have experienced during my life still did not reach the core of my soul. I was still able to recognize good people, but I was not spoilt by their warmth. It was not my mistrust, it was more my analytical thinking and desire to understand the motivations of Zaika, which were still a mystery to me. I asked her directly, "Why do you help me?"

She replied: "Dear Tamarochka! Helping you, I help Russian children who need good children's literature, kind and bright — exactly the way you create it. I want Russian children, including my grandchildren (and I will have them in time), to read intelligent stories and wise tales, not idiotic nonsense, which has been pouring today into the book market."

Well, after such a response it is worth living and creating my stories!

***

Until today, Zaika unselfishly edits and promotes my literary works. Thanks to her, they are widespread, both electronically and on paper. Moscow and all-Russian magazines, which published me, influenced the city Kemerovo publications, and instead of the fresh wind now I had a whirlwind spun — a tornado of real literary success.

When I received the first letter from Zaika, I realized that this person was sent to me by God, and I already anticipated the coming uplift in my literary work. Of course, it took a lot of effort; I threw myself literally into my creative work. I was completely immersed in writing.

My success motivated me, and I wrote more and more. In addition to fiction, I started writing journalistic works — again, it was Zaika who discovered for me a publicist, and who suggested that I ought to write about current affairs. What a joy when your works are in demand, and publishers and readers ask to continue your old stories and you to write new ones! I just prayed to God; and for what I prayed for, that I received in full measure.

***

In April 2004, the second miracle happened — I became a winner of the literary competition announced by Aleksander Gezalov. They sent me a prize — a laptop! This was the first computer in my life! And in the same happy spring, the magazines 'Protect Me!' and 'The Business Lady' published my fairy tales and essay 'The Thorny Way and the Crown of Thorns'.

No sooner had I come to my senses than the third miracle followed in the summer of 2004. Maral Kazakova, the editor of the magazine 'The Country and Us (the publication of the Center for Spiritual and Physical Recovery of Society), who did not even know my full name, published my fairy tale story 'The Belated Waltz of Autumn'. My name was stated as 'T. Cheremnova'.

Something mystical was going on with this fairy tale story. It is not known who put it on the internet. But whoever it was, thank you very much — thanks to this story I became known as a writer.

I would like to reveal how 'The Late Waltz of Autumn' was born. I started writing it in 1982, when I lived in the Prokopyevsk psycho-neurological boarding school. Under my dictation, Luska recorded the beginning, and then I could not go further. And no matter how much I tried to continue it, I just stumbled and could not write a word. Only in 1999, when I was already in Novokuznetsk, one day while I was sitting down in front of my typewriter — the 'Waltz' splashed out in one breath. In 2001 it was published by the Novokuznetsk newspaper 'The Invalid'.

I sent the issue of the journal 'The Country and Us' with my publication to Zaika. She went with it to the editorial office of this just-started journal, where she met with the editor-in-chief, Maral Muradova Kazakova. She told her about me and recommended my other literary works.

Mastering the Computer

I had very little experience in my life with electronic technology, and here I had a laptop. As I saw it, I almost fainted and howled: Holy Father, I will never master it!

And no one was going to sit with me for hours and teach me how to work on the computer. The social worker Ludmila Grigorievna was the sister of our director, but unlike her, she was not arrogant, and treated me with respect. It was she who brought the package with the laptop, then she called her husband; he immediately came and installed the laptop, and then they left. The next time Ludmila Grigorievna showed me how to open a document and type, then she left. I tried to get acquainted with the laptop on my own, but I was still afraid of this machine. I would sit in front of the laptop until I had circles in my eyes, but three weeks later I started to understand it a little bit. I did not escape breakdowns — the trouble of many beginners. How many times the laptop screen would become dark or the system would crash, and I always relied on Ludmila Grigorievna's husband, who would restore my laptop, although he was not obliged to do so.

People were very kind to me — they were attentive and actively helped me. Svetlana Ivanovna Stifanishina, the chairman of the social protection office, asked a professional computer teacher to help me. Her name was Irina; she taught computer science at the Children's Center. But Irina was pregnant and visited me sporadically, because often she had to go to the hospital to care for her pregnancy. She managed to explain to me the windows and how to copy and paste the text. However, most of her teaching time Irina spent trying to understand my laptop, which was outdated, and she was familiar only with recent models. Suddenly, I became the center of attention of the staff and residents of the boarding school — they wondered whether I could master the laptop or not. Yes, it was a challenging task for me, being without education, even without primary school. But I have mastered the laptop.

The Governor Aman Tuleev

The period around the end of 2004 and the beginning of 2005 was something which I never imagined even in my dreams. It was like it brought high acceleration into my life. Events developed so rapidly that I did not have time to comprehend them.

In September 2004, Zaika developed a tumultuous activity. She talked to the editors, Galina Borisovna Rybchinskaia (from the journal 'Protect Me!') and Maral Muradovna Kazakova (from the journal 'The Country and Us'). I name them officially, but for Zaika they were her friends Galochka and Mashenka. And the three of them decided to talk about me to Aman Gumirovich Tuleev, the governor of the Kemerovo region.

Zaika wrote an official letter, in which she listed my publications and merits, and provided links to internet sites with my works and readers' feedback. She mentioned my victory in the literary competition and the prize in the form of a laptop, which I have been mastering. She asked the governor to help me with the internet, explaining how much I needed the internet for my literary work. She also suggested that my works should be recommended for publication to the Kuzbass regional publishing houses producing children's literature. Zaika discussed the letter with Galochka and Mashenka; the three of them put their signatures; then the letter was published on the website of Governor Tuleev, which was open to the public. A similar letter was sent to Sergei Dmitrievich Martin, the mayor of Novokuznetsk. The solid letters, signed by the editors-in-chief of the two Moscow journals and by the writer Olga Zaikina did not go unnoticed.

Tuleev immediately sent a letter to Zaika.

'Dear Olga Eduardovna! I am sincerely grateful to you and everyone who participates in the promotion of Tamara Cheremnova. Tamara Aleksandrovna is a very modest person, and although she has repeatedly contacted our administration, her requests were always concerning other people. I understand that the internet would offer a great opportunity to Tamara Aleksandrovna, in her creative work and human communications. I gave the order to work out the technical side of the internet connection; the issue will be resolved in the near future as part of the program in our preparation for the Day of the Disabled. Respectfully, Aman Tuleev.'

I was so amazed — Aman Gumirovich remembered me!

***

Galina Borisovna Rybchinskaia sent me *her own* money to buy a modem to connect it to my prized laptop. Both she and Maral Muradovna Kazakova encouraged me with their warm letters, and they also took my fairy tales to the publishers of their journals.

I was astounded that I received such attention and care from complete strangers, and sometimes I asked myself: How could it be possible? But it was possible! I tried to think logically. Why would the two Moscow journals be interested in the Siberian disabled Cheremnova when there were plenty of disabled people in Moscow? And these people needed help as well! I wanted to ask those around me: please, pinch me to wake me up!

Our social worker Ludmila Sergeevna, who went to the post office to receive the money transfer from Galina Borisovna, asked me in surprise, "Why did they shower you with money?"

Yes, all this at first glance looked strange — in Novokuznetsk they also periodically give some money to the disabled, but they never gave it to me; by this remark I do not want to offend the local authorities. I explained to Ludmila Sergeevna that Galina Borisovna, the editor of the Moscow journal 'Protect Me!', sent me money to buy a modem for my computer, so I could communicate with my publishers and readers directly. I started believing that all this attention I had received was the deeds of God. After such a long period of misery, which started when I was sent to the orphanage and continued until recent times, only He could shine the light into the darkness, and only He could bring such a heap of joy!

***

The governor Aman Tuleev not only responded to the letter concerning me, but also immediately sent an order regarding the publication of my works to the Department of Culture and National Politics of the Kemerovo region. They even appointed a person responsible for the project — this was Grigorii Shinkarenko, who was contacted by Zaikina. She sent him my works, which by that time were in electronic format. After reading, discussing and approving my works, they decided to publish my novel 'About the Red-Haired Taiushka' as a book.

Then an order came to our boarding school from the Kemerovo authorities to examine my laptop — to see if it would be suitable for internet connection. Ludmila Grigorievna examined the laptop in detail and made a verdict that it was too weak for the internet; it did not have enough memory. And then Aman Gumirovich ordered to allocate money for the purchase of a new laptop. It is necessary to pay tribute to his kindness, and I have to say that he helped not just me but many other disabled people.

***

The book 'About the Red-Haired Taiushka' was published in the spring of 2005. It was a remarkable hardcover edition — with color illustrations and a cheerful image on the book cover depicting a laughing red-haired girl, holding an orange kitten on her shoulder.

The launch presentation of my book 'About the Red-Haired Taiushka' took place in the children's library. At first, I felt like I was in a fog. I was sitting in my wheelchair, deafened by what was happening, not able to think about anything. It was a large children's audience, and so many pairs of inquisitive eyes were looking at me! I had no idea that it was so hard to be the center of the celebration. Then our boarding school librarian, who was leading the presentation, spoke about my book. The children had a chance to look at my book, and they began to ask questions. At that moment I came out of the fog and finally was in accord with reality. I answered their questions and explained some episodes in my book.

Then Lena Medvedeva, who came to my presentation, pushed me in my wheelchair from the library to our boarding school; we were passing the streets of our district. I was proud of myself, and I saw myself as if from the outside — I was dressed in an elegant light suit, which was purchased especially for the presentation. I had a beautiful hairstyle, and I was wearing make-up, which was applied to my face at the insistence of my friends. The sun shone brightly, and passers-by turned around and smiled kindly. I will never forget that feeling — I sensed myself as a slightly tired person who had done a great job.

The appearance of my book 'About the Red-Haired Taiushka' was covered in the newspaper 'The Ilyinsk Times'; I was shown on local television; later the almanac 'The Moscow Parnassus' published an analytical article 'The Magic Tales of Tamara Cheremnova'.

I did not expect that it would not take long for my second presentation — it would take place in the Libtown Almanac. I did not anticipate that in two years my other book would be published — 'A Puppy Walking in Autumn'.

The Internet and New Friends

I had to master the laptop mostly on my own. It was bought with the money allocated by the governor. It was not easy for me to understand this machine, very different from the previous one, which belonged to the older generation of laptops. I learned a little bit from Sergei and Maksim, two computer specialists, who came to me to connect my laptop to the internet. They explained to me the basics and patiently answered my questions. I appreciated their help, and I am still grateful to them.

But not everything went smoothly with the installation of the internet. The director of our boarding school blocked Tuleev's order to connect my computer to the internet. One morning our head doctor came to my room and confessed, "The director has forced me to write a medical certificate that you have serious problems with the coordination of movements and that you will not be able to use the internet. This certificate has already been passed to the local department. Just don't tell her that I told you about this!"

"But what will happen if next time she orders you to shoot me? Will you obey that order too?" I asked him point blank.

"But if I refused to write this certificate, she would kick me out of work..." he said.

I saw in front of me a pathetic, powerless man; I felt sorry for him at that moment.

"You will not tell her?" He was still begging for my promise, standing by my bunk.

"Don't worry, I won't tell her," I promised.

I understood why the director was so opposed to the internet. What if I started complaining about her non-legitimate acts and her harsh practices? After all, it is much easier to communicate on the internet than by regular mail.

At that moment, I wanted so much to go to her office, and look directly into her eyes, not saying anything. Would she stand the scrutiny of my gaze? And then I would say: If I need to complain about you, I will find a way to do it without the internet!

She must have known that the absence of the internet would not give her a guarantee against criticism. Of course, I did not go to her office — I kept my promise given to the head doctor. The idea of connecting the internet to my laptop did not bring any results. But I bought a cell phone with an internet connection, though I only used email, as using other options was too expensive.

I studied manuals and books on psychology — thanks to them and my observations I could read people's characters. I often met people who had similarities with our director; they had the same character. Such people only seemed to be brave; if you are armed with a very disapproving look and asked them about something tricky — they would just fall apart.

I had a chance to reveal the director's character. I had to discuss my participation in the presentation of the collection 'Libtown' which was just released — there were six of my fairy tales under the general name 'The Park of the Lost Childhood'. This publication was just excellent — it had a hardcover, good paper, and high-quality printing. As a matter of fact, other authors whose works were included in this collection were very interesting. The 'Libtown' was published in Odessa, Ukraine. It was my first publication abroad!

Ukraine used to be part of the Soviet Union, but now it is a foreign country. The Libtown collection arrived at the boarding school at the end of 2005. After my friends viewed it and read it, they all decided that such an event should certainly be celebrated. So I went to the director's office to discuss the presentation — where it should take place, what day and time should be chosen, and other details.

The director did not object to the presentation; my literary successes flattered her, because I was a resident of her boarding school. After our discussion, I asked her in a deliberate, calm, even slightly indifferent tone, "Why are you against the installation of the city telephone? Without it it's not possible to connect the modem to the internet. And it was Tuleev's order."

She opened her eyes wide and blurted out, "You can do it, but at your own expense! At your own expense you can order four telephones — it's up to you!"

"I don't need four; I just need one." I smiled, and rolled to my room, congratulating myself on my victory. I was allowed to order the telephone line in my room at my expense — I was satisfied with her ambiguous permission. Now I had to think about where to get the money for this project.

I must give credit to the director — she was a consistent person — when she promised something, she would keep her word. She gave my application, regarding the installation of the telephone in my room, to the librarian and sent her to the telephone office. My monthly payments were arranged in credit. I had some savings — I put aside money from my benefits, and my royalties from publications, and I also borrowed one thousand five hundred rubles.

I am even grateful to the director for procrastination with the internet and for other injustices which had happened before — her cruelty formed in me the ability to resist. And not only she; since the days of the Bachata orphanage and the Prokopyevsk PNBS, I appreciated not only good people, but also unkind people — because thanks to them, I mastered my character and learned how to solve problems independently. And for the physically disabled person it is very important to develop this precious quality — the ability to endure and overcome.

***

In time, I began to post my fairy tales and stories on the internet sites. My readers wrote reviews about my works, they suggested interesting topics, and it was very touching when they gave me advice. They named me 'The Siberian storyteller'. And one geographically savvy reader clarified the name: 'The West Siberian storyteller'. I believe it is a high rank!

***

With the internet, the time accelerated — it was no longer walking but it was flying time; it was rushing like a mustang. I grazed like a cow on the internet, finding more and more new interesting corners and topics, and wondered how I had lived before without it.

I did not just acquire new friends and have conversations with my readers, but I began to search for connections with human rights defenders. Yes, the restless Cheremnova again started fighting for her 'clean medical history'. Was the endless imposition of the diagnosis, which I did not have, and which had blemished my life, not a violation of human rights?

I had applied to medical institutions of different levels, repeatedly requesting to have the wrong diagnosis removed, but all in vain. I even wrote a letter to M.Y. Surabov; at that time, he was the minister of health, but he never responded to my letter.

In 2006, I tried to contact Yuri Sergeevich Savenko — he is a well-known Russian psychiatrist and human rights activist, a member of the Council of Experts of the Russian Commissioner for Human Rights in the Russian Federation. He is also the president of the Independent Psychiatric Association of Russia. He is the editor-in-chief of 'The Independent Journal of Psychiatry'. His main works concern anxious psychotic syndromes, psychotic disorder problems, subjects of psychiatry and the classification of mental disorders. He has his own special approach to mental disorders and is known for his broad social, historical and cultural orientation. I found his phone number and email address, but neither of them was working, apparently; the internet had outdated information.

But if I have a goal, I must succeed. Very often I have to go through many obstacles, but I never stop until I accomplish my task. I took a wide approach — I checked all the links that mentioned human rights. I even sent a letter to President Putin during his direct television communication with Russian citizens. But I received only dry replies, just general words, streamlined phrases, without any specifics. I admit that Mr Putin did not see my letter personally, because the whole country complained to him, and he is just one person. But does he not have his vast administration who could answer? Surely, there are those who lead correspondences of that kind.

'The Spirituality'

In 2007, I received an invitation to publish my works in the children's magazine 'The Little Siberian', published in Krasnoyarsk. It came from Valentina, the volunteer distributor of this magazine. Since it was dedicated to very little children, I refused to publish my works in this magazine. I write for older children and adults. I told Valentina that I was not Korney Chukovsky, whose famous book 'From Two to Five' is so brilliant that I would not dare to compete with him. For very young children it is necessary to write in a very responsive manner, and to achieve this skill one should communicate with them daily, and not only watch them occasionally on the street.

Valentina persuaded and convinced me that if I write for children, I can also write for the young ones. Under her pressure, I agreed and I wrote my first stories for the youngsters substantively. The grandson of Zaika, Temochka, was already grown up, so he became both a hero and a reader of my work from age of two to five.

The publisher liked my fairy tales and offered me a permanent freelance job. Unfortunately, this great job did not last long — only six months — later 'The Little Siberian' changed its leadership, and they were not interested in me as a contributor to their magazine. Oh, my God, what a typical situation — the new broom sweeps out the old authors! However, 'The Little Siberian' had already accepted five of my fairy tales and stories, and they were published. And I still hope that someday I will be invited to work with a children's magazine again.

In the same year, 2007, I met Ekaterina Alekseeva, the editor of the internet site 'The Stoic'. I took part in the online polemic on the topic of culture in the modern world, and she invited me to write a journalistic article.

I was a little bit apprehensive — it was one thing to participate in free discussions on the internet, but to write an article for the site was a completely different thing. But Katia so skillfully made up questions, and in answering them, I was able to write an article. I called it 'And life, and tears, and culture'. I sent it to Zaika; she edited a little and assured me that journalism was also my vocation — I was in heaven.

The article really turned out to be another victory. It was posted in the online magazine, spread on websites, and a year later printed in the magazine 'The Beam of Fomalhaut'. Fomalhaut is the brightest star in the constellation of Piscis Austrinus, the 'Southern Fish', and one of the brightest stars in the sky. 'The Beam of Fomalhaut' was the publication of a group of disabled intellectuals affiliated with the Moscow Center for Socio-cultural Animation, called 'Spiritualization'; the members of its editorial board lived in different parts of Russia. I had a warm relationship with all of them, and I felt like I had crossed another threshold. I felt like I entered a wide bright world, about whose existence I had not known, being secluded in the gray routine of my everyday life. And then a new bright phase of my life began.

***

After getting acquainted and communicating with 'The Spiritualization', I wanted to write something very kind, warm and spiritual. And I decided to write a fairy tale which would be not just for children, but for adults also.

So this was how the novel fairy tale 'A Puppy Walking in Autumn' was born. Writing this story, I was thinking of people who would read my novel — it should give the sense of home and comfort. I wished that every person would find their *own home* and their *own comfort*. Zaika, as usual, edited 'A Puppy Walking in Autumn'. She was flattered because she and her grandson were prototypes of my characters: there is a grandmother with a stroller, from which her grandchild Temochka observes and contemplates the world.

The editorial board of 'The Spirituality' liked my novels, and at the end of the blessed year of 2007, my new book came out in print. It included two novels: 'A Puppy Walking in Autumn' and 'About the Red-Haired Taiushka'. "I did not sell my copyright to the publisher, and 'Taiushka' was republished by 'The Spirituality'; it brought me a great reception. The book cover had an amazing image — it was in color, representing a puppy against the background of the red autumn. There were also charming black and white illustrations inside the book — one could make an animated film on the basis of these illustrations. The book was distributed correctly — it did not go on sale, but the entire circulation went directly to orphanages and boarding schools.

Masha Arbatova

One evening, in the same fruitful 2007, I made myself comfortable in bed, ready to watch my favorite TV show 'Let Them Talk'. I was fond of its presenter Andrey Malakhov; he always invited interesting people who discussed various topics.

Usually I watched this show, standing by my walkers, and thus simultaneously I kill two birds with one stone — I exercised my muscles, which become tense after sitting in front of the laptop, and took part in the 'Let Them Talk' discussion, believing as a viewer, I was also to some extent a participant. But that night I was too lazy to do my physical work; I just wanted to relax...

The program started. Andrei Malakhov presented his guests: "Please welcome Maria Arbatova, a prominent writer and a public figure!"

I saw an attractive woman; she graciously bowed to the audience of the TV studio and to the invisible television viewers which included me. I felt like her friendly bow to the millions of people was directed to me personally.

My relaxed mood disappeared immediately. This was Maria Arbatova, whom I read and about whom I had heard! Abruptly, I changed my position in bed, as if I had been stung by a bee. I stopped viewing the talk show. In two minutes, I was in front of my laptop, typing key words 'maria arbatova official website'. The link opened; I signed up and entered a forum under the rubric 'Hello Everyone!' I wrote my anecdotal bitter story for Maria Arbatova and the forum people: that I have been recognized as a writer, my stories and books have been published for more than ten years, and I am still falsely diagnosed with 'oligophrenia at the stage of debility', and no one could remove this damn stigma from my medical history.

The next day I received responses from Maria Arbatova and the visitors of her site. I received more than three hundred emails. I thought: how will I be able to answer them? How long will it take? Then I found out that I could answer all at once on the site. Maria suggested that everyone who visited her site should read my story. One head is good but many heads are better. I agreed with Maria Arbatova's action: people should know about such injustice; it would prevent other discriminations. I am not the only one who received the diagnosis of 'oligophrenia' which had such a distorted impact on my life. And we decided to fight not just for me, but also for other people affected in the same way.

The atmosphere on the site was friendly, warm and homely. Maria Arbatova was called simply Masha. Masha began working on eliminating my misdiagnosis. At first, she tried to call Mr Savenko, but no one picked up the telephone. She spent almost a day trying to reach him, but no one answered the phone. Savenko's email address also did not work. In general, all the internet information about his contact information was already outdated, and the new was not known to anyone.

Then Masha wrote an official letter to the president, and the state machine started working — a committee arrived to examine my condition. I was surprised to see Gennadii Pavlovich Shiriaev, the former head of the Prokopyevsk psychiatric hospital — he was one of the committee's members! I had seen him only once and very briefly. At that time, he was a black-haired young man, and now I saw a gray-haired man. Gennadii Pavlovich smiled at me. "Tamara! Do you remember me?"

"Yes, of course, you were the head doctor at the Prokopyevsk psychiatric hospital. I am glad you remember me." I also smiled.

I showed the committee members my book, 'About the Red-Haired Taiushka', and told them that I had mastered the laptop and that I surf the internet, that I published my works in magazines and newspapers. And I asked them, no! Rather I demanded — that the diagnosis of 'oligophrenia' must be completely removed from my medical history. No single page which is marked with this horrible diagnosis should be there!

The event of the elimination of this awful thing finally happened, and this was after so many years of refusals. I had a new medical history; it included only new records. This was the end of my suffering, which had continued for so many years. I got rid of this stigma! It was my long-awaited victory! Maria Arbatova and her subscribers congratulated me, and all rejoiced that justice had been done.

However, Mr G. L. Ustiantsev, the deputy chief physician of the Kemerovo Regional Clinical Psychiatric Hospital, sent an angry and contradictory letter to my boarding school. After reading this letter, our director gave it to me, without making any comments.

Here are a few paragraphs from this letter.

'There is no medical documentation in the health system archives, regarding the early period of development of Cheremnova Tamara Aleksandrovna, between the date of her birth, 06.08.1955 and 1962.'

There was a mistake in my date of birthday; it should have been December the sixth instead of August the sixth, but it was a minor thing, just a typo. But the remark that there were no records about my existence before 1962 brought some absurdity. Did it mean that I was not in the USSR at the time? Did I exist at all?

Here is part of a sentence from this remarkable letter: 'According to the medical history of the Chugunash Orphanage of the Disabled... '

Mr Ustiantsev, are you sure that I was in the Chugunash Orphanage? I would like to bring to your attention that I lived in the Bachata orphanage, and the address 'Chugunash' was another absurdity in my medical history. Actually, I have never in my life been in this Chugunash orphanage; it must be a very interesting place.

'We do not have medical documentation which would confirm by whom and when the diagnosis was made, with which she entered the Chugunash orphanage for the disabled people. The medical history was the conclusion of the psychiatrist of the Kemerovo Regional Psycho-Neurological Hospital dated 1962, which says: "Cheremnova Tamara, seven years old, born in 1955, suffers from organic lesion of the central nervous system, spastic tetraparesis, and oligophrenia at the stage of debility. The girl cannot move independently and she cannot serve herself. She needs outside care. She can be in the home for mentally disabled children".'

And here is the killer part:

'As it follows from the medical history, in 1974, at the age of 19, Tamara Cheremnova no longer displayed the mental underdevelopment

— she learned how to read, correctly explained the figurative meaning of proverbs and sayings, she had calm behavior.'

Alas! Does it mean that the idiot cured herself on her own? But such things do not happen — oligophrenia is incurable. The person who suffers with oligophrenia can be adapted to the environment; somehow his or her condition can be improved, and he or she can be taught, but oligophrenia will still remain with this individual forever. And if my 'behavior was calm', why had I been kept in the psycho-neurological boarding school for so many years? Why were they afraid to transfer me to an ordinary boarding school for physically disabled people? They even placed me temporarily to live among violent mentally disabled people!

'Cheremnova T.A. pursues certain goals when she writes her letters. It is dictated by querulant motives, to prove her independence, to draw attention to her, to obtain concessions, which will further entail new complaints and claims.'

The word 'querulant' is derived from the Latin *querulus* which means 'complaining' — it is referred to a person who obsessively feels wronged.

'Regarding the diagnosis of oligophrenia, which she obtained at the age of six, without medical records, it can be assumed that at that time she displayed the lag in her intellectual development. After she learned how to read during her teenage years, she showed sufficient intellectual capacities. At the same time, the gross organic pathology of the brain has led to the formation of characteristic personality traits in the form of egocentrism and rigidity.'

In psychiatry, the term querulous paranoia had been used to describe a paranoid condition which manifested itself in querulant behavior. The concept had disappeared from the psychiatric literature, because it had been misused to stigmatize the behavior of people seeking the resolution of valid grievances. It also appears under the Latin name *paranoia querulans*. The psychiatric term 'querulous motives' also means the pathological desire of the patient to engage in litigation. The phrase about my inherent querulous motives was taken from the psychiatry manual. As for my supposed egocentrism and rigidity, these terms, after I brought them to light, caused a storm of indignation among my friends.

"You are selfish? You always care about other people, getting yourself in trouble! You are the one who is incapable of putting yourself in another person's shoes? This is what you do all the time! You take closely people's problems as your own, you always try to understand and help! You are the one who is rigid? You can't change your opinions and ideas? No one is more flexible than you are! No one rebuilds their personality more successfully than you do! And look how fast you have learned these new technologies — the computer, the internet, and Skype!"

I submitted the letter of Mr Ustiantsev to my readers only to show how my life was documented in medical terms, and I believe my readers will distinguish where the truth is and where the lie is.

The report of Ustiantsev arrived after the false diagnosis of 'oligophrenia' had been officially removed, but unfortunately, it upset me — I was overwhelmed with fears and uncertainty. But at that time, I had someone to help me.

In 2008, the psychologist Irina Yurievna Kurbatova started visiting me. And she became my personal psychologist. Irina Yurievna taught me how to control myself in different situations and how to see other people and their characters. She taught me relaxation techniques, and helped me to get rid of fears and find peace of mind. And now I rejoice every day, even the simplest and unremarkable ones, and pray God to give me such days as many as possible...

Different to Others

When I was young, I tried to find an answer to my question: Why do others treat me this way? I did not do anything wrong, and I tried not to bother people. Then I could not find the answer. But today I know the answer and it is simple — I am not like others. I am unusual for many people; my movements repel, and my unequal eyes and squint aggravate unpleasant impressions. Most people in Russia, for some reason, look squeamishly at crawling invalids who are unable to control their movements.

Here is an example. In December 2009, I was in the neurological department at the Novokuznetsk City Hospital No. 29. I went there to do fluorography. My assistant Olga pushed me in my wheelchair to the office door. The nurse who received patients rolled her eyes and exclaimed in surprise, "Oh-oh-oh-oh-oh-oh-oh!" I did not say anything. I was dragged to the gurney, and then they rolled me to the x-ray machine. I was quite nervous, which resulted in involuntarily violent movements. "Why are they bringing them here?" The nurse on duty expressed her vociferous annoyance. "How can I get her pictures? Call the doctor! Ask him who sent her here!"

There was an awkward pause, and I, who was previously silent as the dead, suddenly dared to make a comment. "And you just shoot me! Then the problem will disappear. No person, no problem. What do you say?"

"I don't know." She shrugged her shoulders.

"By the way, I am a writer; I write books for children," I said.

"Listen to what she just said!" The nurse had already recovered from her embarrassment and turned to her colleague, who raised her head inquiringly. "She says she is a children's writer! She twisted her mouth in an incredulous smile and moved her finger in circular motion at her temple — meaning 'she is insane'.

I had a similar case at the Novokuznetsk Orthopedics Center. The psychologist, who was sitting majestically in her chair, openly mocked my thinking abilities. And none of those who were present cut her off, because no one cared.

This is how people with physical disabilities are treated in Russia. The fact that they are 'different to others' is sufficient to reject them as equals. In Russia, the cultural approach to disability and the understanding that the disabled person is a human being has not yet been instilled.

I understand it is difficult to treat a patient who suffers from a severe disease and has serious motor and speech disorders. I can take myself as an example: my legs do not walk, my hands do not obey. Though my speech is discernible, it can be interrupted by spasticity.

So let us together come up with the installation of some devices which would make it easier for disabled people to live, and then you, healthy people, will have fewer problems with us. When I get to our hospitals, it seems that I am the only one who suffers with cerebral palsy; it seems that I am the only one who has ever been there. Is it true that among all patients with cerebral palsy (by the way, there are about a million of them registered in Russia) it is only I who uses the legal right to back up my precious health?

There are many disabled people who experience similar emotions, because the Russian hospitals and clinics are mostly not adapted — not only for wheelchair users, but even for those who move on crutches.

Joining the Union of Russian Writers

I did not know about Masha Arbatova's far-reaching plans regarding me. In 2008, one day she suddenly invited me to join the Union of Russian Writers. The word 'suddenly' is overused by the authors and usually eliminated by the editors, but here it is appropriate and right to the point.

I was surprised: I, to join the Union of Russian Writers? Is that really possible? I was never sure, either at the dawn of my writing, or even after the release of a number of my books, that I had the right to be called a writer or a literary person. I was not sure about my talent, and besides, I do not have any degrees or formal education. And I preferred the humble, neutral word 'author'. I could not imagine myself to be a member of such a high organization as the Union of Russian Writers, even in my sky-high dreams. After all, the writer should meet with their readers, answer their questions. I was afraid of strangers, and I was a hundred percent sure that the person's appearance meant a lot, and for the first acquaintance the appearance is almost everything.

Thank God my nihilistic perception of the world was wrong. In 2008 I had a literary reception at the Novokuznetsk branch of the Union of Russian Writers. I did not notice anyone among the people who were there who would send me a silent message which I could read as: 'Look at her! She came here in a wheelchair!' On the contrary, people expressed so much benevolence towards me!

But still I rejected the offer to join the Union of Russian Writers. "Masha! Well, where should I go with my crooked snout? I belong only to a freak show! They won't accept me."

"One is not taken into the Union of Russian Writers for beautiful eyes, but for the talent," Masha replied. "And you have more than enough published books to enter the Union."

I gave up and started collecting the necessary documents. I wrote my brief autobiography, collected reviews and compiled a list of publications. It took some efforts to write a list of publications; it was quite long, though I did not include all my publications. I thought: how could I complain that I had not been published sufficiently!

Besides Maria Arbatova, Moscow writers Tatiana Nabatnikova and Gennadii Ivanov gave me recommendations for joining the Union.

***

In December 2009, when my texts and recommendations were approved by the admission committee of the Union and other departments, I was solemnly handed my membership ID. To this day, I do not believe that it has happened to me. It was like a fantasy dream!

The fantasy dream continued. A year later, in December 2010, I received the Governor's Medal for Faith and Kindness along with the impressive monetary prize.

To celebrate my fifty-fifth birthday, the literary reception was held in the Novokuznetsk branch of the Union of Russian Writers. I was afraid of it. While I was taken by car to the city literary cafe, where the anniversary party took place, I was tormented by questions. How will they look at me? Will they accept me? What will they ask? Will my appearance provoke mockery? However, I was tormented by my obsessive question 'How will they look at me?' in vain. For the members of the Union, I was just a normal human person, perhaps not quite like them, but still a human being. The atmosphere was kind and a little bit compassionate, and I felt like a little duck among the swans who felt sorry for the duck. Nevertheless, I saw I was perceived as a professional and colleague.

***

In 2009, the scientific journal 'Life with Cerebral Palsy: Problems and Solutions' was launched — it was intended for us, people with cerebral palsy, and for those who worked with us. The journal had its internet website, and I immediately contacted the editorial office. One of the most valuable points of the online journal was that it published answers to specific questions and had detailed consultations. Ludmila Nikitichna Molchanova, the deputy editor, advised me to get a ticket to go to the sanatorium. I had been asking for a ticket for many years, but I was invariably refused — they would always bring obstacles such as the sanatorium was booked, the service would be too complicated, or I had no need for the sanatorium treatment, and other bureaucratic excuses.

Molchanova's advice proved to be effective; I wrote a letter to the authorities, and in the summer of 2009, I received two tickets — one for me, the other for my assistant. The sanatorium 'The Miner' was comfortable; it was located in the Zenkovskii Natural Park. I took with me Lenochka Medvedeva, and we both had a wonderful vacation and cure.

On my return from the sanatorium, I learned from Zaika that Professor Ksenia Aleksandrovna Semenova, the editor-in-chief of the magazine 'Life With Cerebral Palsy', the world-famous specialist in cerebral palsy, read my novels, 'A Puppy Walking in Autumn' and 'About the Red-Haired Taiushka'. She asked to convey to me her admiration, and wished me to continue writing for children.

***

Thanks to all these kind and attentive people, I felt that all those perennial icicles, which had accumulated during so many years, started melting inside me. I started believing that I could be loved... Everyone wants to be loved: young, elderly, sick, healthy, successful and unlucky. We all need love.

Writing my Autobiography

I came across Leonid Zharov and his wife Svetlana Ermakova, who were both writers from the Tyumen region, on Masha's website and the Live Journal. They were very interested in me, and once they started a conversation with Masha that it would be wonderful if I wrote a book about my life. They believed my life was very unusual, and my life story would be interesting and useful for many people. Masha fervently supported their idea.

Under their communal pressure I started writing my memories. At first, I felt inspired when I described my early childhood, because it was the happiest time when I lived at home, with my family of three generations — my parents, aunts, grandmother and grandfather, and everything was so good. I did not strain a bit; the lines were born themselves, cleverly woven into phrases, and the narration flew... I sent my memoirs to Zaika, and I also posted them on the website of Maria Arbatova.

But when I reached my memories of the autumn of 1962, when I was about seven years old, when they started the process of my registration for the orphanage, I stopped abruptly. I was frightened that I would not be able to describe everything I went through. I did not want to bring these memories or write them down! Some memories even made me feel ill...

I quietly surrendered my position and postponed my work on my autobiography. And to somehow justify myself to Masha and to the spouses Leonid Zharov and Svetlana Ermakova, and also to Zaika, I continued my fairy tale about the witch Shisha, who was the character of the story 'About the Red-Haired Taiushka'. I had an excuse — I followed the wishes of my readers who asked me to continue this story.

But as soon as the story 'Shisha' was completed, Masha again asked me about my work on my autobiography. And she persistently asked this question in her emails. Leaving questions unanswered was not in my nature, and I returned to my autobiography. Now I am so grateful to Masha for her persistence!

***

Since I wrote my autobiographical book in a 'modern' way, that is, sending it by chapters to my regular readers and publishing them on the internet, I had to answer simultaneously my readers' questions and give explanations. The abundance of questions made me happy — this meant I wrote interestingly. And I answered them with pleasure — I also wanted people to know that there is another side of life, very different from their own lives.

My readers said to me that the book, although it describes sad events, is written with humor. However, one of the readers described it as 'gallows humor'. Well, let it be so, especially since I managed to avoid the gallows.

Andrei Tsypliaev, the children's poet from Novomichurinsk, insisted that my autobiographical chapters should be read not only by adults, but also by teenagers and high school students. One of the high school girls gave the 'orphanage' part of my story to read to her ten-year-old sister. While she read this chapter, she was crying. Then she said, "We should send Tamara a kilo of smoked lard and a jar of pickles. These horrible, greedy people didn't give the little unhappy Tamara a piece of lard and a slice of pickle!"

The girl was consoled and assured that Tamara had grown up and become a writer a long time ago, and she does not need the lard and pickles; today these delicacies are sold all over Russia.

***

Long before I finished my autobiographical book, I received an offer from the journal 'The Human Child' to publish the part about the Bachata orphanage in several issues. The journal 'Protect the Child!' also took the chapter about my early childhood for publication. I was so happy!

On December 29, 2010, I was presented with the certificate of the nominee of the international 'philanthropist' award; it came along with a monetary prize.

***

The year 2011 began wonderfully — three of my fairy tales were taken for the 'Anthology of Modern Children's Prose', published by the Academy of Russian Literature and the literary agency of the 'Moscow Parnassus'. My story 'February Dreams' about two clumsy teenagers was included in the collection of prose 'Evenings at the Balcony' which was prepared by Eva Zlatogorova, a children's writer and publisher.

Instead of Postscript

When I decided to write this book, I thought with horror: what can I tell my readers? I spent most of my life being locked up in four walls, living in terrible conditions, and in fact, in a prison regime. Well, would it be interesting to readers? My life experience consisted of limitations and my struggle against them. I was accidentally limited physically by my fate, and I was also limited financially, mentally and spiritually by people. Even despite my constant dependence on others, without whose assistance I could not eat, drink, and write even a few lines, I was able to achieve a lot in my life.

I want to tell you, my dear readers, about something that I have learned through my suffering and bitter experience. Never lose hope, as there are no hopeless situations. In any desperate situation there is always a hidden little door, which you just have to find. Don't be lazy, ask God to help you, and just start your work. Start from zero, and believe me, you will succeed. You only need to start…

Some people who will read this book will probably be horrified by my life; they may think: 'If I were born as an invalid, I would not be able to live such a squalid life until old age!' Yes, sometimes it brings a lot of pain when you realize you do not have in your life that which others have. I would like to have a family; I would like to be loved. God forbid, you learn what real loneliness is! Actually, I am an ordinary woman inside, and in my case, it was a forced loneliness! And my soul can long for someone like anyone's soul…

Oh, how much I do not want to stand out among others! Oh, how I want to get up and run barefoot on the grass, especially on a summer evening, when the ground is warm, soft and tender. And how I want to feel myself light and beautiful — at least for one hour, or for half an hour, or at least, for ten minutes!

But like all of us, I came to this earth with a mission — to show that even in such a deplorable condition it would be possible to live with dignity and overcome many obstacles. And probably, if the soul has endured great suffering in this world, it will be greatly rewarded later. The soul is given by God as material that man improves on his own, and sometimes one life is not enough for this.

After I finished this book, I felt like I had lived my life anew. I can dip the pen in my own blood if I choose when I write about my suffering, but now I am looking at my past life from the outside, analyzing events and summing up. And making the last point, I can say firmly and confidently: I have succeeded in my life!

www.ingramcontent.com/pod-product-compliance
Lightning Source LLC
Chambersburg PA
CBHW021140080526
44588CB00008B/137